Founding editor: J.
General ed:
JAMES C. BULMAN, CAROL CHILLINGTON RUTTER

Coriolanus

Manchester University Press

Already published in the series
Geraldine Cousin *King John*
Anthony B. Dawson *Hamlet*
Mary Judith Dunbar *The Winter's Tale*
Jay L. Halio *A Midsummer Night's Dream* (2nd edn)
Michael D. Friedman *Titus Andronicus*
Andrew Hartley *Julius Caesar*
Stuart Hampton-Reeves and Carol Chillington Rutter *The Henry VI* plays
Bernice W. Kliman *Macbeth* (2nd edn)
Alexander Leggatt *King Lear*
James Loehlin *Henry V*
Scott McMillin *Henry IV, Part One*
Lois Potter *Othello*
Hugh M. Richmond *King Henry VIII*
Margaret Shewring *King Richard II*
Virginia Mason Vaugha *The Tempest*

Shakespeare
in
Performance

Coriolanus

ROBERT ORMSBY

Manchester University Press

The right of Robert Ormsby to be identified as the author of this work
has been asserted by him in accordance with the Copyright, Designs and
Patents Act 1988.

Published by Manchester University Press
Altrincham Street, Manchester M1 7JA, UK
www.manchesteruniversitypress.co.uk

British Library Cataloguing-in-Publication Data is available

ISBN 978 0 7190 7867 5 *hardback*
ISBN 978 1 5261 3945 0 *paperback*

First published by Manchester University Press in hardback 2014

This edition first published 2019

The publisher has no responsibility for the persistence or accuracy of URLs for any
external or third-party internet websites referred to in this book, and does not guarantee
that any content on such websites is, or will remain, accurate or appropriate.

CONTENTS

LIST OF ILLUSTRATIONS

SERIES EDITORS' PREFACE

Recently, the study of Shakespeare's plays as scripts for performance in the theatre has grown to rival the reading of Shakespeare
as literature among university, college and secondary-school
teachers and their students. The aim of the present series is to
assist this study by describing how certain of Shakespeare's texts
have been realized in production.

The series is not concerned to provide theatre history in the
traditional sense. Rather, it employs the more contemporary
discourses of performance criticism to explore how a multitude
of factors work together to determine how a play achieves
meaning for a particular audience. Each contributor to the
series has selected a number of productions of a given play and
analysed them comparatively. These productions – drawn from
different periods, countries and media – were chosen not only
because they are culturally significant in their own right but also
because they represent something of the range and variety of the
possible interpretations of the play in hand. They illustrate how
the convergence of various material conditions helps to shape a
performance: the medium for which the text is adapted; stage-
design and theatrical tradition; the acting company itself; the
body and abilities of the individual actor; and the historical,
political and social contexts which condition audience reception
of the play.

We hope that theatregoers, by reading these accounts of
Shakespeare in performance, may enlarge their understanding
of what a play-text is and begin, too, to appreciate the complex
ways in which performance is a collaborative effort. Any study
of a Shakespeare text will, of course, reveal only a small propor-
tion of the play's potential meaning; but by engaging issues of
how a text is translated in performance, our series encourages a
kind of reading that is receptive to the contingencies that make
theatre a living art.

J. R. Mulryne, Founding editor
James C. Bulman, Carol Chillington Rutter, General editors

PREFACE

Coriolanus is a relentlessly ugly play, one that seethes with
mutual hatred that is barely discernible from mutual dependence. Martius' scorn for most human relationships does not
easily win theatregoers' sympathy, but there is a terrible urgency
in his obedience to the laws of the three suicidal pacts by which
he is bound. He serves a city whose People and Tribunes he
despises as a disease and who despise him in kind. Martius is
'proud to hunt' (1.1.234) Aufidius, whom he loathes 'Worse than
a promise-breaker' (1.9.2), but he offers the Volsce his naked
throat as a sign of their alliance.[1] He is gruesomely loyal to a
vampiric mother, whose infantilizing pride in her son manifests
itself as a longing to have his blood shed. Shakespeare sweeps us
along on a verbal tide of '[f]ractured, harsh rhythms, dissonance,
[and] repellent imagery' that 'bespeak a calculated assault upon
the senses' (Ripley 13). As John Ripley, the foremost chronicler
of *Coriolanus'* stage history, remarks, the main characters'
'passions are crude and elemental', and the ending 'brings no
comforting insight', just 'a deafening crash as irresistible force
meets immovable object' (13). Despite such searing bleakness, it
is not exactly the case that the play 'has never been very popular'
(Vickers 7), nor is it particularly true that '[i]t is seldom acted',
not even in 1912 when A.C. Bradley made the claim (25). *Coriolanus* 'has had in fact a considerable and very varied stage
history', comments Brian Parker (Introduction 115), and, whatever the tragedy's harshness or difficulties, its 'career [in
performance] ... is an account of a theater establishment irre-
sistibly drawn to its acting opportunities' (Ripley 32). These
opportunities are numerous, and help explain why the title role
has attracted so many established leading actors over the
centuries. But there is more to it than that. *Coriolanus* has been
reconfigured by adapters as diverse as Nahum Tate, Bertolt
Brecht, Günter Grass and John Osborne. In its long post-
Restoration stage history, the play has been many things: it has
served diverse political agendas; advanced actor-manager
careers; helped mark the turn to Elizabethan modernism; and
helped mark the turn to Shakespearean textual 'purity'. In the

[x]

last third of the twentieth century it was given radically different treatment by 'directors' theatre' directors, it has been turned into educational television programming, and, in 2011, appeared as an action film. As with all of Shakespeare's plays, artists have long used *Coriolanus'* narrative, language and characters as raw material for their own purposes, shaping this material to make it resonate with particular audiences at particular times and locales. The results of their shaping this raw material, especially since the Second World War, is the subject of this book.

ACKNOWLEDGEMENTS

I would like to thank the following people for their intellectual, moral and material support while I was working on *Coriolanus*: John Astington, Peter Ayers, Rob Conkie, Brad Crombie, Sarah Eichert, Irene and Bernie Frolic, Edwin and Krisztina Heathcote, John Jowett, József and Irma Juhász, Barbara Hodgdon, Peter Holland, Gordon Jones, Margaret Jane Kidnie, Alexander Leggatt, Luella Massey, Mónika Nagy, George and Margaret Ormsby, Domenico Pietropaolo, John Ripley, Veronika Schandl, Annette Staveley, Alison Turner and members of various seminars at the Shakespeare Association of America and at the American Society for Theatre Research's Shakespeare in Performance Working Group. I would also like to thank staff at the British Library's Sound Archive, D-Films in Toronto, ExMachina Theatre Company in Québec City, the Folger Shakespeare Library, the Globe Theatre archive, the Katona József Theatre in Budapest, the National Theatre archive, the New York Public Library's Billy Rose Theatre Collection, the Országos Színháztörténeti Múzeum és Intézet in Budapest and the Shakespeare Birthplace Trust. I greatly appreciate Cambridge University Press allowing me to reprint a version of 'Québécois Shakespeare goes global: Robert Lepage's *Coriolan*', which appeared in *Shakespeare Survey* 64 (2011). I am very grateful for the funding from Memorial University of Newfoundland, the Society for Theatre Research and the University of Toronto that allowed me to undertake research for this book. Each stage of my writing has benefited from Jill Levenson's encouragement and commentary, and my task would have been impossible without her. Matthew Frost at Manchester University Press has been tremendously helpful in bringing this book to completion. Special thanks are due to series editors Jim Bulman and Carol Chillington Rutter; their patience, insight and generously constructive feedback greatly improved every aspect of this volume. Elizabeth Ormsby and Ágnes Juhász-Ormsby endured the writing process with more grace than should be expected of anyone. This book is dedicated to Ágnes.

CHAPTER I

Introduction – *Coriolanus* from the seventeenth to the twentieth century

The play in the early modern theatre

Coriolanus resonated for a Jacobean London audience through performance, assuming it actually was performed in the early seventeenth century. In fact, there is not much that we know for certain about the tragedy in early modern England, and Ripley sensibly warns that '[a]ny attempt to recreate a Jacobean performance of *Coriolanus* is largely a speculative venture' because 'not a scrap of solid evidence related to the play's original staging has emerged' outside the 1623 Folio's pages (36). The play's date of composition and performance is usually placed somewhere between 1605 and 1610, when it might have been acted at the Globe theatre, though, according to later seventeenth-century documents, it was supposedly staged in the private indoor theatre at Blackfriars, which the King's Men secured for their own use in 1608 (George, '*Coriolanus* at the Blackfriars?' 491; Parker, Introduction 87; Ripley 372 n.10.). Exactly when it could have played at Blackfriars is unclear, though Parker, who believes that *Coriolanus*' 'sardonic tone, long passages of constitutional debate and heavy use of legal terminology' would have appealed to the indoor theatre's wealthy clientele, suggests a date somewhere between 1608 and 1610. It was thus, possibly, one of the first dramas to be performed by the King's Men at Blackfriars (Parker, Introduction 86–88). Of course, it could have played both at the Globe and at their new venue, and, despite his own cautionary words about recreating the original production, Ripley argues that the 'neutral canvas' of either theatre's performance space 'allowed [*Coriolanus*'] calculated groupings, patterned entrances, and mannered posings to shape the narrative with uncompromising clarity', while its indeterminate action and harsh language 'steadily alienated the sensibilities and challenged the interpretive powers of an audience situated above, below, and around it' (51).

What kinds of resonances, then, would *Coriolanus* have had for the alienated audiences who surrounded its neutral canvas? For those who see the play as 'Shakespeare's most detailed analysis of politics' (Vickers 7) or as 'hugely, indeed grotesquely, political' (Jagendorf 232), it should come as no surprise that a large body of criticism exists elucidating the play's topicality. The Plebeians' complaints have been repeatedly analysed in light of grain shortage riots across early modern England, especially in the Midlands in 1607, where Shakespeare was involved in the malting business (Eastman; Hindle; Sharp; Wilson). Coriolanus' aristocratic disdain for the Plebeians' desire to have a voice in Roman politics has been linked to Jacobean absolutism, to the nature of electoral franchise in Tudor and Stuart England and to conflicts between Crown and Parliament (Goldberg; Marcus; Miller, 'Topicality'). The hero's hatred of dissembling self-display has been connected to the rhetoric of antitheatrical tracts that circulated in the late sixteenth and early seventeenth centuries (Lehnhof; Ormsby; Sanders). *Coriolanus* supposedly entered into debates about the purveyance of goods for the royal household (Zeeveld), union with Scotland (Garganigo), increased autonomy for municipal authorities (Marcus, Shrank) and the question of military support for Protestantism on the Continent (Wells, 'Manhood'). Certain characters in the play ostensibly represent (directly and indirectly) politicians in Shakespeare's England, including King James (Miller, 'Topicality'), his son Prince Henry (Wells, 'Manhood'), the Second Earl of Essex (Sharp) and Baron Brooke, Fulke Greville (Wilson).

While such a list of political subjects illuminates concerns that are central to the culture of which *Coriolanus* was a part, scholarship on the play's topicality reveals that the tragedy's politics extend far beyond a mere litany of allusions. When Stanley Cavell, eschewing a strictly topical reading, writes that the play 'is about the formation of the political, the founding of the city, about what it is that makes a rational animal fit for conversation, for civility' (165), he vaguely but judiciously describes the play's politics as one of fundamental human transaction. Parker is more specific when he argues that Shakespeare dramatizes politics as 'a triple interaction between three forces: individual character; that individual's institutions, including the family which is the basic institution; and society as a whole, which is at the same time the product and the cause of the other two. Hence the cultural knot between mother and country which Coriolanus cannot untie, and of which Volumnia is as much victim as the agent' (Introduction 11). Yet *Coriolanus* is also about politics *as performance*. It is about the formation of the political in the sense of people agreeing to perform in mutually binding social acts with civility or, in the First Citizen's words, to act 'kindly' (2.3.71). Out of the binding relations that Parker discerns emerge the play's political specificity and its connections to early modern England. These political connections, of course, are filtered through Roman characters and history (or legend) and are arrayed in *Coriolanus* as a series of tremendous performance 'opportunities', as Ripley puts it. These opportunities include the performance of military feats, processions, the staging of election to office and intensely personal supplications, all of which are connected to Martius' self-consciously performative identity.

Shakespeare structures *Coriolanus* to introduce in the first three scenes the hero's crucial relationships to the Citizens and the Tribunes, Aufidius and the Volsces, and Volumnia and his family, but the remainder of the first act is dominated by military action. It is Martius' performance in the battle scenes that transforms him into Coriolanus, and solidifies the impression of his singularity. This military singularity would have been all the more pronounced for Jacobean spectators if the role had been taken by the company's leading man, Richard Burbage, who, Parker notes, was a 'crack swordsman' (Introduction 107). The battles allow Martius to extend his self-definition through the attempted negation of his relationship to his fellow Romans. Twice Shakespeare gives the lead actor an opportunity to prove himself a 'tear-throat' (Parker, Introduction 107) by berating the other Roman soldiers, just as he had berated the Roman Citizens in 1.1: immediately before the two sides fight, he threatens to turn his comrades into the enemy and cut them down if they do not fight well (1.4.28–29); just after the Romans are beaten back, he unleashes a characteristic stream of invective, cursing the men whom he now calls 'Boils and plagues' (1.5.2). Shakespeare also singles out Martius by giving him emblematic action and gestures to perform in the thick of the fight. According to the Folio stage directions, he twice (1.5 and 1.7) emerges alone from Corioles covered in blood; both are potentially spectacular entrances that could be seen as symbolic 'of triumphant re-birth' (Adelman 152) from within the town after which he is renamed, a form of performative self-authoring that implicitly codes the theatre's tiring-house space as a womb, thus mitigating Volumnia's claims of maternal ownership of her son.

Admittedly, reconstructing the stage business in this way is a conclusion more likely to be arrived at upon reflection in the study than by witnessing quickly unfolding action in the theatre but the emblematic quality of another of Martius' battlefield transformations would have been readily legible for the Jacobean spectator. Specifically, when the Roman soldiers wave their swords and hoist Martius aloft, he is both literally and symbolically superior to them. His words, 'O, me alone! Make you a sword of me?' (1.7.77), help turn him metaphorically into an inanimate singular killing instrument that does not have to participate as a human in human affairs. Subsequently, he seems to prove his uniqueness, his lack of need for others by overcoming his enemy Aufidius, who is, by contrast, shamed by the help he gets from the other Volsces. Yet the theatrical effects of the fight for Corioles would not have depended on Martius alone; the other actors would have provided the performative context for his singularity. The hero performs with murderous virtuosity amidst a swirl of thrilling, bustling activity. Shakespeare sweeps the action of the battle forward rapidly in a handful of relatively brief scenes that are filled with alarums and flourishes as the Romans parley, fight, retreat, advance, march on to the stage with drums and trumpets and celebrate their victory. The actors playing the soldiers would have provided Jacobean theatregoers with the visceral excitement of their collective voice and actions, in ways that emphasized their *connection* with Martius: lifting him up and shouting in unison as they waved their weapons would have made a 'sword' of Martius, but one that the soldiers wielded in hoisting him; when they 'cast ... up their caps and lances' and first cried 'Martius' (1.10.40.1–2) and later 'Martius Caius Coriolanus' (1.10.67), their soldierly voices ringing out in either the Globe or the Blackfriars theatre would have powerfully demonstrated their endorsement of Martius' place among them. In other words, the theatrical effects of his exceptionalism

[4]

would have been produced in conjunction with his fellow Romans, and it is this reliance on others to fulfil his performances that he finds so hard to accept.

Coriolanus' link to others in the play as those who witness and 'complete' his performances almost as if they were themselves audience members is especially pronounced in Shakespeare's use of processions or ceremonial entries, types of public performance not unfamiliar to early modern Londoners. The entry in 2.1 might well have reminded early modern theatregoers of James I's 1604 Coronation entry to London, which David George suggests Shakespeare himself probably saw ('*Coriolanus'* Triumphal Entry' 163), and which Anthony Miller remarks was characterized by a 'studiously classical iconography' (273). Whether or not this procession did actually remind seventeenth-century spectators of a specific royal entry, the processions of Act 2 suggest the 'politically integrative function' of the historical quasi-dramatic triumphal entries that were supposed to convert military victory into civic cohesion (Miller, 'Domains' 269). In both 2.1 and 2.2 the processions are designed to depict Coriolanus' centrality to Rome. In 2.1, the entry would have stressed Coriolanus' military identity: he wears the garland of victory, enters between the generals Cominius and Titus Lartius, and is surrounded by soldiers. Although the public procession through the streets is narrated by Brutus and the Messenger, Coriolanus is still very much the centre of Rome's rapt attention. In 2.2 the emphasis shifts to civilian life. Coriolanus enters the Senate accompanied by his general Cominius but he is also surrounded by Patricians, the Tribunes and Lictors, representatives of Roman law, not war. In both Act 2 processions Coriolanus is praised for his former military service, and in the latter he is presented to the Senators (as quasi-audience members) for them to appraise his worthiness for political office. In both scenes, Coriolanus rejects the attention, even exiting the Senate/playing space in 2.2 to avoid the ceremonial praise.

The early modern audience might not have immediately seen in Coriolanus' rejection of praise the topicality of James's and the English aristocracy's aversion to 'contaminat[ion] by' a 'new model of social relations created by' London's rising mercantile class (Miller, 'Domains' 281), but the staging of the three processions in the last two scenes would have made clear to the original theatregoers the consequences of Coriolanus 'import[ing] the military ethos into the city' rather than 'le[aving] it outside', as should have been the case in historical triumphal entries (Miller, 'Domains' 269). Volumnia's 5.5 entry mirrors Coriolanus' earlier ones, but does so with telling differences. Jacobean spectators would have seen something similar to the procession from 2.2, as Volumnia and the other women enter with political representatives (Senators and Lords). Thus, although she 'is greeted with the marks of a triumphator', her 'triumph marks [a] bloodless victory' (Miller, 'Domains' 276) in the sense that her diplomacy won Rome its respite. As the 'triumphator' who processed across the Blackfriars or Globe stage, she also would have exceeded the martial bonds that linked her to Coriolanus by superseding him; she is the one heralded in this ceremonial entry as 'the life of Rome' (5.5.1). Supplanting Coriolanus, though, entails his sacrifice (Miller, 'Domains' 277), so her victory is not wholly bloodless, and the duality of the triumph may have been reflected in performance by the procession's accompaniment by both 'martial and non-martial instruments' (Parker, Introduction 100). Volumnia's transformation into the processing Roman victor her son had once been adds an irony to Coriolanus' entry to the Volsces in 5.6, the victorious nature of which had already been undercut with the dramatic irony of Aufidius' plotting at the top of the scene. Unlike his mother's entry, Coriolanus appears with drums and colours, aural and visual cues for the early modern theatregoers signalling Coriolanus' attempt to provide a military façade for the non-military victory – the treaty – that he gives the Volsces. That is, for an early modern audience relatively familiar with public pageantry, the banners and martial music would have been the outward, readily legible theatrical signs of the irony that, in contrast to the warlike conflict he brought back to civilian life in Rome after beating the Volsces, he now brings the Volsces negotiated peace in the guise of warlike victory. Shakespeare completes this gestural irony in Coriolanus' funeral procession. Aufidius' act of standing on Coriolanus' corpse would have established bluntly and powerfully for Jacobean spectators the Volsce's superiority over his dead enemy while amplifying the irony of the fact that Coriolanus' 'murderer ... speaks his eulogy' (Parker, Introduction 115). Shakespeare maintains this conflicted atmosphere moments later when the

[6]

'dead march' plays for the defeated hero being processed off the stage, 'his blood-soaked corpse ... borne aloft by Aufidius' and three other Volsces, 'reflect[ing] ironically that earlier emblematic gesture in 1.6, when an equally blood-soaked Martius was brandished like a sword by beaten Roman soldiery as their fetish against defeat' (Parker, Introduction 115).

Coriolanus' uneasy reliance upon other characters as quasi-audience members who bear witness to political ceremonies analogous to those in early modern England characterizes the theatrically intense and complex action during and immediately after his election as Consul in 2.3. While Coriolanus' election to the consulship is a threat to Brutus' and Sicinius' power, the Tribunes' election is, according to Oliver Arnold, 'a disaster for the people' (192), because it is a form of political containment, not enfranchisement for the Plebeians: 'they agree to lay down their "strong arms" in exchange for *voices* in the political system' (198, emphasis in original), and thereby give themselves over to the power of their representatives. Arnold argues that the disenfranchising elections in *Coriolanus* are modelled upon early modern English parliamentary selection ceremonies in which the voters had no real power because normally they were simply presented with candidates whom they had to affirm (187). The Third Citizen succinctly describes the restrictions on their role in legal process of electing Coriolanus Consul in similar terms: 'it is a power that we have no power to do' (2.3.4–5). But this Citizen continues by coding their power to elect as public display that involves a physical violation of Coriolanus' body: 'if he show us his wounds and tell us his deeds, we are to put our tongues into those wounds and speak for them' (2.3.5–7). This metaphorical violence, which turns Coriolanus' once-heroically active and performing body into a passive one that is acted upon, may be a vivid reflection of the anxiety that early modern elites had about the electorate, but the wounds have both political and theatrical significance. Just as Coriolanus depends upon the People's voices to affirm his identity as Consul, so the actor playing him (Burbage or otherwise) relies upon the theatre audience (Jacobean or otherwise) to affirm his subjectivity or his status as a character. As Cynthia Marshall argues, the wound ceremony 'require[s] collusion ... from the audience' in the playhouse (101): the audience's knowledge that the wounds are false creates a sense of theatrical distance from the performance; they become 'real' (101) only when a 'viewer who imagines the wounds completes the theatrical circuit and, in a certain sense, creates the character by incorporating his or her thoughts and feelings' (107). Such contentions about the theatre are not necessarily specific to early modern performance, but, by crafting a ceremony that openly mirrors seventeenth-century elections, one that requires Coriolanus to act a part that is judged by a group akin to the Blackfriars or Globe spectators, Shakespeare was arguably positing that actual human identity, like Jacobean politics, is inherently theatrical; like the effect of subjectivity in the theatre, both are formed through transaction with an audience.

This line of argument about the scene's complex metatheatricality is, perhaps, another instance of knowledge derived from scholarly reflection after the theatrical fact, but, if early modern audiences saw an image of themselves as theatregoers and voters in the Roman Citizens in 2.3, 3.1 and 3.3, Shakespeare reveals the Citizens' political power (directed by the Tribunes), in theatrically exciting ways. In 2.3 seventeenth-century spectators watched the Tribunes 'stage managing' the Plebeians in planning to remove Coriolanus' Consulship. In 3.1 the People manifest their political power as a participatory quasi-audience but once more they give themselves and their political support over to the direction of Brutus and Sicinius: they reply with unified voices to Sicinius' 'Hear me, people, peace!' with 'Let's hear our tribune! Peace! Speak, speak, speak!' (193–194), to Brutus' 'Aediles, seize him' with a collective 'Yield, Martius, yield' (214–215), and they support their representatives with the physical violence of the 'mutiny' (229).[2] The theatrical vitality of the Citizens' unified, near-choral speech is even greater in 3.3, though the Tribunes' plotting at the start of the scene leaves no doubt that the People's collective power is again being channelled by their elected representatives. In this scene, the Citizens appear to lose the individuality that they demonstrated at the start of 1.1 and 2.3, when they were fractious but able to conduct fairly rational debates; now the Citizens cohere as a group merely to paraphrase closely the Tribunes. In particular, they intone 'It shall be so' five times, a repetition that takes on a mindless, chanted quality (107–108, 120). To the extent that their chanting actually provided a chilling effect in the Jacobean playhouse, one related to their unified identity as a dangerous mob

[8]

of indistinguishable 'fragments' (1.1.220), the metatheatrical violence of the tongues-in-wounds metaphor would have become a powerfully embodied theatrical fact. Shakespeare thus likely offered seventeenth-century spectators compelling confrontations that, ironically, invited the theatregoers to see themselves in the Plebeians-as-audience while playing on a perception of the Jacobean political elite's contempt for early modern voters as nothing more than affirmative voices that exist to do that elite's bidding.

Whatever theatrical power such 'public' scenes had on the early modern stage, some of the play's most potentially dramatic action occurs as (virtually) private encounters or supplications. In 4.5, when Coriolanus turns himself over to Aufidius, the Volsce conveys intense personal emotion in his erotically charged speeches, beginning with Aufidius' rapturous 'O Martius, Martius!' (102). Aufidius maintains this erotic tone by comparing this meeting with Coriolanus to seeing his wife on his wedding night and by revealing his almost sexual dreams of hand-to-hand battle between the two men. However, Aufidius' passionate declamation follows Coriolanus' highly theatrical supplication: he builds suspense by slowly revealing his identity, removing his scarf to show his face, and in an overtly theatrical gesture proffering his throat for the cutting. Shakespeare stresses the theatrical nature of this action by having Aufidius comment on Coriolanus' costume and by having the two servants step forward at the end of it and comment on the performance as if they were discussing a play at the interval. The emphasis on gesture and guise echoes Volumnia's urgent pleading with her son in 3.2. The emotional intensity of their encounter is the result of their personal connection: when she chastises, 'Thy valiantness was mine, thou suck'st it from me, / But owe thy pride thyself' (131–132), he is clearly wounded by the charge of filial impiety, replying at once 'Pray be content. / Mother, I am going to the market-place' (132–133). Yet their interaction – or performance – is watched by others on stage (Cominius and Menenius), which is appropriate since Volumnia instructs her son how to persuade spectators with carefully calculated gestures and demeanour.

Shakespeare dramatizes the power that such performance can have when Volumnia tries out her own supplicating gestures on Coriolanus, during what is arguably the play's emotional high-point, the women's embassy in 5.3. Although she kneels in deference to Coriolanus, she repeatedly berates him by playing on his filial duty, and the performance leads to one of the most potentially poignant moments in Shakespearean drama, Coriolanus 'hold[ing] her by the hand, silent' (5.3.183). Of course, the ironic disjunction between her kneeling and belligerent words echoes her son's ultimately unsuccessful performance in the vote scene of 2.3. Yet the disjunction between physical disposition and speech here exemplifies the fact that Volumnia is both Coriolanus' nurturing mother and the woman who transmits to him 'the masculinist, militarist ideology of Rome' (Kahn 147) and she makes this point explicitly by comparing his assault on his homeland to treading on her womb (5.3.124–125). It is impossible to know whether or not Jacobean theatregoers recognized that Shakespeare was extending a classical tradition of militarist mothers depicted in texts available at the time. It seems safer to say that they could have understood the scene to depict yet another performance within the fictional action of the play where a witness to that action parallels the actual spectatorship of the theatregoers. As the Plebeians used Coriolanus' public performance in 2.3 against him, the witness, Aufidius, will accentuate the political nature of Volumnia's connection to her son by turning the private performance between family members into an act of treason against the Volsces. Shakespeare thus remains constant to what he had revealed in the play's processions and vote scene, scenes that seventeenth-century spectators might have recognized as dramatizations of their own experience. That is, there is no world elsewhere for the individual, isolated hero; even the play's most intimate, personal attachments are, at bottom, political, and the political is, fundamentally, a matter of performance.

Political debates, analogous to those performed in *Coriolanus*, played out historically in the seventeenth century as the English Civil War, including the 1649 execution of Charles I. Of course, this political cause had the theatrical effect of closing the public playhouses in 1642 for nearly twenty years, until shortly after the restoration of Charles II. When *Coriolanus* made its next appearance, early in the third decade of Charles II's reign, the play's political identity would sharpen considerably, as it became a vehicle for partisan polemic. Over the next three hundred-plus years, many or most productions were less explicit about their partisan politics, though such productions never lacked political import. The rest of the introduction is devoted to a survey of *Coriolanus* stagings, both overtly and covertly political, from the Restoration to the early twentieth century. My account of these productions draws on numerous sources but is significantly indebted to Ripley's magisterial study of the play in performance. A large part of what distinguishes this volume from Ripley's is a reversal of emphasis; his focus is mostly on pre-1940s productions; this book is primarily concerned with those of the postwar era.

Coriolanus as polemic: 1682–1749

The first known production of *Coriolanus* is Nahum Tate's version of the play, *The Ingratitude of A Common-Wealth*, staged in early 1682 at London's Theatre Royal, Drury Lane. Often remembered as the man who scripted a happy conclusion to *King Lear*, Tate inaugurated seven decades of polemical *Coriolanus* productions by using his adaptation to participate in contemporary debates about the balance of power between a single ruler and the general populace. In 1681 Charles II was embroiled in a years-long quarrel with a faction in Parliament about the official exclusion of his Roman Catholic brother James, Duke of York, from succeeding to the throne. Sentiment against James had grown in reaction to the Popish Plot, a false conspiracy supposedly devised by Catholic forces to assassinate the king. Those MPs seeking to exclude James from the succession, a group that developed into the Whig party, were defeated in their efforts to make the Exclusion Bill law by a combination of Charles proroguing Parliament and the House of Lords finally rejecting the legislation passed by the Commons. The theatres, under the patronage of the Crown, backed their king, and, as Tate's title suggests, he reworked the play to support the royal (or Tory) cause, making it but 'one of a number of dramatic contributions to an anti-Whig propaganda campaign waged by the Tories between 1680 and 1683' (Ripley 55). Indeed, Tate explicitly stated that '*The Moral ... of these Scenes*' is '*to Recommend Submission and Adherence to Establisht Lawful Power, which in a word, is* Loyalty' (McGugan 3).

Instead of making explicit topical allusions, Tate reveals his sympathies by 'improving' Martius' behaviour, by making the

[11]

Tribunes and the Plebeians less attractive, and by generating pathos through the suffering of the hero's family. Tate maintains his focus on the conflict between Coriolanus and the People by minimizing the conflict between the Romans and the Volsces; of the some fifteen scenes he removes from Shakespeare's play, Tate scripts only two battlefield scenes and deletes Shakespeare's 1.2, in which Aufidius discusses the military situation with the Volscian Senators. Throughout, the Tribunes are more tersely cynical, their lines having been significantly reduced. The Citizens are especially fickle, and reveal their dangerous mutability in Tate's 4.3, when Rome learns of Coriolanus' planned invasion; they end the scene by '*Haling and Dragging off the* Tribunes' to their apparent doom (McGugan 79). Coriolanus, meanwhile, is 'improved' through his familial relationships. Volumnia bends him to her will in Act 3 and in the women's embassy by appealing to his patriotism, stressing his love of country more than to any infantilizing debt he owes her. While downplaying any perverse connection to Volumnia, Tate plays up Coriolanus' wholesome connection to his child and wife. Coriolanus asks for his son to be brought to him during his exile leave-taking but, after a stirring speech to Young Martius, he asks that the boy be removed because the emotion is too much to bear. Martius is also closer to Virgilia, especially during the women's embassy, when she pleads far more emotionally with her husband than she does in Shakespeare's script. However, Tate saves the most violent family passions for his final scene. Having learned, upon their triumphant return to Rome, that Aufidius' henchman Nigridus (one of Tate's innovations) intends to kill Coriolanus, the family goes back to Coriolanus, who has remained with the Volsces. They are detained by Aufidius, who plans to rape Virgilia; a dying wife is eventually reunited with the expiring Coriolanus, and Volumnia, driven insane by her grandson's brutal torture, brings Young Martius to his father for a final round of pathos-heavy lamentations. Tate's additions to this scene not only reveal the chaos that ensues from factionalism but are meant to generate pity for the man who should have been respected by his countrymen for the service he rendered them.

Although it is not certain who acted in the production, or how the production was received, we can discern a number of things about its staging in conditions very different from those in which Shakespeare worked. Besides employing women in the professional public theatre of the Restoration, the indoor performance space was unlike the encompassing space at the Globe. The stage projection was an apron of less than twenty feet, and much of the action took place within the area behind the proscenium arch. Restoration scenic design vaguely indicated location using painted flats that could be slid on and off stage in grooves in the stage floor. Ripley argues that Tate made good use of what forestage there was by massing Plebeians on the apron during the uprising of 1.1, during the Citizens' dialogue with Coriolanus when seeking the Consulship, and when the People dragged away the Tribunes (Ripley 65–67). Putting the unruly Citizens up close to the theatregoers contributed to Tate's polemic, giving the spectators a visceral sense of 'the risks inherent in popular suffrage' (Ripley 67). Tate made frequent use of discoveries, in which flats were opened to reveal tableaux. In 2.2 a white toga-clad Coriolanus was discovered and visually elevated by being set off against a group of Senators who surrounded him. For the tableau of Menenius embassy in 4.4 the discovery revealed 'Coriolanus seated in State, in a rich Pavillion' (McGugan 79). He was once again at the centre of attention, surrounded both by likeminded '*Guards and Souldiers with lighted Torches, as ready to set Fire on* Rome' and '*Petitioners as from the* Citty' whom he disdainfully rejected (McGugan 79). After Coriolanus turned down Menenius's request, a trumpet sounded, and the tableau began to move, '*Advanc*[ing] *with their Lights*' (McGugan 80) to torch Rome. However, their advance was dramatically checked by the entrance of Coriolanus' family '*in Mourning*' (McGugan 80), enacting a stark confrontation between the hero's military instincts and his familial duty. The final scene, too, began as a discovery of '*The* Lords *of* Corioles, *as set in Councel*' (McGugan 96) but it was the carefully plotted action that was most important to driving Tate's agenda here, as he stacked the corpses at the end to build sympathy for the hero. Aufidius gloatingly planned to rape Virgilia before Coriolanus' eyes but recanted and, in the interest of poetic justice, died almost as soon as he saw the self-wounded Virgilia brought in. Similarly, when Nigridus boasted of torturing Young Martius, Tate amplified the pity by having a '*Distracted*' (McGugan 103) Volumnia bring on the bloodied boy but deliver more poetic justice by dispatching

Nigridus before running off stage. With the dead Virgilia on one arm and his son's corpse in the other, Coriolanus delivered his sad farewell to the world, offering a glimpse of something that will become familiar in future stagings of *Coriolanus*, even ones quite differently politicized from *Ingratitude*: the emphatic focus on the plight of the individual hero, the star of the performance, whose familial bonds bring to the fore his personal and emotionally charged suffering.

John Dennis's *The Invader of His Country* took the play in virtually the opposite direction, shaping it into Whig polemic. Dennis probably started writing *Invader* in 1708, two decades after James II (who survived the Exclusion crisis to come to the throne in 1685) was deposed and replaced by his daughter Mary and her husband, William of Orange (Ripley 71). By the time *Invader* finally appeared at Drury Lane, the exiled James had been defeated at the Battle of the Boyne (1690) when trying to invade Ireland, his son James (the 'Old Pretender') had made an unsuccessful invasion attempt in Scotland in 1708, and another Scottish Jacobite uprising had failed in 1715. During that time the Hanoverian king George I had taken the throne, and the Whig party had begun its ascent. Dennis underscores the political thrust of the play against invaders like the Stuarts in his dedication to the young Whig Lord Chamberlain (and future prime minister), Thomas Pelham-Holles. In that dedication Dennis complains of Drury Lane's theatrical managers (Colly Cibber, Richard Steele and Barton Booth, the last of whom played Coriolanus) in political metaphors, angry both that they closed the production after only three performances and that they postponed the production for a year in 1718 when 'a Double Invasion' from Sweden and Spain seemed imminent, and which Dennis wanted his play to answer 'in the Cause' of England (A3). The Prologue, meanwhile, relates that Shakespeare's '*Masterstrokes*' needed to be '*brought to as much Order*' (B3) as possible, indicating that Dennis's political message would be conveyed according to neoclassical principles.

He cut the play to ten scenes in accordance with the neoclassical pursuit of the unities of action and place. The Plebeians behave more bravely in battle than they do in Shakespeare's play but their comic mugging and cowardice in 2.3 would have primed theatregoers to see them as a violent rabble in Act 4, hauling away the Tribunes to be thrown from the Tarpeian rock.[3]

The treatment of the People did not dignify the democratic process but neither would Coriolanus have made a positive impression on those spectators passionate about political enfranchisement. In particular, Cominius is given the role of his chastising instructor, lecturing him at the end of the first act that they live 'in a Free State, a State / That's so much founded on Equality' (11). Yet Dennis was not interested in a complexly ignoble autocrat for a hero and sought to exalt and generate sympathy for him in performance. In Act 4, the arrival of Booth's Coriolanus at the Volsce Senate was given a spectacular edge when it was revealed as a discovery. Coriolanus' betrayal of Rome was signalled by Booth moving, at the request of John Mills's Aufidius, from the forestage, where he first entered the scene, to the upstage area, where the Senators were gathered. However, Booth's Coriolanus was also glorified visually here, when the Senators rose as a group to welcome him with a cheer, accentuating his singular heroic stature. Coriolanus' interview with the women (Mary Porter as Volumnia and Sarah Thurmond as Virgilia), meanwhile, was held in private, as Mills exited shortly after they arrived. The scene, complete with Porter's Volumnia offering of the dagger with which her son could kill her (70), was thus staged to heighten the power of the admirable familial bond which motivated the hero. Dennis extended this private emotion to the confrontation between Coriolanus and Aufidius; Booth and Mills were alone on stage together when Coriolanus killed his old foe. The stage then began to fill again with several Volsce Tribunes seeking revenge for Aufidius' death, and the women, off stage, added horror to the confrontation by shrieking as Booth killed three of the Tribunes before a fourth ran 'him thro' the Back' (77). The women re-entered the instant Booth collapsed and they amplified sympathy for him in their final emotional exchange. The production concluded on a clear note of poetic justice: John Thurmond's Cominius arrived to serve as the author's mouthpiece, excusing Coriolanus' invasion but ensuring that theatregoers understood the wages of his sin by reminding them that anyone who invades his homeland will receive their own justice at the hands of 'their perfidious Foreign Friends' (79).

Written during the final attempts at a Jacobite uprising, James Thomson's *Coriolanus* (1749) was, according to David Wheeler, 'the last of the [eighteenth] century's overtly political' versions of the play (292). Thomson probably began writing his *Coriolanus* in 1742 but left it off until 1745, the year that Charles Edward Stuart, son of the 'Old Pretender', landed in Scotland to raise an army in support of the Jacobite cause (Ripley 82). Although the hopes for the return of the house of Stuart were defeated along with 'Bonnie Prince Charlie' at the Battle of Culloden in 1746, parallels between Coriolanus and the invading heir aspirant would still have been current in 1749, when the play was finally staged at Covent Garden, with James Quin in the title role. While the Covent Garden run lasted 'a more than respectable' ten performances, the production was originally meant only to be a one-off benefit to discharge the by-then deceased Thomson's debts (Ripley 93). However, Ripley argues that, while Thomson was a 'Whig propagandist', this *Coriolanus* was 'less partisan' than some of his earlier work and that the play is less remarkable for its politics than for its 'radical affirmation of neoclassical aesthetics and its innovative and spectacular stagecraft, both of which were to have their influence on subsequent stage realizations of Shakespeare's text' (83).

Thomson maintained a neoclassical unity of action by removing Shakespeare's first three acts so that the production began with Quin's Coriolanus arriving at the Volsce camp as they await the Roman reply to their peace offer (they are on the verge of attacking Rome). He maintained a unity of place by setting all the scenes among the Volsces, with minor changes of location often indicated by discoveries. After Quin's Coriolanus offered himself to Lacy Ryan's Tullus Attius (the Aufidius figure) and Rome rejected the peace offer, Thomson's new Volscian character, Galesus (whom Coriolanus had reportedly saved during battle), played by Denis Delane, warned Coriolanus not to be overly vengeful in retaliating against Rome. Thomson adds his own nefarious Volsce officer, Volusius, who works on Tullus' jealousy of Coriolanus' military success and would continue to do so in performances well into the next century. Thomson also designs his own spectacular discoveries that glorified the hero. On stage this meant that suspense was built up for Quin's appearance in Act 1 by having a soldier tell Ryan's Tullus of a stranger who was sitting 'majestic ... in solemn silence', making the soldier feel 'As if the presence of some God had struck' him (215), and then revealing Quin in this pose for spectators to admire. In Act 2 the actor was elevated in another discovery

[16]

when '*the* Volsican *States*' who '*rose and saluted* Coriolanus' were revealed (231). The final discovery, which opened Act 5, was the production's most dramatic. It revealed the Roman women in mourning dress entering among the soldiers, thus creating a divide between Coriolanus' familial and comradely loyalties. Thomson established this contrast so the theatregoers could witness Quin's Coriolanus weaken overtly: '*when he perceived his mother and wife, after some struggle, he advanced and went hastily to embrace them*' (268). Thomson here followed the neoclassical requirement of a fundamentally noble hero, using the pathos of the ensuing encounter to help sanitize Coriolanus. Peg Woffington's Veturia (Thomson's name for Volumnia) and George Anne Bellamy's Volumnia (Thomson's name for Virgilia) worked on his loyalty to them and to Rome, and Thomson's stage directions carefully detail Coriolanus' agitated demeanour as the women were to wear him down in performance. This wearing-down included the moment when Woffington's Veturia wielded her dagger, which Quin's Coriolanus said she should turn on him 'to reconcile [his] fighting duties' (277). The ensuing action turned back to political concerns. Coriolanus and Tullus quarrelled and, when the former refused the latter's offer of a safe return to Rome, Ryan called in Isaac Sparks's Volusius and the Conspirators cowardly dispatched Coriolanus. The production ended with a reassertion of neoclassical poetic justice: echoing the author's moralizing sentiments, Delane's didactic Galesus stepped forward to remind the audience of the action's political import in a way that upheld Coriolanus' individual virtue. Addressing himself as much to the Volsces as to those in the auditorium, Delane pronounced Coriolanus the 'glory of his age', whose lone 'blot' was that 'He rais'd his vengeful arm against his country', for which crime 'the righteous gods have chastis'd him' (286). It is a fitting eulogy to a production that had sought both to be topical and to celebrate a less complex heroic individualism than the one that Shakespeare had offered his early seventeenth-century patrons.

Coriolanus in the age of the actor-manager (and beyond)

Thomson's script, with additions from Shakespeare, forms the basis of Thomas Sheridan's *Coriolanus: Or, The Roman Matron*, productions of which arguably represented what would prove to be a long-lasting shift in the nature of *Coriolanus* revivals. Ripley suggests that, beginning with Sheridan in middle of the eighteenth century and continuing through to the end of the nineteenth century, 'actor-managers opted to contain' the tragedy's 'potential political subversiveness' (95). It was not that the eighteenth century lacked urgent political and military struggles that could readily inform *Coriolanus* stagings: ongoing conflict with France until the close of the Napoleonic era and the cataclysmic unfolding of the French Revolution provided plenty of real-life events capable of generating anxiety about the kinds of domestic and foreign strife dramatized in the play. Between Sheridan, whose version dominated production from the 1750s to the 1780s, and John Philip Kemble, who developed Sheridan's innovations in his own masterful performances, the play became a vehicle for actor-managers who were increasingly able to control all aspects of theatrical presentation. Ripley contends that 'the *Coriolanus* revivals of Sheridan and Kemble, to the immense satisfaction of their middle- and upper-class audiences, celebrated the individualistic struggle of an antique military figure, while largely suppressing the class conflict which animates Shakespeare's narrative' (96). Furthermore, by the time Kemble retired from the theatre with a last turn as Coriolanus, the tradition of the hero's individualistic struggle became closely associated with powerful actor-managers. It is this association that would pronounce itself for decades, and it is to Kemble's productions that I will now turn.

John Philip Kemble's productions of *Coriolanus* between 1789 and 1817 are among the most significant in the play's career on stage. Kemble 'singlehandedly canonized the text played in the theater' for more than a century and 'created the visual tradition which, with minor variations, accompanied the play until World War I' (Ripley 114). Kemble's production was not overtly topical but he did use it to make 'a commanding statement against the desirability of popular participation in the political process' (Sachs 195). As Michael Dobson remarks, during 'the era of the French Revolution', all cultural matters, 'including that of the authority and allegiances of Shakespearean drama itself, were inescapably politicized' ('Kemble' 62). Added to fear of unrest and bloodshed generated by the Revolution was the danger posed by Napoleon's armies, and evidence of this politically tense atmosphere was the fact that Kemble removed the play from his repertoire between 1798 and 1805, returning it to the stage in 1806 after threat of a French invasion of Britain had passed. In fact, to the extent that Kemble regarded 'Coriolanus [as] the kind of severe, antique hero of ancient times who would provide ... a moral example in an era of political and social upheaval' (Ripley 116), associations between the role and his own role as actor-manager at Covent Garden were politicized. Kemble's star power was crucial to filling the high-capacity theatre, especially after he rebuilt it after it burned down in 1808. Star power gave Kemble great control over every aspect of his productions, a control he wielded brilliantly, as his 'unusually developed visual sense' (Dobson, 'Kemble' 62) helped him fill the refurbished theatre with crowd-pleasing spectacle. Yet the classically inspired theatre, designed as 'a true temple of dramatic art' (Dobson, 'Kemble' 92), also revealed the actor-manager's class bias; Kemble added many expensive boxes to the new auditorium and raised all ticket prices, leading to the Old Price Riots, rowdy protests that lasted for sixty-seven nights, interrupting performances. Dobson ('Kemble') suggests that Kemble's role as Coriolanus 'could only serve to remind his audiences of his defiant assertions of managerial privilege throughout' the protests (99). However, he is remembered not for his similarities to the arrogant Roman but for the production's spectacle and his epic acting style.

Kemble altered Sheridan's text by adding some Shakespeare and removing some Thomson in order to reduce the variety of others' opinions about Coriolanus, thereby keeping the spectators' attention centred on him.[4] For instance, while Kemble restored cuts traditionally made to Shakespeare's 1.1, he did not restore everything. Menenius had virtually no relationship to the People; instead, he entered with Martius, and it is Martius' anti-Plebeian scorn alone that would have registered in the theatre. Similarly, while Kemble's text has two battlefield scenes, Aufidius is absent from both, so that in performance the hero's military success and transformation into Coriolanus would have had nothing directly to do with any worthy antagonist who might compete with Martius for the theatregoers' admiration. Coriolanus' vote-seeking and the Tribunes' subsequent manipulation of the People are curtailed in the text, though these alterations were probably made to move to the banishment episodes quickly; indeed, Kemble cut 3.3 to move swiftly to the dramatic exit line 'There is a world elsewhere', the new ending to the scene being Sheridan's innovation. By cutting Shakespeare's 4.1–4.3, Kemble was able to proceed almost directly from that powerful exit line to his discovery at Aufidius' house, ensuring that very little interfered with the star's big moments. Finally, Kemble's text maintains the manipulative Volusius, but he did not include Galesus, removing the chance to moralize about Coriolanus' sins. In Kemble's script, Aufidius merely watches while Volusius and the Conspirators murder Coriolanus, and if the Volsce's final speech, taken mostly from Shakespeare, was received by audiences as cynical, this perception would probably have been amplified by the few added lines of praise for the hero slain in an uneven fight.

Kemble designed the production, too, conspicuously to revolve around his own performance. Kemble's address to the audience at the end of his retirement performance as Coriolanus in 1817 offers us a sense of what had motivated this and, indeed, all his performances, namely the 'union of propriety and splendour in the representation of our best plays, and particularly those of the divine Shakespeare' (*An Authentic* 6). Dobson explains this comment by arguing that Kemble 'was the supreme Platonist of the English Shakespearean tradition, committed to making visible in performance the ideal forms which for him were only imperfectly embodied in the plays' printed texts' ('Kemble' 62). The revelation of these 'ideal forms' was connected to both Kemble's and Siddons's 'cultivat[ing] what became known as "the grand style"' (of acting), 'characterized by a deliberate and majestic step, a statuesque grace of action, and formal, stately declamation' (Ripley 117). Although this style is not always discernible in the prompt-book, what that document does reveal is the way that Kemble arranged the action to provide a milieu on stage highly favourable to majestic and statuesque gracefulness. The majesty suggested by the classically inspired interior of Covent Garden itself was reflected in the production's painted backdrops, which offered detailed architectural vistas of Rome. Although the paintings were supposedly inspired by Kemble's informed admiration for the classical past and his own era's fine arts, the scenes were not, strictly speaking, historically accurate. Rather, in keeping with Kemble's conservative biases, the backdrops were idealized images of imperial Rome, evoking a sense of imposing grandeur that had little to do with the early republic's messy squabbles over plebeian enfranchisement. Against these backdrops, he staged massive processions that projected great military power. The ovation procession in Act 2 celebrated Rome's might under Coriolanus' leadership. Broken into four divisions, the procession included priests, boys and girls but was dominated by those carrying the spoils of war, prisoners, silver and gold eagles, banners and soldiers. As each division entered, three shouts rang out, and at the appearance of the fourth division, which was brought up at the rear by Coriolanus, the musicians began playing Handel's 'See the Conquering Hero Comes!' from his opera *Julius Caesar* (Ripley 129). Kemble staged a more modest military procession in Act 4 when Coriolanus was about to attack Rome. This procession was perhaps less than a fifth the size of the ovation but nevertheless gave theatregoers a lavish impression of the power that Coriolanus commanded. The final procession occurred at the top of Act 5, immediately preceding the arrival of the women's embassy. It seems to have been comprised of more than two hundred supernumeraries, and, if so, would have extended the tradition of starkly contrasting the women's humble entrance in mourning costume with the overwhelming presence of the Volsce forces.[5]

Kemble remained throughout a dignified figure who achieved many of his great effects as a static presence, a stasis that suggested his constancy, set as it was against the stage imagery, both painted and living. In the second-act victory ovation Kemble halted under the triumphal arch; theatregoers were invited to see him, framed by the structure associated with his military glory, as the lone and perhaps aloof conquering hero, master of all who passed before him. He modified the by-then traditional discovery of the exiled Coriolanus at Aufidius' house to exalt himself more remarkably than any actor who had yet performed this scene. Kemble was revealed posing next to a statue of Mars, a *coup-de-théâtre* that inspired one of the most famous images of *Coriolanus'* stage history, Sir Francis Bourgeois's *John Philip Kemble as Coriolanus Beneath the Statue of Mars*. The scene presented theatregoers with the most blatant of comparisons between the hero and his divine namesake, though they might have wondered if the statuesque living man (the actor or the character) was, in fact, the model for the statue. Ripley points out, furthermore, that the blocking was designed so that 'the star occupie[d] center stage at all times, and the action in which he [was] engaged [was] the exclusive focus of interest' (125). Such blocking was evident even during the women's embassy, arguably the emotional high-point of the production. After the Volsces entered in procession, Coriolanus and Aufidius seated themselves. Once the women made their entrance, Kemble hardly moved at all, except to stand, sit and kneel; the women did almost all the moving, with each shift in the emotional debate between them signalled by their approach to and retreat from Coriolanus.

Kemble's productions from 1811 onwards left powerful impressions on his audiences. While relatively slight attention was paid to the Tribunes and the People, Sarah Siddons (Kemble's sister), who played the Roman matron between 1789 and 1811, attracted response befitting her status as the greatest actress of her age. The sense of her ability to overpower audiences with her emotion is discernible in reaction to her performance during the ovation, where 'her action lost all grace, and, yet, became so true to nature, so picturesque, and so descriptive, that, pit and gallery sprang to their feet, electrified by the transcendent execution of the conception' (qtd in Ripley 141). The greatest praise, unsurprisingly, was reserved for Kemble, and reaction to his farewell performance is a kind of apotheosis of the admiration he generated over the course of his career in the role. A portion of the response was reprinted in *An Authentic Narrative of Mr. Kemble's Retirement from the Stage*, which also records the speeches given by worthies attending Kemble's retirement dinner shortly after the final performance. The 'admiring thousands' who crowded into Covent Garden 'simultaneously rose to welcome' Kemble's 'entrance, and the reiterated thunders of their salutations, for a considerable time arrested the progress of the play' (*Morning Chronicle* 24 June 1817, qtd in *An Authentic* 12). They were rewarded, apparently, with a 'performance ... such as to gratify and afflict beyond any thing of the kind we ever witnessed ... and as a greater treat cannot be imagined, more sincere regret could not be felt than was proved by all present, while reflecting that such transcendent excellence would delight them no more' (*The Morning Post* 24 June 1817, qtd in *An Authentic* 20). This transcendent excellence could be expressed only in superlatives: 'On Monday night we finally parted with the Master of the Tragic Scene – the most

[22]

graceful, majestic, and classical pillar, which, for the last 20 years, has supported the Fane of the Tragic Muse – Mr. Kemble bade adieu to the stage and the public' (*The News* 29 June 1817, qtd in *An Authentic* 30). Such comments reflect not simply an appreciation of Kemble's exceptionalism but the passing of an age.

Ripley, however, makes a case not for a passing age but for the perpetuation of 'The Kemble Tradition' for nearly a century in England, following the actor's retirement. What undoubtedly remained constant in major English *Coriolanus* stagings were certain spectacular scenic conventions, which predated Kemble considerably, and the traditional diminution of overtly partisan politics in favour of the actor-manager's performance of individual greatness, which Kemble had perfected. Edmund Kean's 1820 production at Drury Lane (under the managership of Robert Elliston) employed a purportedly authentic pre-imperial Roman scenography, which supposedly inspired Charles Macready's and later Henry Irving's attempts at architectural authenticity in their scenic design (in 1838 and 1901 respectively). Macready re-accentuated the spectacle of Thomson's Senate scene, where Roman Senators provided living scenery to glorify Coriolanus, and the scene became crucial to both Irving's staging and Samuel Phelps's productions in the 1840s to 1860s. Sir Frank Benson's touring productions between 1893 and 1919 had fewer resources than Kemble or Irving but Benson took the belief in scenic authenticity even further by employing as his designer Lawrence Alma-Tadema, the same academic painter who helped create Irving's pictorially realistic backdrops. Yet, as Ripley is careful to note, efforts to repeat Kemble's lofty stature 'became softer focused' in the following one hundred years until it 'threatened to disappear forever' (160). Indeed, there was significant variety in the acting styles of *Coriolanus* productions and in the conditions under which they were staged in performances up to the First World War. Edmund Kean, whom Ripley acknowledges was a challenger to the Kemble tradition, played Coriolanus with a kind of vital intensity that reflected the character's individual psyche more than any patrician beliefs (Ripley 158). Charles Macready's acting was arguably closer in certain ways to Kean than he was to Kemble when he played the hero at Covent Garden in 1838, while Samuel Phelps supposedly emphasized his military heroism and his tender feelings for his family

[23]

in performances during the middle of the nineteenth century (Ripley 164, 181). The tremendous talents of the sixty-three-year-old Irving and his Volumnia, Ellen Terry, meanwhile, were ostensibly ill-suited to the tasks they had set themselves in staging the play at the Lyceum Theatre, where the production was retired at the end of the season (Ripley 184, 198).

Although there were fewer notable American than English actor-managers who took on Coriolanus in the nineteenth century, the great American star Edwin Forrest is the performer most comparable to Kemble, if only for the stature he brought to and attained in the role. *Coriolanus* was performed in the United States as early as the 1760s, and was kept before American audiences in the nineteenth century by a number of actors originally from Britain, such as Thomas Abthorp Cooper, William Conway and Thomas Hamblin. Forrest worked with both Conway and Hamblin, and was deeply influenced by Kean. However, Forrest's best-known connection to a fellow Coriolanus is his rivalry with Macready, which embodied contemporary class-inflected tensions between American and English perceptions of cultural self-worth. The rivalry came to a head in the 1849 Astor Place Riot: Forrest and Macready were scheduled to play Macbeth on 10 May at the Broadway Theatre and Astor Place Theatre, respectively; when Forrest's largely working-class supporters violently protested outside Macready's venue, soldiers were called in and opened fire, wounding and killing dozens. The incident seems appropriate for the powerfully built, charismatic and sometimes publicly violent Forrest, who enjoyed the hero-worship of his numerous, and sometimes publicly violent, fans. His fame resulted from his tremendous vocal power and control, his exuberantly physical performance of heroism, the perpetuation of the 'myth of Forrest as a symbol of America [itself] drawing strength from inner resolve' (McConachie, *Melodramatic* 85), and his 'reputation for sincerity and the near identity between his own public image and the image of [his] protagonists' (McConachie, *Melodramatic* 114). Any contradictions between Forrest's devotion to republican democratic ideals and his occasional return to Coriolanus between the 1830s and the 1860s might be explained by the fact that he crafted his celebrity persona in melodramas which were supposedly meant to 'assert the equality of all men', but which were really designed to 'empower a charismatic hero and reduce the people to the status

[24]

of victims' (McConachie, *Melodramatic* 91–92). Probably his mastery of theatrical melodrama led him to shape his *Coriolanus* into 'the moral and social crusade of a Roman frontiersman against a rabble of degenerate ruffians', thereby playing on nineteenth-century fears of 'uncontrolled antebellum economic expansion and urbanization', which led to a 'perceived decline in moral integrity' (Ripley 218).

The text that Forrest used for his New York, Boston and Philadelphia performances in 1863 and 1864, when his technique had fully matured, was indirectly based on Kemble's, though, as the prompt-book reveals, he made a few of his own remarkable additions to the action.[6] Forrest set the action in imperial Rome (flattering American aspirations as a transcontinental power) and staged the by-then conventional spectacular scenes, all intended to magnify Coriolanus' eminence: the massive Act 2 ovation was developed through several sections and included the singing of 'See the Conquering Hero Comes!'; Forrest staged the Senate scene as Macready had, though with fewer supernumeraries than his rival managed; the hero was discovered in Act 4 standing next to the statue of Mars; and the women's embassy was staged as a magnificent discovery. Forrest added to the role a fearless military demeanour in the battle scenes in order to show off his physical prowess. Reflecting his own persona's split between common man and hero-celebrity, he turned the ovation into a delicate balancing act between populism and tyranny by having throngs of Citizens cheer his entry while other Citizens actually drew his victory cart on to the stage themselves. Immediately following his assassination, when Coriolanus was surrounded by throngs of soldiers so the audience could not witness the killing, Forrest created for the hero an aura of elegiac mystery. First, his funeral procession exited, then solemnly crossed over the stage again against a black backdrop. After the procession exited a second time, the backdrop lifted to show a moonlit grove, with Coriolanus' body on a pyre, which was surrounded by a huge crowd that included Senators, soldiers, choristers, Aufidius, Volusius and Coriolanus' family. The choristers sang a dirge for the hero, the priests lit a fire, and, as the body (a dummy) sank into the trap, solemnity and dignity sank into spectacular melodramatic excess: 'A phoenix r[ose] from the flames', signalling that Coriolanus' death was, in fact, a regenerative sacrifice with cosmic resonance. If Forrest's Coriolanus were to stand as a moral exemplar against social decay and if he were to devise a down-to-earth build-up to such a larger-than-life pay-off, he had to take the edge off his anti-democratic sentiments. He did so in part by emphasizing the hero's tenderness for his family, particularly when giving in to his mother in the scene before he is banished and during the women's fifth-act embassy. Forrest got around Coriolanus' anti-democratic bias, meanwhile, by ensuring that the Plebeians he came into contact with were despicably craven and malicious, and that he turned on them only when he had been pushed too far.

While Forrest did not overtly share Kemble's patrician biases, both men enjoyed a celebrity that would have enduring effects on *Coriolanus'* future in the theatre, though the American's fame is perhaps the more telling. Specifically, the hero-worship that allowed Forrest to extend the star-centred tradition of *Coriolanus* 'contradicted the democratic rhetoric' associated with so much of his acting career, exposing 'a central tension in the culture of Jacksonian America' (McConachie, 'Forrest'). Analogous tensions between avowed political convictions and the desire for both spectacle and charismatic lead performances would characterize much of *Coriolanus'* production for the next 150 years. Such tensions were not especially evident in stagings of the play during the 1920s and 1930s, when *Coriolanus* was pushed in the direction of modernist and 'Elizabethan Methodist' techniques (Ripley 240–269). These productions, by directors like William Bridges Adams at Stratford, Robert Atkins at the Old Vic and Nugent Monck at Norwich, did not particularly rely on star actors, nor were they tremendously influential in and of themselves, but they were part of a broader movement to help to restore (to varying degrees) the Shakespearean text, to introduce swift scenic changes that enhanced the flow of the action and to move beyond the constraints of the proscenium enclosure. If many directors avoided specific messages about class, war and enfranchisement, there were some notably political productions. These include Dominic Roche's 1935 modern-dress staging in Manchester and the far more widely publicized 1933–34 staging at the Comédie Française in Paris, which was politicized when it became the pretext for right-wing elements to criticize the leftist national government. The scenic innovations of the early twentieth century would evolve into oft-reiterated aspects of *Coriolanus'* theatrical vernacular, and disavowal of the play's politics in performance would continue until the 1960s, when the lessons of the Berliner Ensemble would be transmuted into the drive for contemporaneity. Although the productions of the 1920s and early to mid-1930s did not have many famous or powerful principal actors, the thirst for charismatic star performances – even in productions marked by explicit political import – would persist for the next eight decades.

CHAPTER II

Olivier's *Coriolanus*

Laurence Olivier's spectacular death plunge at Stratford-upon-Avon's Shakespeare Memorial Theatre (SMT) in 1959 provides *Coriolanus* and postwar British theatre with one of its most striking and best-known images. Having been impaled by Volscian spears, the fifty-two-year-old Olivier, incredibly, dived headfirst from a rocky ledge more than ten feet above the stage. Angus McBean's photograph recreating this scene shows the actor in his short dark wig facing the audience hanging upside down and limp-limbed, held at the ankles by the Volsces on the ledge, who had grabbed Olivier as he fell. The hero's arms and legs are almost fully exposed by his brief Roman tunic-cum-breastplate, and a partial cloak stretches even further to the stage adding to the image's pendulum effect. Meanwhile, Anthony Nicholls's Aufidius, long-haired and dressed in dark furs like his comrades to suggest the Volsces' relative barbarism, lifts his dagger for what looks like a final blow. Fearlessly swashbuckling, the astounding fall was vintage Olivier, a daring development of his death scene twenty-one years earlier at the Old Vic theatre when his Coriolanus tumbled down a flight of stairs, silencing astonished audience members (Ripley 274). Both death scenes arguably embody what John Ripley calls the 'romantic style' of production that provided audiences in the 1930s and 1950s with escape from the harsh realities of 'a depression, the rise of fascism, World War II, and its aftermath', by feeding '[t]he public's appetite for film stars in romantic stage roles' (270). The 1959 fall also embodied Olivier's second take on the Roman general because, despite the necessity of the supporting actors holding him in place upside down, the audacious moment was precisely calculated to show off both the hero and the star who played him. The production's director, Peter Hall, was soon to begin transforming the SMT into the supposedly ensemble-driven Royal Shakespeare Company (RSC) when he became artistic director at Stratford the following year, but in 1959 the SMT was still a star-centred theatre and *Coriolanus*, which exemplified the star system, was the highlight of that celebrity-filled season. Although Olivier was matched with the venerable Dame Edith Evans as Volumnia and although the cast was filled with a number of Britain's next generation of leading actors (including Albert Finney, Vanessa Redgrave and Ian Holm), there is no doubt the production revolved around its star. Decades later, Olivier would write, 'the audience must be respected' even if '[t]hey can be manipulated', which 'they enjoy' and which 'is why they are here; but they must not be handled clumsily' (*On Acting* 28). He knew why Stratford theatregoers were there, to be manipulated *masterfully*, to give themselves over to the qualities that made Olivier the foremost actor in the English language: a virile physicality, a control of Shakespeare's language and a magnetism that conveyed a stirring sense of his protagonist's consummate heroism.

In 1959, the SMT celebrated its one hundredth season by taking 'the stars policy' to the point of '*reductio ad absurdum*' (Beauman 232).[1] Besides Olivier and Evans, the season included performances by Charles Laughton, Paul Robeson, Sam Wanamaker and Mary Ure (as Virgilia). Sally Beauman points out that the pursuit of first-rate and celebrated performers, who would appear for only one season at Stratford before returning to more lucrative work in London theatres and on film, hindered the SMT's ability in the 1950s to plan very far ahead or to achieve much continuity in the company's identity from one year to the next (216–218). Yet the SMT's artistic director, Glen Byam Shaw, knew well top stars' drawing power from the 1955 season, when Olivier and his celebrity wife, the actress Vivien Leigh, created overwhelming interest in and box office success for Stratford by appearing on stage together in *Titus Andronicus*, which went on to a lengthy London and European tour. Although the excitement generated by the celebrity couple was missing in the 1959 season (their marriage was falling apart), Olivier was, more than any other actor at the SMT that year, able to provide the star status that the company relied upon. He is undoubtedly *the* towering figure of twentieth-century British performance; by the time of his death in 1989, he had played over one hundred and twenty stage roles, had acted in more than fifty movies and in fifteen television programmes, had directed nearly forty plays and six films, had served as the artistic director of the Chichester Festival, was the founding artistic director of Britain's National Theatre, and was a Tony, BAFTA, Emmy and Academy award-winner (Holden 6). But even thirty years earlier, he had no equal. In addition to success in the commercial West End theatre and Hollywood, he already had a distinguished Shakespearean career, had starred in and directed films of *Henry V, Hamlet* and *Richard III*, had just finished filming the Roman epic *Spartacus*, had starred as broken-down music-hall performer Archie Rice in the stage version of 'angry young man' John Osborne's *The Entertainer* and was shooting this last work for the cinema during the days when performing in *Coriolanus* at night. His many successes rested not just on his athleticism, his discipline, his technical command of body and verse, his ability to disappear into a role but also on his tremendous, even dangerous charisma. As critic Kenneth Tynan writes, 'Watching Olivier, you feel that at any moment he may do something utterly unpredictable; something explosive, possibly apocalyptic, anyway unnerving in its emotional nakedness … deep in his temperament there runs a vein of rage that his affable mask cannot wholly conceal' (*Profiles* 204).

The unabashed veneration of individual celebrity performers at the SMT in 1959 may have exemplified escapist Shakespeare but the season was, in fact, highly politicized before it even began. With Paul Robeson playing Othello, it could not be otherwise, as the American actor brought the full weight of Cold War politics into the theatre with him. Owing to Robeson's outspoken criticism of colonialism worldwide and of racism in the United States, and because he was a vocal supporter of the Soviet Union, the US State Department had withheld his passport from 1950 to 1958. During that eight-year period of blacklisting, he had a famously heated exchange with members of the House Un-American Activities Committee (HUAC), when he refused to answer whether or not he was a communist. Playing against Robeson in 1959 was the Iago of Sam Wanamaker, another blacklisted American who, like Robeson, was the target of FBI and MI5 surveillance, but who had decided in the early 1950s to pursue a career in Britain.[2] Signing Robeson was a coup for Byam Shaw, who had tried to cast him in the company's 1958 *Pericles*. *Othello* was also a triumph for many in the British arts community who had lobbied on other occasions to have Robeson perform in Britain when the US government was restricting his travel. Olivier himself had declined to add his name to a 1957 London County Council (LCC) petition to invite Robeson to England, an act that might be seen as consistent with the view of Olivier as the essentially conservative artist who had directed and starred in the 1944 'wartime propaganda' film of *Henry V* (Whelehan and Cartmell 58). Whatever the romanticized nationalism of his *Henry V*, made when Britain was in a fight for its survival with the Axis powers, the reason Olivier gave the LCC was less a matter of overt political convictions than it was of pettily 'professional' motivations; he wrote that he would himself like to play Othello in the near future (Coleman 331).

Olivier's film work immediately before and during the *Coriolanus* run, meanwhile, implied a complicated political identity, as the personal convictions of his characters in these works represent fraught relationships to national histories analogous to those relationships that played out behind the scenes at the SMT. His turn as Rice in Tony Richardson's film of Osborne's *The Entertainer* is a downbeat meditation on contemporary Britain's fading greatness. Aware that he 'stood for everything that the young generation at the Royal Court', where the stage version first played, 'would find most objectionable' (Olivier, *Confessions* 219), Olivier embraced the portrayal of Rice's bleak desperation in a work that linked the vanishing music hall tradition with the death rattle of British imperial aspirations that the 1956 Suez crisis represented (though, according to Richardson (116), Olivier imposed cuts on the script that reduced unpatriotic sentiment for later runs of the play). His supporting role in *Spartacus*, shot just before the 1959 SMT season and released shortly after, is more readily comparable to *Coriolanus*. In that film, written by the blacklisted screenwriter Dalton Trumbo, Olivier plays Marcus Crassus, a Roman general and politician who despises the republic, seeks power for himself and ruthlessly crushes the slave rebellion led by the film's star Kirk Douglas, as Spartacus. While Olivier wished to show some of his character's self-doubt and vulnerability, his thoroughly villainous Crassus, in service to a viciously oppressive state, was far from his Henry V in Trumbo's near-allegory of HUAC's anti-communist witch hunts. For all Crassus' Coriolanus-like anti-plebeian sentiment on screen, those involved in the shooting recall the battles off screen taking place between Olivier and another of the film's British stars, Charles Laughton, who had greater Hollywood success than Olivier but was suspicious of his motives (Holden 337, Munn 187–189, Ustinov 300–301). Michael Blakemore, who played a Roman Senator in *Coriolanus* and the mechanical Snout in *Dream* with Laughton, by contrast, offers in his memoirs a non-celebrity view of the backstage environment at the SMT in 1959, which he remembers as a rigidly hierarchical space where the indignities of the theatrical star system were constantly imposed upon plebeian-like non-principal actors. Blakemore conjures a democratically minded Laughton not unlike the latter's populist Senator Gracchus in *Spartacus*, but paints an unflattering portrait of Peter Hall deferring to Olivier and ignoring actors lower on the playbill (211–234). While Blakemore's is just one perspective, others have cast the relationship between Hall and Olivier in terms of a director taking on or giving in to the star of the theatrical establishment (Fay 107, Holden 339). The social critiques in *The Entertainer* and *Spartacus* might be understood to be motivated by the same impulses that animated changes to British Shakespeare which Hall was about to make with an ensemble-oriented and nationally subsidized RSC. Nevertheless, the pseudo-imperial relationships of central and peripheral actors in the star system, which had prevailed in the performance of the national poet at Stratford, would prevail for at least one more year with particular force in a *Coriolanus* dominated by Olivier's overwhelming charisma.

To be fair, Hall's cuts to the text, approximately six hundred lines in total, give some credence to the director's purported efforts to convince his star to apply his charisma to a complex characterization by maintaining Coriolanus' lines of false modesty, which he claims Olivier had told him were cut in his 1938 production (Hall, 'The Job' 120–121).[3] Hall left most of Coriolanus' expressions of distaste for praise in his prompt-book, and Olivier evidently came around to the director's way of thinking, noting that the 'secrets' they discovered in the text and that they primarily worked on had to do with 'the business of his [Coriolanus'] not being able to accept praise although his great fault was pride' (Cook, *Shakespeare's Players* 94).[4] Yet it is difficult to regard many of the textual alterations as part of any concerted effort to diminish significantly the audience's sympa-

[32]

thies for the hero, despite Olivier's later contention that the hero is 'a very straightforward reactionary son of a so-and-so' (Cook, *Shakespeare's Players* 94). Many of the deletions remove other characters' perspectives on Coriolanus: gone is the dialogue between the two officers at the start of 2.2, Hall cut the whole meeting between Adrian and Nicanor (4.3), and he removed fifteen lines from the Volscian serving men's discussion of Coriolanus in 4.5.[5] Furthermore, much of the Tribunes' scheming lines from 1.1, 2.1, 2.2 and 2.3 are missing, as is much of their dispute with Menenius at the start of 2.1, all of which arguably improves our view of two of Coriolanus' main enemies. Of course, removing others' perspectives also allows more time to focus on the hero himself, and more significant than the cuts are the scenes that Hall left largely untouched. He kept most of Martius' invective against the People in 1.1 (though some of his lengthy diatribes are scaled back in 3.1) and all of his angry words against the People are intact in 3.3. Similarly, Coriolanus' meeting with Aufidius in 4.5 and his conflict with the Volsce general in 5.6 are barely altered, and the lengthy exchange between mother and son in 5.3 is cut by only a dozen lines. By streamlining the various perspectives on the action while maintaining the vast majority of dialogue in such scenes, Hall allowed his star to give full expression to the conflicts with his three principal antagonists: the People (led by the Tribunes), Volumnia and Aufidius.

Olivier's first entrance, made at the same perch on Boris Aronson's set from which he launched himself into space at the hero's demise, signalled Martius' complete dominance over the People. The permanent set left little open ground on the SMT's proscenium-arch playing space: broad steps painted to look like multi-coloured mosaics ascended several feet to a platform backed by column-framed rust-red gates; a second staircase led from the first to the higher centre-stage platform fronted by the death-leap ledge; beneath the ledge, stage-level doors with jagged ends could open and close like a fanged mouth; other columns, short stairs, bas-relief figures and geometrical patterns meant to imitate carved stone in various hues of brownish-grey and brownish-red rounded out the evocation of a vaguely classical and richly but not gaudily coloured scene.[6] As Laurence Kitchin comments, the set's divided spaces did not encourage 'ceremonial entrances between ranked guards of honour ... neither could a dense mob assemble nor a marching column gather impetus' (143). But the stage architecture did allow for an easy spatial depiction of hierarchical relationships, which Olivier and Hall took full advantage of for Martius' initial verbal assault on the People. After Harry Andrews's Menenius worked the crowd of angry Citizens, eliciting their laughter when he belched during the 'Tale of the Belly' and when he mocked Albert Finney's First Citizen as the rebellion's great toe, Olivier's entrance came unexpectedly. In Kitchin's memory, he did not seek applause from a drawn-out march onstage, rather, '[t]here, like the apparition of an eagle, he suddenly was' (143). From this superior position, Martius, wearing a dark, short, sleeveless tunic and sandals that showed off his respectably athletic arms and legs, verbally savaged the People below him. Yet Olivier immediately demonstrated that he had no need for the protection of his lofty spot by slowly descending the stairs and passing through the crowd as he heaped scorn on them. Although the People hissed when Olivier called them 'geese' (171), sneeringly drawing out the long vowel, he was unconcerned by this feedback. The sound recording registers the steady flow of his scathing contempt, an even rhythm occasionally slowed by such ejaculations as 'Hang ye!' (180), 'They say?' (188) and Olivier's tremendously rolled 'r' on his bellowed 'frrrrrragments!' (221).[7] Proving that the enraged People are merely a trifle to him, Olivier responded to the Messenger's news that 'the Volsces are in arms' (223) by laughing lustily before remarking 'I am glad on't. Then we shall ha' means to vent / Our musty superfluity' (224–225). To drive home this point, Olivier interrupted his exit from the scene, turned to the Citizens and laughed at them before saying 'Nay. Let them follow. / The Volsces have much corn' (246–247); after he invited them, 'Pray follow' (250), he sarcastically queried 'Ah?' and laughed derisively as the People groaned in frustration.

Because the evidence is scant for a number of scenes involving the Tribunes, it is difficult to gauge Coriolanus' relationship to the People and their representatives. On the one hand, the Tribunes' third-act victory over Coriolanus was depicted as short-lived and hollow. The sound recording reveals them as utterly smug when they first greet the People in 4.6, and Robert Hardy's Sicinius priggishly remarked to Andrews's Menenius that 'Coriolanus is not much missed' (13), to which Andrews could only reply in a small voice. Yet, as soon as news of Coriolanus' invasion was confirmed, the Tribunes crumbled, no longer sure of themselves at all; Andrews and Paul Hardwick's Cominius hurled invective at the People's now-uncertain representatives and, by 5.1, the Tribunes had become fearful and desperate. On the other hand, in 2.3, Coriolanus seemed the 'reactionary son of a so-and-so' that Olivier found him, well deserving of his defeat at the Tribunes' hands. At the start of the scene the Citizens debated amongst themselves in a serious but friendly way their political duties and responsibilities; however they may have behaved earlier as civilians (the incomplete recording is silent on that matter), they seemed rational here. Dressed in a long, loose, coarse-fibred gown of humility and a broad-brimmed sun-hat, Olivier, meanwhile, gave a demonstration of his own virtuoso abilities, suggesting that, while this Coriolanus may have been a straightforward reactionary, his arrogance was splendidly multi-faceted. He played part of the scene for humour, getting laughs on his snide 'Bid them wash their faces / And keep their teeth clean' (59–60), and on the ironic riposte 'You should account me the more virtuous, that I have not been common in my love' (93–94). Olivier's performance in the scene was remarkable for his quick reversal of tone. One moment he petulantly spoke, 'Ay, but not mine own desire' (65) and the next he recovered himself and calmly said, 'No, sir, 'twas never my desire yet to trouble the poor with begging' (68–69). He maintained this carefully measured calm delivery when begging Julian Glover's Third Citizen, 'Kindly, sir, I pray let me ha't' (74), but once he had the vote he sought, he immediately sent the Citizens away with a curt, dismissive 'I have your alms: adieu' (81). Finally, after reflecting on how it is better to die than to beg for the People's voices and steeling himself for his final rhetorical push in which he angrily recounted his past military deeds, he paused dramatically before first shrieking 'Your voices!' (129) and then calmly uttering, 'Indeed, I would be consul' (130). For a scene premised on the hero's loathing for acting a part he would rather not play, this Coriolanus was exceptionally chameleon-like in his utter disdain for the People and their ceremony. Still, no matter how contemptuous Olivier's hero was, it is hard to tell how manipulative the Tribunes were and how fickle and gullible the Plebeians were in the rest of the scene simply because, although much of the Tribunes' cynical, plotting dialogue remains in the prompt-book, the sound recording does not capture most of the dialogue after Coriolanus exits in the scene. This omission is typical of the recording, and it is richly ironic that the tape does not give a clear sense of how much Hall balanced the celebrity-protagonist's ugly behaviour with that of his antagonists because the tape operator himself was apparently focused on the stars of the production.[8]

It is more obvious from the remaining evidence that Hall devised grand, dramatic confrontations in 3.1 and 3.3 which afforded Olivier further opportunities to display his talents for ostentatious rage but which also revealed that the Tribunes and the People were not entirely mismatched against the hero. The drama in 3.1 derived in large part from the physical confrontations: Coriolanus first threw off and then shook Hardy's Sicinius on 'I shall shake thy bones / Out of thy garments' (178–179); the first extremely loud struggle with the Plebeians ended with Coriolanus crossing stage left and unsheathing his sword, ready for death; the second ended with the People chased off through the central gates threatened by the drawn blades of Olivier, Donald Eccles's Titus Lartius and Hardwick's Cominius. Neither Peter Woodthorpe's Brutus nor Hardy's Sicinius was particularly menacing or manipulative in the scene, but they conveyed the fairness of their cause, speaking with the self-assurance of righteous anger, and the Plebeians sounded like a force to be reckoned with, bellowing their assent at the Tribunes' accusations. Olivier met their charges with more virtuoso vocalization, switching suddenly from incisive reason to profound hatred, his voice, in Kenneth Tynan's words, like 'soft steel that can chill and cut, or melt and scorch' (*Curtains* 241). The frenetic activity was missing from Hall's 3.3, where the drama and conflict derived almost entirely from the verbal sparring. The Tribunes' initial cynical plotting to incite Coriolanus' ire remained in the script, but in the recording Woodthorpe and Hardy do not sound merely like 'parodie[s]' of the Tribunes, nor do the people seem to have served only 'as an intensifier of excitement' (Ripley 291). Rather, Woodthorpe and Hardy again spoke with what sounded like real conviction, matching Olivier's vituperation with their own, and, once more, the People powerfully and loudly ratified their representatives' dicta. Admittedly, it was Olivier who, once more, stood out for his modulation of voice, instantly shifting from breathless disbelief on 'traitor!' (67) to violent fury on 'The fires i'th'lowest hell fold in the people!' (68). Then, as the Plebeians bellowed, 'It shall be so!' (119), echoing Brutus' sentence of exile, Olivier ascended the steps to return to the perch on which he first appeared in the production, towering over his enemies for a second time. Although Olivier's superior position here did not carry the same weight as it did in 1.1, since he was now on the verge of exile, he imposed his *actorly* command of the scene in his departing speech. In the first half of this diatribe, Olivier was restrained, his voice perfectly measuring out the iambs in 'You common cry of curs' (120) but later slowing his tempo to draw out, in an almost serene voice, his loathing for the Plebeians on 'I banish you' (124). In the second half of the speech, he gradually wound himself back up into a bellowing rage, concluding by first shouting, trumpet-like, 'thus I turn my back' (134), and pausing for three seconds before quietly and slowly but portentously intoning, 'There is a world elsewhere' (135). Of course, this superbly controlled conclusion simultaneously looked back to his denunciation in the first scene and ahead to the final one, Olivier's violent shriek on the penultimate line followed by the dramatic falling away of the second anticipating the cruel physical action of the thrust blades and the hero's silent plunge in 5.6.

Whatever command Olivier's Coriolanus had over his opponents in Act 3 had been fully established in the first-act battles. Roberto Gerhard's music for the fight at Corioles, a series of extremely loud drum bursts, trumpet blasts and cymbal crashes, was matched by the enthusiastic shouting of both sides' soldiers, and provided a sense of the thrill of battle. Olivier's hero, now with breastplate, heavy shield and black cape, was in his element here, excited by the prospect of a fight, and singled out by action calculated to show off his individual soldierly skill. With the Roman army gathered at stage level for the start of the battle, Olivier rousingly declared, 'He that retires, I'll take him for a Volsce, / And he shall feel mine edge' (1.4.28–29) before running up the stairs alone, through the Volsce army, to the top platform, the better to display himself, as he immediately killed two enemies. He concluded the scene in the same showy manner: the gates at the middle platform several feet above the stage opened to discover Olivier battling the Volsces by himself. There is no sound recording for his lone struggle with Nicholls's Aufidius, but the archived fight plan shows them to be well-matched initially, with an even number of thrusts, parries and cuts before Olivier disarmed his antagonist. Apparently, it was not sufficiently valiant for the star merely to have Nicholls saved by other Volsce soldiers. Instead, Olivier killed one rescuer, chased off the other two, magnanimously returned Nicholls his weapon and exited. Nicholls's disgraced Aufidius was left with the consolation prize of chastising and shaking off the two cowardly Volsces who returned only once Martius was gone. Olivier stood out, furthermore, by inspiring the others to join the fray. Although his 'O, me alone! Make you a sword of me?' (1.6.76) drew comradely laughter from the other Romans who held him aloft on their shoulders, his lusty 'If these shows be not outward, which of you / But is four Volsces?' (1.6.77–78) elicited from them an excited cheer. They quickly followed him into the fight, where they easily got the better of the Volsces, putting them to flight. Yet Olivier also gave ample scope to Martius' scorn for the common soldiers when they did not live up to his heroic standards. Before running through the open gates in 1.4, he ranted in a saliva-filled growl, 'Mend and charge home, / Or, by the fires of heaven, I'll leave the foe / And make my wars on you' (38–40). He similarly derided the Roman spoil-takers, sneering at them with deep contempt, 'See here these movers that do prize their hours / At a cracked drachma' (1.5.4–5). As in the final scene's fall, Olivier's attitude in this scene was not necessarily just a matter of Martius' supreme status, but reflected the actor's awareness of his supreme place in the company, his own high standards and his commitment to the production. According to Blakemore, Olivier one day turned to some yawning actors in rehearsal 'and muttered, "Not enjoying this line of work, boys?" The sly menace of his line was undisguised' (223).

The command of Olivier's Martius was built up the better to render spectacular and pathetic his defeat at both Volumnia's and Aufidius' hands. At the time Edith Evans played Volumnia, she was appreciated primarily as a comic actress. She had already played a show-stealing Nurse against Olivier and John Gielgud in a 1935 *Romeo and Juliet*, and would have been widely recognized in 1959 for her portrayal of Oscar Wilde's comically monstrous aristocrat Lady Bracknell in *The Importance of Being Earnest*, especially her turn in the 1952 film version of the play. Although she must have cut an impressive figure in her full-length metallic gown and cloak and fringed head-band, there was little of the monstrous mother figure in her first several scenes as Volumnia. In 1.3, her high-pitched quavering voice on the audio recording makes her dialogue sound very formal and calculated, and she spoke seriously but not overly sternly with Ure's Virgilia. Similarly, she delivered such lines as 'Then his good report should have been my son' (20–21) with pride but not with heartless indifference to Martius' death. She was more overtly humorous in 2.1, drawing laughter from the audience when scolding Ure's Virgilia for her squeamishness, firmly rebutting her daughter-in-law's fear of Martius' possible injury with 'O, he is wounded, I thank the gods for't' (119). Hall used the scene to reveal Martius' bonds to his family; in his military regalia that now included a laurel wreath and a white cape, Olivier spoke lovingly when he greeted Ure (demurely dressed, as she was up to 5.3, in a long diaphanous white frock and simple white head-band), embracing her and then pausing for effect before kissing her. He showed a more complex relationship to Evans's Volumnia, first kneeling to her and saying with gratitude, 'You have, I know, petitioned all the gods / For my prosperity!' (168–169). Yet, according to Kitchin, Olivier actually flashed Evans 'a long smile with the spoilt son's immodest complacency' (145), and briefly showed his childish side by petulantly telling her as he exited the stage, 'Know, good mother, / I had rather be their servant in my way / Than sway with them in theirs' (199–201). He carried these conflicted emotions into 3.2. For most of that scene, Evans met his petulance with firm reason, driving Olivier's hero into self-conflicted fits of contrasting tones characteristic of his speech elsewhere in the performance. One moment he angrily demanded, 'Must I / With my base tongue give to my noble heart a lie that it must bear?' (100–101), the next calmly relenting on 'Well, I will do't' (101). Olivier worked this conflict for humour, drawing laughter when reversing himself, first pausing before his throwaway line, 'I will not do't' (120) and switching again for comic relief when he gave in to Volumnia on 'Pray be content: / Mother, I am going to the market-place' (130–131), which the audience on the sound recording laughed at heartily. The build-up of his childish dependence effected by alternating anger and comedy was here not just another opportunity for Olivier to display his virtuosity but led to a dramatic peak that served as a turning point when Evans could reveal Volumnia's resolve. At the end of Olivier's emotional appeal to her, Evans hardened, commenting harshly 'Do your will' (137) as she exited, effectively abandoning her son on stage.

Evans deepened her portrayal of Volumnia's resolve in 4.2, a scene that prepared the way for her ascendancy in 5.3. The actress relentlessly assailed Hardy and Woodthorpe's Tribunes, who opened the scene smugly discussing Coriolanus' exile. Evans unleashed her fury upon them with an emotional conviction that she lacked earlier in the performance, her contempt for the Plebeians and their representatives as thorough as her son's when shouting, ''Twas you incensed the rabble!' (4.2.33). The compelling rage of her final lines, 'Leave this faint puling and lament as I do, / In anger, Juno-like. Come, come, come' (4.2.52–53), was met with applause but it also cast an aura of dread over the moments leading up to the interval, a portentousness underscored by Andrews's fearful 'Fie, fie, fie' (4.2.54) and by the ominous pounding of a drum. By concluding the production's first half with Evans's star turn, Hall suggested that Volumnia was taking over her son's power (or, perhaps, that all along he had been channelling hers), and that the subsequent action would hinge upon her. This suggestion became manifest in 5.3, where Coriolanus' spirit was spectacularly broken in the course of Olivier and Evans matching one another's bravura performances. At the top of the scene, Olivier spoke to Nicholls's Aufidius in a businesslike way but the moment he perceived his family's entrance (the three women now covered in black shawls), he reverted to his wild vocal fluctuations, moving from a restrained intensity when commenting on the women's bowing to him (27–33) to a shrieked 'I'll never / Be such a gosling to obey instinct, but stand / As if a man were author of himself / And knew no other kin' (34–37). But Olivier carefully delineated Coriolanus' failure to disobey his instinct for the familial bond, cutting back and forth between a breathy 'O, a kiss / Long as my exile, sweet as my revenge!' (44–45) to Ure's Virgilia, to nearly hissing his disbelieving 'What's this? / Your knee to me?' (56–57) when Evans knelt, but immediately bellowing, 'Then let the pebbles on the hungry beach / Fillip the stars' (58–59). In the first of Volumnia's long supplicating speeches, Evans exuded a constancy of spirit in a calm and even but emotionally powerful delivery that Olivier made sure his hero could never fully manage. When her strategy did not work, she became more like her son, or, rather, Evans became more like Olivier. In the first long section of the speech, she slowly increased her emotional intensity but slowed her pace and lowered her volume for 'Think'st thou it honourable for a noble man / Still to remember wrongs?' (154–155). She repeated this rhythm twice more to build towards an emotional climax, loudly exclaiming, 'Down ladies; let us shame him with our knees!' (169) but then spoke, 'Down: an end' (171) with a soft quavering voice. She induced guilt by harshly declaiming, 'This fellow had a Volscian to his mother; / His wife is in Corioli, and his child / Like him by chance' (178–179) but then quietly speaking, 'I am hushed until our city be afire / And then I'll speak a little' (181–182). Drawing out the similarities between mother and son (or between the two stars) led to the hero's explicitly personal, individual collapse. Silently holding Evans's hand, Olivier also borrowed from his own 1955 performance in *Titus Andronicus* when he maintained a long silent pause between cutting off his own hand and releasing a horrible wail. Now he paused for over twenty seconds, an excruciating and dramatic interval that did not end in a wail but with Olivier's quiet yet greatly moving 'O mother, mother! / What have you done?' (182–183). Volumnia's emotional attack had its desired effect, as Olivier showed Coriolanus twice overcome by his feelings and twice forced to pull himself together.

Coriolanus' relationship with Aufidius, too, was explicitly a battle between two powerful individual personalities, and Nicholls exploited the same emotional vulnerability that Evans's Volumnia did in order to finish off his rival. Kitchin asserts that 4.5 was the climax of the production and implies that it was a silent precursor to Coriolanus' awareness of his sealed fate in 5.3: Olivier's glazed eyes and 'premonitory misgiving in the way he eventually shook hands' indicated that '[w]hatever integration of character Marcius had possessed fell apart at that moment' (144). While it is hard to read Kitchin's impressions of the live performance into the extant evidence, and while there were more emotionally wrought moments later in the production, the meeting in 4.5 was highly charged and their alliance did expose the psychological weakness of Olivier's Coriolanus that would be so potently displayed in 5.3. The two men unfolded their feelings to one another in 4.5 in an emotional but evenly spoken exchange of lengthy speeches, though Olivier's angrily growled 'I also am / Longer to live most weary, and present / My throat to thee and to thy ancient malice' (97–99) suggested the anguish that his offer truly cost him. Nicholls's initial blissful 'O Martius, Martius!' (104) belied both the ominous pauses before and after his penultimate sentence, 'Your hand', and the quiet power of his concluding 'Most welcome!' (150), and the portent of these words lingered as the men exited the stage hand in hand. Hall then further primed the audience for Coriolanus' final breakdown in 5.6 by emphasizing the dramatic irony on either side of the women's embassy, in 4.7 and at the start of 5.6. In the former scene, Nicholls concluded Aufidius' cynically candid talk with his lieutenant on a hushed but electric note of vengeance: 'When, Caius, Rome is thine, / Thou art poor'st of all; then shortly art thou mine' (56–57). In the latter conversation with his Conspirators, Nicholls conveyed Aufidius' ignobly self-interested resentment about Coriolanus taking his place among the Volsces, and his disdain for the exiled Roman weeping at Volumnia's pleading was absolute.

Having carefully established Aufidius as the more dishonourable of the two, Hall made sure that he remained so at the production's conclusion. In the wake of Aufidius' conspiratorial dialogue, Olivier's confident, smoothly flowing opening speech to the Volsces made his Coriolanus appear particularly naive, and, though he seemed genuinely confused when Nicholls called him traitor, he soon realized the trap, shrieking, 'Martius?' (87). Like Evans's Volumnia in 5.3, Nicholls wound his victim into his trap by imitating Olivier's fluctuating speech patterns, spiking his own otherwise fluid and rapid accusatory speech with the scornfully shouted 'Ay, Martius, Caius Martius!' (88), 'in Corioli' (90), 'rotten silk' (96) and 'at his nurse's tears / He whined and roared away your victory' (97–98). But Olivier was the one who put on the final soaring rhetorical display to match his heroic ascent to the perch for his swan dive. Reaching the top of the first set of stairs, Olivier shouted, 'Boy!' and followed it with a breathless 'O slave!' (104) before building his volume over several lines. He immediately repeated this performance after mounting the second set of steps, looming high above his enemies for the third and last denunciation from his spiritual eyrie. Now he shrieked and drew out the vowel on '"Booooooy"!' (113), and once again muted his speech only to build to a crescendo for the line of vowel-stretched words, 'Alooooone I did it. "Booooooooy"!' (117). Shortly, he desperately bellowed, 'O that I had him, / With six Aufidiuses or more – his tribe, / To use my lawful sword!' (128–130), the Conspirators stabbed him, and he made his famous fall. Once he performed the harrowing leap, Olivier remained the undisputed star to the end. Even as Coriolanus was apparently dead, Olivier, now lying on the ground, reached out to seize Nicholls's foot when he stabbed Coriolanus a second time, and the Volsce had to shake off his enemy to free himself, perhaps echoing his personal defeat in Act 1 when he shook off his cowardly would-be rescuers. Nicholls's Aufidius was explicitly denied any further measure of victory because the audience watched him try ignominiously to jump on the corpse but fail to do so when the Senators restrained him, refusing him his opportunity to insult the dead hero's body. At the conclusion, Olivier's Coriolanus was elevated one last time, carried on the Volsces' shoulders up the first set of stairs through the gates, his funeral procession dignified by the slow, solemn pounding of bass drums.

The critics' response, collectively, revealed a journalistic community largely in tune with the star system. While reviewers made brief remarks about the Plebeians, the Tribunes and Menenius, they expended much more energy focusing on the two principal celebrities in the cast. On the whole, they were divided about Evans's Volumnia. For some, she was 'playing ... with a saintly and majestic brevity' (*Daily Mail* 8 July 1959), she proved 'overpoweringly dominating as Coriolanus' ferocious mother' (*Evening Standard* 8 July 1959) and she gave 'glorious testimony to the fortitude of Volumnia' (*Morning Advertiser* 11 July 1959). For others, 'she lacked the savage, ruthless, cannibal guts of a Roman mum on a blood kick' (*The Spectator* 17 July 1959), perhaps because 'she found the massive scale of Volumnia unsympathetic, for she delivered her great plea for Rome in uniformly subdued, almost flat accents' (*New Statesman* 18 July 1959). Reviewers spent most of their space discussing Olivier's performance in terms of an idealized portrayal of individual greatness, with the majority regarding it as a triumph in a difficult, unsympathetic role. Olivier added to his Old Vic turn 'all kinds of happy human subtleties', delivering 'a wonderful, completely rounded, marvellously spoken performance which achieves the feat of giving warmth to a notoriously icy character' (*News Chronicle* 8 July 1959). He 'developed and heightened' the excitement of 'those famous spring nights at the Old Vic in 1938' by showing 'the wilful egotist, obstinate patrician, stand[ing] before us like a statue from marmoreal Rome given nobly authoritative life' (*Birmingham Post* 12 August 1959). Olivier's 'innate majesty' as 'Caius Marcius is apparent as soon as he walks among the people soon after the beginning and the reckless, uncontrollable pride and prejudice which are to deprive him of the prizes deserved by his valour and his profound love for Rome are brilliantly expressed' (*Morning Advertiser* 11 July 1959). The star's 'presence dominates the stage no matter what is happening or who is talking. He has a kind of animal magnetism, controlled by his wonderful interpretive intelligence' (*New Statesman* 18 July 1959). Yet there were criticisms. Some felt Olivier's virtuosity unbalanced Shakespeare's political equilibrium by giving 'Coriolanus a studied romantic charm which weighs the argument unfairly against the mob' (*Evening Standard* 8 July 1959). Others believed that Olivier's actorly 'tricks' interfered with the character. Alan Brien complained, 'I would ask for less consciousness on Olivier's part that every word is putty and can be moulded to his whim. I would ask for less technique – instead, I would like to feel that the lines are mastering him occasionally' (*The Spectator* 17 July 1959). What was worse, according to T.C. Worsley, was that the technique was becoming hackneyed: despite his 'technical feats', his 'performance did not seem to be an act of creation of a character but rather an act of selection precisely from the superb repository he has been building up in this decade. But he has added nothing to it and it is surely time that he did' (*Financial Times* 8 July 1959).

Hall's biographer, Stephen Fay, considers the critical disrespect for Olivier's 'charismatic performance that typified the 1950s' to be 'a clue to changing attitudes to reputation and to new fashions in acting' (107), but it was not the first time that Olivier had put off reviewers with his idiosyncratic style, and there was more to the changes coming than 'fashions in acting'.[9] In Ripley's words, by the early 1960s, 'theatrical romance was displaced by calculated ugliness, escape by confrontation, the hero by the antihero, and emotional intoxication by politics, psychoanalysis, and [later] postmodernity' (298). Part of these changes, which were already under way, emerged from the well-founded criticisms of postwar England's fading power that Olivier himself embodied as Archie Rice in *The Entertainer*. Other changes to come both at Stratford under Peter Hall and at the National Theatre under Olivier's artistic directorship were closely connected to an increased reliance on the nation officially underwriting the costs of big-institution theatre, which coincided with a shift away from the star system. The desire for 'political' Shakespeare would also be seen in the rise of the call for 'relevance', a development often attributed to the influence in Britain of the Polish critic Jan Kott's writings. But awareness of the potential for a more political performance that was expressed through a new kind of overt theatricality was partly due to the palpable influence of the Berliner Ensemble, the East German company that had already toured to London in 1956 and that would do so again with their *Coriolanus* at the National Theatre's Old Vic in 1965, two years into Olivier's tenure there. Yet Ripley's assertion that the hero would be replaced by its antithesis is not strictly true. Just as Olivier was directly involved in so many of the changes to British theatre and Shakespearean performance coming in the following decade, so would directors, actors and critics aspire to create and witness the type of profound emotional experience that the star provided in the 1959 *Coriolanus*. It is this tension between the impending departure from and desire for the charismatic heroism that Olivier delivered that I will explore in the following chapters.

CHAPTER III

Coriolanus and Brecht, 1951–71

At the turn of the twenty-first century, Antony Tatlow recalled the Berliner Ensemble's 1964 German staging of the Bertolt-Brecht-inspired *Coriolanus* that the company would mount the following year in London on the National Theatre's Old Vic stage: 'It made the hopelessly conventional English Shakespearean productions appear vacuous, abstract, and theatrical, merely rhetorical, dramatic fashion shows for superficial flourishings of language, lazy stylizations lost in histrionic rodomontade' (159). Tatlow's description of Brecht's practices (developed by the Ensemble, which he founded in 1949 in East Germany) as a revolutionary force that exposed the supposed emptiness of British Shakespeare's flaws echoes the enthusiasm with which the company's work was received in London on both its 1956 and 1965 tours. The enthusiastic response to the 1965 *Coriolanus* is further reflected in the frequency with which Brecht and *Coriolanus* were brought together on British stages in the 1960s and early 1970s. In 1971, Manfred Wekwerth and Joachim Tenschert, who co-directed the Ensemble's production, returned to the National Theatre to direct an English-language Brecht-inflected version of the play. One year earlier, the Royal Shakespeare Company had staged Günter Grass's *The Plebeians Rehearse the Uprising: A German Tragedy*, a play that critiques Brecht's supposedly compromised political stance by fictionalizing the director's rehearsal of his *Coriolanus* adaptation during the 1953 East Berlin workers' uprising. Brecht's techniques are also discernible in the RSC's 1972 *Coriolanus* in Stratford-upon-Avon and its significantly altered 1973 London transfer, which are the subjects of the next chapter.

Yet accounts of Brecht's status in Britain are ambivalent.

Typically, they emphasize the tremendous impact of the Berliner Ensemble's 1956 and 1965 tours, tours that overwhelmed London audiences with their theatrical élan just as the 1964 *Coriolanus* in Berlin had thrilled Tatlow. At the same time, most authors of these accounts insist that the British journalists, playwrights and practitioners who embraced Brecht's formal theatrical techniques also disavowed or transformed his political (i.e. Marxist) and theoretical writings. Whether because of a 'traditional British xenophobia' or 'a basic distrust of the intellectual, typical of British art circles' (Eddershaw 1, 3–4), the English purportedly adopted the outward signs of Brecht's 'epic' theatre – techniques designed to inhibit theatregoers' overly emotional identification with the actors, such as anti-illusionistic fully lit bare staging with hints of realism and performers who appear to comment on their roles by not disappearing into them – but without Brecht's full political commitment to employing such 'alienation' devices to develop a critical response in the audience that would allow them to understand and thus alter the social forces that shape individuals' lives. Consequently, the British supposedly created for themselves 'a Brecht whose priorities are emotional, personal, intuitive, practical and British' (Rebellato 150). The irony of such a situation is evident: 'Deprived of their political dimensions Brecht's "novelties" were treated as isolated artistic devices that could be incorporated unquestioningly into the dominant bourgeois theatre in order to revitalize it while originally they were meant to work against it' (Germanou 213).

Brecht's *Coriolanus* underwent significant changes before it arrived on the British stage in 1965 and experienced further transformations on that stage. *Coriolanus'* varied identity was the result of the different historical and theatrical contexts to which it was adapted, contexts that were created in the relationships amongst various theatre practitioners, Cold War politicians and audiences, including British theatre reviewers. In this chapter, I will trace the development of the Brecht-related *Coriolanus*es – from the playwright's adaptation to its later German and English productions to Grass's adaptation of the adaptation – in relation to these evolving contexts. The evolution of *Coriolanus* did, frequently, involve a depoliticization or diminishment of Brecht's Marxism as the play was moved closer in production to versions that privileged traditional forms of

Shakespearean performance and 'bourgeois' values. Yet, at the same time, *Coriolanus'* identity in production was undoubtedly also politicized by its development within East Germany, where the overt politicization of art could not be avoided, and by its British reception, which frequently coded Brechtian theatre as an ideologically hostile and distinctly foreign threat to Shakespeare.

Brecht's *Coriolanus*

Brecht returned to Germany in 1948, following a decade and a half of exile that began with the rise of Hitler in 1933. Having fled, in stages, across Europe, Russia and to America, he took up residence in Switzerland in 1947 as a refugee with few clear prospects. However, within months of returning to Germany, Brecht had negotiated working conditions for himself in the country's Soviet-occupied zone that would allow him to solidify his reputation as the twentieth-century theatre's most influential practitioner-theorist. Shortly after the tremendous early successes Brecht achieved with the state-subsidized Berliner Ensemble, he began the drawn-out process of working on *Coriolanus*.[1] Brecht published an initial version of the adaptation's opening scene in 1952, and a year or two later was working on the 'Study of the First Scene of Shakespeare's "Coriolanus"'.[2] This analysis of the play's opening action is written as a dramatic dialogue between Brecht and members of the Berliner Ensemble, reflecting the company's collaborative working methods. Although Brecht was still contemplating the *Coriolanus* adaptation in 1955, he did not complete it before he died in August 1956. This unfinished script was not published in German until 1959 and apparently the only early German production of the adaptation was mounted not by the Berliner Ensemble but by Hans Koch in Frankfurt, West Germany, in 1962.[3]

As Brecht's play is only about 60 per cent as long as Shakespeare's, and about 17 per cent of this material is new (Subiotto 150), it is not difficult to see why some critics have analysed the adaptation's relationship to Shakespeare's play in terms of an artistic falling off. Ruby Cohn is representative of those who understand Brecht to have reduced the scope or grandeur of the original tragedy, arguing that his desire to elevate the Plebeians and prove Coriolanus' dispensability to Rome resulted in an adaptation that 'converts Shakespeare's tragedy to melodrama with its reductive good-evil ethos' (374).[4] Certain changes Brecht introduced do appear to make Coriolanus and the Patricians less appealing and important than they are in Shakespeare's script.[5] Coriolanus first enters to confront the Plebeians with a group of armed men, making him seem cowardly or less singularly dangerous, the Roman women no longer have a victory procession as they do in Shakespeare's 5.5 and, in Brecht's 5.3 (Shakespeare's 5.4), the Patricians are reported to be abandoning Rome as Coriolanus and the Volscians advance upon it. Other changes seem designed to improve the Plebeians: Brecht introduced a 'Man with Child', who adds pathos to the opening scene with his description of the desperate circumstances in Rome; the Plebeians are hardly quarrelsome at all in the prelude to voting for Coriolanus as Consul; and Brecht makes them less petty by not having them plan to jeer at Coriolanus as he leaves Rome for exile. The greatest change to the Plebeians is that, in Brecht's 5.3, unlike the craven Patricians, the People unite to defend the city, and it is this show of solidarity and resilience that finally convinces Coriolanus to abandon his assault on Rome with the Volscians.

Rather than seeing such alterations simply as an exercise in melodramatization, however, it is more productive to understand Brecht's changes for the ways that they shift emphasis from the individual character to the political and social forces that shape character, a shift driven by Brecht's Marxist convictions. Although Brecht did not come to adapt the first-act battle scenes, scenes in which Coriolanus displays his monumental individual military prowess, his other changes downplay the exploration of Coriolanus' individuality.[6] For instance, Brecht maintains the Adrian–Nicanor encounter from Act 4, but in the adaptation they become a Roman (Laetus) and Volsce (Piger) who are less interested in Coriolanus' banishment than they are in the mundane routines of daily life. The adaptation, furthermore, reduces the centrality of Aufidius' and Coriolanus' personal *agon*. Not only does Brecht diminish Aufidius' conspiratorial dialogue at the top of 5.6 and entirely delete Shakespeare's 1.2, in which Aufidius expresses his enmity for Martius, he greatly shortens their meeting in Act 4 at Antium and removes the Servingmen's dialogue about the dining Volsce Lords and Aufidius fawning over Coriolanus. Brecht's most overt change, returning the action to the Roman Senate at the play's end for an additional 5.7, saps Coriolanus' assassination of its climactic quality. When news of Coriolanus' death reaches the Senate, Brecht does not allow Menenius' request for a memorial inscription and permission for Coriolanus' family to wear mourning clothes to interrupt the legislators' deliberation about building an aqueduct. The extra scene is thus not merely a denouement but a blunt assertion that daily civic life will continue unimpeded by the individual and familial concerns of its Citizens.

This is not to say that Coriolanus becomes entirely hateful or one-dimensional. Brecht originally wanted Ernst Busch, 'the great people's actor', to take the role, intending his Coriolanus to be 'Not too likeable, and likeable enough' ('Study' 263). Indeed, the song that Brecht gives Coriolanus to sing when asking for the People's votes (2.3) may make him appear cynical about 'selling' himself to the People, yet it is also a typical Brechtian alienating device designed not only to create an analytical attitude in the audience but to provide a star actor like Busch with an opportunity to flaunt his talents. Furthermore, Brecht does make it clear that Coriolanus' skills are, for the moment, necessary to Rome. As the People gather to witness Coriolanus ask for their votes in 2.3, the Second Citizen explicitly recognizes the hero's value to Rome, calling the general 'a neck with a goiter'; 'A neck is indispensable even if it has a goiter. The goiter is his pride' (2.3). In Brecht's version, it is Coriolanus' realization that social necessities have changed and that he has become dispensable which leads him to his tragic decision to halt the march on Rome. By rewriting Shakespeare's 5.4 to portray the Plebeians' resolve to defend Rome, and by placing it before the Roman women's visit to Coriolanus (thus reversing the order of Shakespeare's sequence), Brecht makes Volumnia's personal appeal somewhat extraneous. More importantly, Brecht has Volumina explicitly inform her son that, because the People are no longer submissive, he faces the very real threat of defeat. It is Volumnia's report of this change in the Citizens of Rome, as much as her maternal chastisement (which Brecht greatly reduces from her speeches in this scene), that causes Coriolanus' personal anguish when he cries 'O mother, mother! What have you done?' (142).

Coriolanus may, in the process of emphasizing the social forces that shape the hero's individuality, 'present the Plebeians as wronged, aware, and finally brave and united' but Brecht appears more concerned with 'improving' the Tribunes, portraying them as the People's selfless representatives who lead the move towards political awareness. He removes almost all the Tribunes' self-interested scheming against Coriolanus in 1.2 and 2.2, and in 2.3 they no longer cynically cultivate the People's uncertainty about electing Coriolanus as Consul. In Brecht's 4.3 (Shakespeare's 4.6), after Menenius and Cominius blame the Tribunes for Coriolanus' impending invasion in front of a group of frightened Citizens, Sicinius stands firm, encouraging the People not to fear the Patricians' accusations which, he says, mask their desire to see Coriolanus reinstated in Rome (130). Then, in 5.3 Brutus selflessly places his cunning in the service of Rome by encouraging Volumnia's embassy to Coriolanus so that the People will gain crucial time to prepare for the invasion. Having demonstrated their political insight and military resolve, Brecht finally elevates the Tribunes to a position of power that Shakespeare reserved for the Patricians. In the adapted 5.3, Cominius and Brutus form an alliance on behalf of the groups they represent to oppose the invasion, and, instead of the Roman women's victory procession in Shakespeare's 5.5, Brutus *speaks for* the People in Brecht's version of the scene, commenting chorus-like on the Citizens' power in turning away Coriolanus and the Volsces (143). Finally, during Brecht's additional closing scene, it is the Tribunes who move to return the land taken from the defeated Volsces and it is Brutus who rejects Menenius' request to memorialize Coriolanus and moves that the Senate proceed with current state business (146).

If examining the shift from the individual to the political within *Coriolanus* helps explain Brecht's adaptive strategies, focusing on the political contexts in which Brecht worked on the adaptation is also instructive. Darko Suvin convincingly portrays the adaptation as a 'wish-dream and counter-project to the failed plebeian revolutions in Germany after both World Wars' and as an indictment of Joseph Stalin's dictatorial cult of personality and his blackmailing of Soviet society with his supposed irreplaceability as a great organizer and military leader (*To Brecht and Beyond* 197, 200). For Suvin, 'The confrontation of the two tribunes and Coriolan is', partly, 'a confrontation between the pristine revolutionary impulse ... and – as Brecht hoped – the resurgent democratic Leninism of the plebeian masses with the once – but now no longer – useful bloody stage of Stalinism' (*To Brecht and Beyond* 201). The implication of this argument is that Brecht uses *Coriolanus* to establish politically committed artists like himself as 'Leninist' representatives of the people, figures who could instruct the workers to become a counterforce to replaceable tyrants like Stalin who jeopardize the future of Marxism. This is a wholly plausible implication, given Brecht's desire to develop a critical faculty in his audiences that would lead to social awareness and thus positive democratizing political change.

Yet any identification that Brecht may have felt with his idealized representatives of the People would have been complicated by the playwright's awareness of the difficulties such tribune-artist figures faced in communist East Germany, especially during the early 1950s when the Stalinist purges within the Soviet Union had begun to spread to the German Democratic Republic (GDR) (Völker 337–338). At this time, when Brecht and his colleagues were working on *Coriolanus*, Brecht perceived GDR functionaries to be targeting the Ensemble for not conforming to the dictates of socialist realism, the government-sanctioned aesthetic (Hayman 354, 365–366). Indeed, authorities in 1951 made a great display of forcing Brecht and Paul Dessau (who provided the music for the Ensemble's *Coriolanus*) to rewrite their co-devised opera, *The Trial of Lucullus*, about a Roman general who, far more explicitly than Coriolanus, fights wars for personal gain. Brecht became even more aware of his compromised position in the GDR after 17 June 1953 when officials manipulated his ambivalent statements about Soviet tanks crushing the workers' uprising to make them appear like words of support for the Socialist Unity Party's (SED) leader, Walter Ulbricht (Hayman 369). These events proved that, despite the thaw that followed Stalin's death three months earlier, the SED leadership did not intend to relinquish its power to the people, nor did it intend to be swayed on crucial political matters by artists who took it upon themselves to speak for the people.[7]

Although Brecht could not succeed in openly critiquing a government willing to maintain power by recourse to the Soviet military, he was able to thrive artistically during the last three years of his life, winning prestigious awards for his work and a permanent home for the Ensemble at the Theater am Schiffbauerdamm in 1954 (Völker 369–376, Hayman 379–388). With help from his wife, Helene Weigel, he acquired a degree of artistic freedom and succeeded in pursuing the kind of work he wished to produce by solidifying personal and professional relationships within the SED cultural hierarchy (Völker 370–371, Hayman 375, Setje-Eilers). With the blessing of the same cultural authorities, the cosmopolitan Brecht established the Ensemble as Europe's finest theatre company by leading it on hugely successful tours in Western Europe in 1954 and 1955. Although he died shortly before the company's first tour to London in 1956, Brecht had demonstrated the value of his canny 'sceptical commitment' (Völker 337) to East German socialism, a commitment which rested on adapting himself to changing conditions within the GDR and simultaneously on acquiring prestige in the capitalist West to secure himself against persecution at home. It was a lesson that the next generation of tribune-artists at the Berliner Ensemble, under the guidance of Weigel, Wekwerth and Tenschert, would remember when they reworked *Coriolanus* and toured it to London in 1965.

The Berliner Ensemble adapts Brecht's adaptation

The years between Brecht's death in 1956 and the Berlin premier of the Ensemble's *Coriolanus* in September 1964 represent a time of political and artistic consolidation for the GDR. This period witnessed the collectivization of the country's agriculture and industry and, in 1961, completion of the Berlin Wall to stop movement between the two Germanys, especially the huge number of those leaving the GDR for the West. Sealing off East Germany's borders also had implications for the study and performance of Shakespeare in the GDR. In 1963, the Deutsche Shakespeare-Gesellschaft (the German Shakespeare Society) split into Eastern and Western groups shortly before the one hundredth anniversary of the society's founding in 1864.[8] At the same time, communist cultural authorities strengthened conservative nationalist views of Shakespeare in order to shore up their legitimacy. Once fighting ended in 1945, Germans, who had long considered Shakespeare a substitute national poet, treated the dramatist's works as a kind of traditional refuge from modernity and the modern war that had left their country devastated (Habicht 160). Subsequently, those responsible for cultural policy in the GDR developed this traditionalism into a rhetoric about 'a new Renaissance ... possibly emerging with new values and new humanist objectives', leading to 'an ahistorical fixation on the Renaissance as a social model' (Hamburger 177). This attitude came into sharp focus during the 1964 celebrations for the four hundredth anniversary of Shakespeare's birth when the Secretary for Culture, Alexander Abusch, delivered a nationally broadcast speech entitled 'Shakespeare: Realist and Humanist, Genius of World Literature' (Gunter 114). Abusch's comments, which treated the playwright as a 'constituent force in the formation of modern Socialist society', signalled that the official attitude was that Shakespeare was 'a cultural monument, to be admired and praised but not to be critically examined' (Gunter 114). The playwright thus 'assumed a legitimizing function' within the socialist state and, officially, productions of his plays were meant to show 'that all social conflicts had been resolved and all past humanist endeavours had been realized in the socialist reality of the 1960s' (Sorge 106). Directors in the mid-1960s, whose experimental productions significantly critiqued this attitude, could face serious reprimands from the authorities.[9]

In his persuasive account of the Berliner Ensemble's *Coriolanus*, Suvin argues that the process of political and cultural consolidation greatly influenced co-director Manfred Wekwerth's approach to the production. Committed Marxist intellectuals like Wekwerth had to come to terms with an authoritarian communist regime whose 'revolution' was dictated from above (rather than by the masses) and the fact that the Ensemble could critique a Stalin-like cult of personality 'but only if they stripped it of prefigurative applicability to their own situation' ('Brechtian' 150, 152). Echoing those who accuse British practitioners of depoliticizing Brecht, Suvin writes that the result of this political situation was 'a disbelief into the possibility of an integral plebeian democracy', hence Wekwerth and Tenschert's return to 'Shakespeare's one-sided stress on the Hero' ('Brechtian' 138). This strategy of adapting Brecht's adaptation was especially visible during the production's Corioli scenes in which Suvin accuses the Ensemble of using 'the technical devices of estrangement' in the battles 'for theatrical bewitchment' and thus establishing 'a horizon of mythical estrangement' that 'is unusable for critical understanding' ('Brechtian' 145). Evidence

[54]

for the London staging, however, invites a more complicated reading of the production than the one Suvin provides.

Although the Ensemble script is based on the 1959 version, their version did partially reverse Brecht's changes to the Citizens and the Tribunes. To an extent, the Citizens were less willing to fight, less organized and less politically aware. Unlike Brecht's Citizens in his 1.1, Wekwerth and Tenschert's did not distribute weapons amongst themselves at the start of the performance, the Citizens in the Ensemble's Scene 7 were more impressed with Coriolanus' usefulness to Rome than they are in Brecht's corresponding 2.3, and in the Ensemble's Scene 10 the People were no longer represented by chairmen of their 'electoral districts' who prepare voter lists as they had been in Brecht's 3.2. Yet the German-language sound recording of the 1965 London production at the Old Vic reveals that the People were frequently spirited and reasoning individuals.[10] In the opening scene, the Citizens debated among themselves with conviction about their uprising, and gave as good as they got from Wolf Kaiser's confidently derisive Menenius. The same is true in Scene 7. At the start, they debated calmly and rationally their role in Coriolanus' subsequent scar-showing ceremony, and they held their own against the Coriolanus of Ekkehard Schall, who delivered his lines querulously. They seemed especially composed in comparison to Schall's mockingly bitter performance of his song about begging the People for the Consulship. The Tribunes of the Ensemble's script, too, are less politically significant than they are in Brecht's text. At the end of Brecht's 1.1, the Tribunes tell the Citizens that they will continue to fight for their political interests in Rome while the People are away at war with the Volsces but in the Ensemble script the Tribunes simply hoped the gods will protect the People. In Brecht's 3.2, the Tribunes magnanimously commute Coriolanus' death sentence because of his service to Rome but this incident is cut from the Ensemble's Scene 10. Finally, Wekwerth and Tenschert cut Brecht's 5.5, in which Brutus remarks upon the Citizens' power to turn away Coriolanus' invasion of Rome, and reduced the Tribunes' dialogue and importance to the Senate's proceedings in the final additional Scene 17 (Brecht's 5.7). On the recording, Günter Naumann's Brutus and Martin Flörchinger's Sicinius sound like rational political agents working in the People's interest. Their judicious conversation about the dangers that Coriolanus posed to Rome, once the city had been infected with its victory over the Volsces, was counterpointed with the offstage Romans madly chanting 'Caius Martius Coriolanus!', echoing the crazed militarism of the battle scenes. The chant resounded again at the scene's close, after Bruno Carstens's Cominius praised Coriolanus to the Senate in an ugly and blood-thirsty voice; again, the Tribunes, by contrast, rationally debated the dangers of Coriolanus winning the Consulship. Naumann and Flörchinger were calmly resolute when banishing Cori-olanus and successfully reassured the Citizens when news of Coriolanus' invasion arrived (Scene 15); unlike Shakespeare's mutable Citizens, Johannes Conrad's Faber shouted confidently his affirmation that they were right to banish Coriolanus. For the rest of the production, Naumann and Flörchinger spoke with a businesslike toughness of mind, telling Kaiser's Menenius that the People would indeed stand against Coriolanus (Scene 15b), and forming an alliance with Cominius, not in desperate tones of self-preservation but sounding like dedicated leaders (Scene 15d). In the final scene, Naumann's Brutus had the last word, matter-of-factly countering Kaiser's proposal to honour Cori-olanus with the suggestion that they continue their routine business, which the Senate proceeded to do.

Wekwerth and Tenschert also partially undid Brecht's dimin-ishment of Martius by altering a number of telling details.[11] In the Ensemble's Scene 5, Coriolanus was described as having twenty-seven wounds (as he does in Shakespeare) rather than the nine he has in Brecht (2.1), and at the play's conclusion there is no proposal to allow Coriolanus' family to wear mourning clothes for ten months, and thus no need to reject the particular proposal, a rejection that so clearly underlined Coriolanus' indi-vidual dispensability in Brecht's adaptation. In the production, Schall made his first appearance alone, not with a group of armed men as Martius does in Brecht's text, and thus seemed more singularly brave than he would have done with an entourage. Significantly, the Ensemble script re-emphasized Martius' individual *agon* with Aufidius by restoring Shake-speare's 1.2 (Scene 2) and Aufidius' conspiratorial planning with his henchmen named Spurius and Calvus in the Ensemble Scene 16, action that Brecht had removed entirely. In the production, Hilmar Thate's Aufidius was frequently a rational antagonist to Schall's emotional protagonist. When speaking to Willi

Schwabe's Spurius, Thate was calculating and confidently analytical about suiting himself to the time in order to defeat Coriolanus (Scene 15a). Whereas Schall spoke with an angry desperation that regressed to pleading when his exiled hero offered himself to Thate's Aufidius, Thate's ecstatic gasp at the start of his long speech gave way to an artificial auctioneer-like rattling delivery that sapped the speech of its emotion. During their final encounter, however, both actors furiously shrieked their lines; their delivery seemed almost to be a parody of their warrior-hatred and power-hunger, though whether it served an alienating purpose is unclear. Weigel's brittle-voiced Volumnia, too, was a rational foil to Schall's erratic hero. When arming him, her calm delivery revealed that her admiration for his military prowess was guided by reason, not rapture (Scene 3). She maintained her calm when reasoning with Coriolanus to humble himself before the People, her rational demeanour driving Schall to scream his near-hysterical acquiescence to her (Scene 9). She was just as rational for most of the women's embassy, shouting only when she derided Coriolanus for misunderstanding the smoke from Rome, which she explained was from the forging of weapons. Although Weigel did rant that Coriolanus was disloyal to his family and to her, and although Schall admitted with great emotion that she was responsible for Rome's victory, it was evident that it was not the maternal bond that mattered but her explanation of the smoke that undid him, since he stared at the signal in disbelief, unable to rouse himself to fight, even though Thate's Aufidius urged him on to battle.

Most importantly, Wekwerth and Tenschert turned their attention to the battle scenes, and their focus on this action indicates their effort to portray Coriolanus' development as a hero useful to Rome during wartime, though, as I argue below, the directors developed him according to Brechtian principles. The battle scenes were undoubtedly the most visually impressive aspects of the production's scenography, which appeared to be typically Brechtian in its monochromatic minimalism. Photographs show the white bare stage platform and walls, lit in a constant full-strength white light, dominated by a revolving archway that represented Rome with a white stone façade on one side and Corioles with a black wooden stockade on the other.[12] Additional scenic elements, such as benches for Senators and captured armour hung up on display stands for Martius' victory procession, were brought on the stage and struck as required. Similarly, a tent façade was added to the black stockade to represent Coriolanus' encampment in preparation for attacking Rome. The actors had Roman-inspired costumes of trousers and tunics, helmets, leather breastplates, togas and (for the Patrician women) Roman matronly dresses. Both stockade and performers could be rotated 360 degrees by the large white revolve placed in the centre of the stage, and scene changes occurred behind a half-curtain, a standard Brechtian device that allowed spectators literally to witness the theatre's means of production. Under Wekwerth and Tenschert's direction, the combat included plenty of carefully choreographed, exciting violence. Photographs show two long lines of Volsce and Roman soldiers in pitched battle, grappling and thrusting swords at each other. Other images depict Roman soldiers ascending ladders to enter Corioles while Volsces push the ladders away with long poles. These battles, furthermore, provided Schall tremendous opportunity to flaunt Coriolanus' physical prowess. Certain photographs reveal him calmly standing in the middle of the combat as the Romans climb siege ladders into Corioles; others show him at the centre of the pitched battle or besting individual opponents. The sound recording conveys much more forcefully the frightening power that Londoners encountered in the battles. When the Romans and Volsces first clashed outside Corioli's gates, drums and cymbals crashed repeatedly in accompaniment to an apparently amplified and deep-voiced chant of 'Au-fi-di-us!' This frightening cacophony, which steadily grew in volume, assaulted theatregoers' senses for more than three minutes (Scene 4). This sound was embellished for the second conflict, after Martius emerged from the city. To the drums and cymbals was added a double chant: now 'Cai-us Mar-tius!' answered the bellowed 'Au-fi-di-us, whoo-oo-ooo!' This call-and-response venerated the two military leaders but the overall effect was thrilling and overwhelming, and, to an extent, offered the kind of mystifying portrayal of primal war-lust that Suvin describes.

But did these battles *necessarily* betray Brecht's ostensibly politically useful forms of alienation? In fact, the directors' rearrangement of the first quarter of the script suggests a counterforce to any 'mythical estrangement' that the stage combat may have encouraged. Wekwerth and Tenschert redistributed dialogue from Shakespeare's 1.3 (Virgilia's conversation with Volumnia and Valeria) and 2.1 (Menenius' conversation with the Tribunes) amongst the battle scenes, creating an alternating sequence of 'domestic' scenes in Rome and skirmishes at Corioles. The resulting episodic arrangement of incident is a hallmark of Brechtian or 'epic' narrative structure and the stark juxtaposition between calm and tense action is meant to encourage the audience to reflect upon and analyse the differences.[13] Breaking up Shakespeare's 1.4–1.10, scenes which trace Martius' heroic rise in a largely uninterrupted manner, had the additional effects of decreasing the momentum of his transformation and of making this transformation less apparently inevitable. The hero's rise was further qualified by the creation of the Ensemble's Scene 3, in which Volumnia dresses Martius for battle, taking lines from Shakespeare's 1.3 and six lines from Act 4 of *Antony and Cleopatra* in which Cleopatra helps Antony put on his armour. The scene served a Brechtian alienating purpose insofar as the specific allusion to Shakespeare's earlier tragedy ironized any erotic aspects of the relationship between mother and son, including Volumnia's destructive lust for the glory that will accrue to her in her son's injury, a desire that she explicitly articulated at length in the dialogue preceding these lines in the Ensemble production. Furthermore, the battle chants were repeated later in the production, after Coriolanus' exit in a triumphal procession when he returned to Rome (Scene 6), and at Antium the 'Au-fi-di-us' chant resounded just before Coriolanus encountered Aufidius' men. As noted above, the former chant counterpointed the Tribunes' serious concerns about Coriolanus. The latter chant, meanwhile, was undercut with irony, as two of Aufidius' officers entered, drunkenly intoning the chant and proceeded to urinate as they discussed the effects of alcohol. In the production's penultimate scene, Coriolanus' entry was accompanied by the 'Coriolanus' chant and Aufidius exited in a victorious procession accompanied by the 'Aufidius' chant, leaving the corpse of Schall's Coriolanus on the stage. Although this switching of chants might suggest an essential, mystified spirit of war that is integral to human nature, the final scene, as I remarked earlier, returned audiences to a Rome that had rid itself of an unnecessary warrior. In other words, they were able to see that the warring spirit is changeable, and that the mundane but crucial business of life can be conducted without it.

Other elements of Wekwerth and Tenschert's scenography embody a markedly Brechtian treatment of Martius' character. For example, in the first ten scenes of the production, the directors tracked Martius' development into Coriolanus by carefully establishing parallels in the action through visual military cues. Such cues are a form of the Brechtian 'gest', that outward manifestation of an attitude or bearing which is meant to clarify and make legible the social forces that condition human behaviour.[14] Specifically, *Coriolanus'* visual cues externalized the militarism of Rome as it had conditioned Coriolanus. In Scene 2, the audience watched Thate's Aufidius prepare for battle, and in the following scene Weigel's Volumnia dressed Schall for battle. Schall wore this armour throughout the battle of Corioles and in his duel with Thate until Scene 8, at the end of the fighting, when he entered with Aufidius' captured helmet, which he threw to his comrades. Scene 10 began back in Rome with two soldiers hanging up captured armour for display, a prelude to Schall's Coriolanus being carried on stage in procession, at which point he handed Weigel his sword, completing the arch of action begun with her dressing him in Scene 3.[15] The penultimate scene reversed the trajectory of Martius' victorious transformation into Coriolanus begun in Scene 3 and completed Aufidius' parallel (but deferred) trajectory begun in Scene 2. Schall entered held aloft by cheering Volscian soldiers but, after he was killed, they held Thate's Aufidius aloft, cheering as they exited through the archway. Not only did these military symbols provide a gestic tracking of character but they made perfectly legible the fact that Coriolanus' military prowess is, finally, dispensable for both the Romans and the Volsces.

If the Ensemble's script and scenography suggest a hedging between Shakespeare and Brecht, there is no direct evidence that the company designed the production specifically to fulfil Secretary for Culture Abusch's hopes for Shakespeare's socialist future. Nevertheless, the Ensemble members proved to be experts at managing top officials' opinions of the company's work in the 1950s and 1960s, especially when it came to deflecting perceptions of potentially unflattering parallels between their productions and the frequently brutal reality of life in the GDR (Setje-Eilers). Certainly, the manner in which members of the company explained *Coriolanus* to communities outside the GDR was consistent with Abusch's sentiments. In interviews and (as I discuss below) in programme notes, Weigel, Wekwerth and others in the Ensemble largely avoided making topical statements about East Germany or their specific political agenda. Instead, they described their adaptation in only the most general socialist terms, and consistently and carefully signalled their efforts to remain 'faithful' to Shakespeare.[16] This stance – of insisting upon a respect for Shakespeare's intentions, while evolving him according to quite vague socialist principles rather than using him for specific political critiques – is not simply, as Suvin would have it, a betrayal of Brecht's beliefs. On the contrary, it is an extension of a very Brechtian compromise, and reflects the Ensemble members' appreciation of their mentor's pragmatic willingness to practise the high stakes diplomacy required when making theatre at the geographical centre of the Cold War. The stakes involved in producing Shakespeare in an environment of compromise between political ideals and political reality became fully – and fatally – clear during and shortly after the Ensemble's August 1965 London tour.

The Berliner Ensemble's *Coriolanus* in London: Its contexts and reception

At the end of October 1965, *The Times* reported that the Ensemble actor Christian Weisbrod had been found dead in an East Berlin church earlier that month (27 October 1965). Two months prior to this report, Weisbrod and the Ensemble tailor Rolf Preisser caused a minor sensation by defecting to the West German embassy in London as the company's English tour drew to a close. Although the actor reportedly committed suicide by swallowing pesticide after trying to rejoin the Ensemble in Berlin, his death followed interrogation by East Germany's notorious Stasi secret police (Smith, 'Brecht, the Berliner Ensemble' 321). Whatever its cause, the actor's death is a grim reminder of the tense diplomatic battles waged mostly behind the scenes of the Ensemble tour. West Germany had long pressured its North Atlantic Treaty Organization (NATO) allies to limit East German travel visas to their countries, with the result that Britain's Foreign Office tried, unsuccessfully, to block the Berliner Ensemble's 1956 London tour but did prevent the company's proposed tour to the Edinburgh Festival in 1956 and 1963 (Smith, 'Brecht, the Berliner Ensemble' 311–318). In 1963, public criticism over banning such renowned artists from travelling to a supposedly democratic country caused sufficient friction within the Cabinet that the Prime Minister Harold Macmillan himself expressed exasperation at being 'bullied' by the West Germans (Smith, 'Brecht, the Berliner Ensemble' 317–319). The government eventually announced, in March 1964, that an easing of visa restrictions would occur in exchange for two imprisoned American pilots who had been shot down in the GDR (Smith, 'Brecht, the Berliner Ensemble' 320).

None of the political forces that generated the strife which took place in the British Cabinet, amongst NATO allies or between the capitalist West and communist East, were directly reflected in the Ensemble's discussions of their work. Instead, company members depicted their performances to London theatregoers in terms of an almost apolitical theatrical aesthetic, providing only an imprecise socialist gloss on their work. These efforts to accommodate themselves to British audience expectations for the performance of Shakespeare are clear in the *Coriolanus* programme, a document that was especially important for introducing the production to English theatregoers who, by and large, did not speak German. The programme note describing the Ensemble, for instance, relates that they strive to embody Brecht's dictum that 'What has to be done is to develop two arts: an art of acting and an art of watching'. Such nebulousness about the company's fundamental principles, which masks any pointedly Marxist impetus for their work, is mirrored in the programme's explanation of Brecht's approach to adapting the play. This note states that Brecht found Volumnia's pleading speech in Act 5 'strangely uninspired' but that 'Brecht regarded Shakespeare far too highly to' think that he did not have an ulterior motive for this lack of inspiration. Having searched for this motive, and amazed at 'how much Shakespeare's realism yields', Brecht was able to discover the play's 'true story': the People must pay the price for Coriolanus' selfish duel with Aufidius, but they resist Coriolanus once they realize he is expendable, and it is this Plebeian resistance that actually breaks the protagonist's will. This Plebeian-focused exegesis undoubtedly runs contrary to a traditional heroic understanding of Coriolanus but its political import is euphemistic at best, shrouded as it is in an admiring analysis of Shakespeare. Such statements could simply be regarded as the company's effort to find common ground with audiences who were likely to be hostile to Marxist ideology. Yet, even in the avowedly socialist paper *The Daily Worker*, Wekwerth explicitly portrayed their production as faithful to the playwright, insisting that their *Coriolanus* is 'not a rewritten Shakespeare, but a rescued Shakespeare, based on an entirely new and truer translation Brecht had made' (Leeson, 'How They Carry'). Thus, in explaining themselves to the British public, the Ensemble drew on respect for Shakespeare as a form of shared understanding, and they treated the performance of this deeply political tragedy as a partially depoliticized forum where differences between bourgeois capitalist audiences and the world's most famous communist theatre company could disappear.

Certain English reviewers re-enforced the company's depoliticization of *Coriolanus* by explaining the production in terms of naturalist acting assumptions about generating emotionally convincing and moving individual personalities. In other words, they discerned in the production 'a Brecht whose priorities are emotional, personal, intuitive, practical and British'. Ensemble actors were praised for 'put[ting] to shame every other company in the world for the conviction with which they invest their work' (*Daily Mail* 11 August 1965) and for creating 'moments ... of almost unbearable poignancy' (*Financial Times* 11 August 1965). Schall in particular was singled out for his '[s]uperbly controlled and measured' performance, for the 'explosive force' of his acting 'that is shattering in its impact' (*Stage* 12 August 1965) and for going out of his way to 'show us a man without patience, a grown-up "mother's boy"' (*Daily Mail* 11 August 1965). More often, this depoliticizing strand of reception centred on an appreciation of the aesthetic power of the fight scenes at Corioli, bearing out Suvin's critique of the 'theatrical bewitchment' generated by the Ensemble's presentation that was 'unusable for critical understanding'. Reviewers valued 'the gymnastics of the individual combats [which] are breathtaking' (*Jewish Chronicle* 20 August 1965), while the group battles were praised as 'spectacular', filled with 'ritualism' (*The Observer* 15 August 1965), and, 'staged with marvellous precision and tremendous dramatic power', became 'a great event in themselves' (*Stage* 12 August 1965).

Simultaneously, however, other aspects of the London reception politicized *Coriolanus*. In particular, reviewers confronted the production's political import by attributing to Brecht those elements of the production they deemed too narrowly ideological to qualify as Shakespeare. These critics sought to protect Shakespeare from the German playwright's ideological influence, labelling Brecht a 'proselytizer' (*Scotsman* 16 August 1965) who was 'blinded by pet political passions' (*Press and Journal* 21 August 1965). They insisted that Shakespeare, who had so much 'respect for individual magnitude' (*The Times* 11 August 1965) and who was anything but 'a convinced Prole' (*Daily Telegraph* 11 August 1965), received a 'rigidly perverse treatment' (*The Times* 11 August 1965) by the Ensemble 'in order to twist the story to Marxian purpose' (*Glasgow Herald* 14 August 1965). Not only would this *Coriolanus* 'not be recalled as a contribution to Shakespeare' (*The Illustrated News* 21 August 1965), but only 'a dramatist with a command of language as sublime as Shakespeare's' could 'invest his [Brecht's] crude propagandist tracts with any interest for people of sense and sensibility' (*What's On* 19 August 1965).

Much of the negative response to the battle scenes makes it clear that such politicization was a matter not simply of declaring the impossibility of a Marxist Shakespeare but of keeping German Shakespeare in its place. Several critics treated the combat as antithetical to a 'native', roughly Stanislavskian playing style that values the 'realism' of the illusion that action is occurring for the first time. Critics who were put off by the apparent 'calculation and patience and drill that' went into the battles which 'seem to work at the push of a button' (*Glasgow Herald* 14 August 1965) implicitly critiqued the East German company's purposefully choreographed artifice, and one reviewer specifically connected the Ensemble's nationality and its 'calculated' style: 'I get the impression that these players are automatons like Prussian troops on parade never varying from one performance or manoeuvre to another' (*Press and Journal* 21 August 1965). This xenophobic tone was even more pronounced in the comments of those reviewers who saw the battles' 'theatrical bewitchment' as evidence of some primal German bloodlust: Schall was the 'embodiment of the bullet-headed Junker ... never far from violence' (*The Times* 11 August 1965), and there was 'a power not ourselves [i.e. not English] which makes for a wickedness' in the combat scenes (*Sunday Times* 15 August 1965). Just like those who portrayed the combat as the work of automata, these critics equated the non-naturalistic mystical performance style they perceived in the battles with the production's foreignness. Irving Wardle wrote that this violence 'outclasses anything we have seen in the Royal Shakespeare's *Wars of the Roses*' because it is 'more barbarous and terrifying than any representation of naturalistic combat' (*The Times* 11 August 1965) and J.W. Lambert went so far as to declare that the Ensemble's presentation had nothing to do with Brechtian emotional distance but actually conjured the mesmerizing violence of Nazi rallies: 'we were plunged into a nightmare of drums and guns, marching songs, chanted slogans, and superbly spoken intoxicating rant' (*Sunday Times* 29 August 1965). In this theatrical attack on 'the guts' that induced a 'frenzy of applause, hands red and bruised with clapping, feet numb with stamping, eyes at once glazed and blazing', it was, he claims, '[i]mpossible not to hear now a dreadful ironical echo – and from the other side of the wall into the bargain – of that very Germany of the 1930s from which Brecht was forced to flee' (*Sunday Times* 29 August 1965).

The contradictory impulses that animated both the production and reception of the 1965 *Coriolanus* defy easy categorization. *Coriolanus* did not merely represent a 'simplistic Marxism' that failed as a 'substitute for the mature, if maddening political complexity of the original' (Ripley 311) because the performance context itself produced such politically complex results. The Ensemble's combined profession of fidelity to Shakespeare and to vaguely articulated Marxist principles was met by an ostensibly depoliticizing understanding of performance that both incorporated Brecht's politically motivated theatrical theory and served as an exclusionary, reactionary force. This force revealed, with an explicitness that East German actors could simply not afford, the severity of the political and military conflicts between Axis and Allies and their NATO and Soviet Bloc successors that the Ensemble's performances in London were meant to cover over. Although nothing as momentous as Christian Weisbrod's death occurred when Wekwerth and Tenschert returned six years later to direct a company of National Theatre actors in *Coriolanus*, the same contradictory theatrical and political currents shaped the creation and reception of this English-language production.

Shakespeare and Brecht reprised at
the National Theatre in 1971

In the spring of 1971 Christopher Plummer withdrew from rehearsals as the lead in the National Theatre's *Coriolanus*, apparently over artistic differences with Wekwerth and Tenschert. A gossipy *Times* 'Diary' article published three weeks before *Coriolanus* opened at the Old Vic on 7 May reported (without referring to any sources) that the directors planned to stage an English version of their Ensemble script but that those at the National expected them to stage Shakespeare's script (14 April 1971). Denied a second chance to present a purportedly 'near psychotic' and 'parasit[ic]' Roman hero to London audiences, the directors apparently had to rewrite the play twice (*The Times* 14 April 1971). Benedict Nightingale was equally severe in his review, claiming that Plummer – who was replaced by Anthony Hopkins – chose to leave 'rather than pervert his performance in the manner the directors demanded' (*New Statesman* 14 May 1971). Are these charges of near-psychosis, parasitism and perversion confirmation that the National's *Coriolanus* was caught up in the 'Press War' as the East German magazine *GDR Review* later claimed (W.T., *Coriolanus* 57)? Was the response an aspect of 'the class struggle, something which according to the bourgeois Press no longer exists' (W.T., *Coriolanus* 57)? Perhaps, but printed reaction indicates that the British press was no more conscious of being part of any class struggle than it had been in 1965. In fact, while Wekwerth and Tenschert altered the 1971 script to bring it closer to Shakespeare's text, this later production reveals an intensification of the forces embodied in the 1965 *Coriolanus*.

Wekwerth and Tenschert described the 1971 *Coriolanus* as a compromise between Brechtian principles and a certain understanding of Shakespearean performance, though they positioned themselves closer to Shakespeare than they had in 1965. To be sure, the directors emphasized their Brecht-inspired approach to the theatrical representation of social relations and an analytical apprehension of character. When Wekwerth asserted that 'The first instance of democratic and historical thinking' in the play is when the People 'free themselves from the myth that this man [Coriolanus] is indispensable' (*Morning Star* 4 May 1971), or that in 'choosing between the people and a single [military] specialist, however necessary he may be, the decision must be in favour of the people' (*Morning Star* 4 May 1971), he expressed obvious, if generalized, Marxist attitudes about the production. At the same time, Wekwerth and Tenschert aligned Brecht's theory with Shakespeare's dramaturgy while making Brecht's ideas more comprehensible in 'British' terms that equate Shakespeare with emotional plausibility and complexity. Tenschert was careful to stress, even more than company members had been in 1965, Brecht's desire to remain faithful to Shakespeare, remarking that 'the starting point for [their] production of the Shakespearean version at the National Theatre' in 1971 was Brecht's conviction that, eventually, 'it would be possible to convey this interpretation using Shakespeare's original text' (*Morning Star* 4 May 1971). Furthermore, the co-directors revealed an interest in making 'The poetic nature of the hero's loneliness ... emotionally accessible' (Programme) and qualified their Brechtian conviction that the hero 'destroys himself by using his great services as a means to blackmail his fellow-citizens' (Programme) with recourse to the cliché of the playwright's grasp of psychological complexity: 'Motives in Shakespeare are as numerous and complex as the refractions of light in a prism' (Programme).[17]

Continuity between the Ensemble's *Coriolanus* and the 1971 *Coriolanus* is particularly evident in the latter production's appearance. The set was once again a bare stage with a revolve at centre stage and a reversible building with the black stockade for Corioles and a white Roman wall (now brick rather than stone).[18] The armour, togas, weapons, gowns and props are virtually identical in pictures of the two productions, and in comparing these pictures it is clear that, despite some minor facial differences, even Schall and Hopkins look remarkably similar; both are stocky, with large round heads, strong jaw lines and powerful necks. The photographs also show actors adopting identical gestures and blocking: in one image that appears in both sets of archival pictures, Schall and Hopkins enter Rome carried on a chair in the post-Corioles procession, their arms extended upwards in victory; Weigel's and Constance Cummings's Volumnias hold aloft Coriolanus' sword in both pairs of hands and Renate Richter's 1965 and Anna Carteret's 1971 Virgilias reach up to the victor. As in the 1965 staging, furthermore, Wekwerth and Tenschert tracked Coriolanus' development through the gestic use of military symbols in 1971, from Aufidius' and Martius' arming in Scenes 2 and 3 respectively, to Martius throwing the Volsce's captured helmet to his comrades in Scene 8, to the Lictors hanging up battle spoils in Scene 10, to Aufidius' defeat of Coriolanus and the victory procession exit in the assassination scene. Finally, the directors employed the powerfully menacing battle chants of 'Au-fi-di-us' and 'Cai-us Mar-tius' to largely the same effects as they had in the earlier London staging.

Changes to the 1971 production, however, demonstrate an even more significant retreat from Brecht's adaptation than Suvin discerns in the Ensemble's *Coriolanus*. The 1971 script is not a translation of the Ensemble's German text but employs Shakespeare's language throughout. Furthermore, although important features of the Ensemble's script – Volumnia's arming of Coriolanus in Scene 3, the alternation between domestic and battle scenes early in the production, the deletion of the women's victory procession after their embassy to Coriolanus – remain in the 1971 text, Wekwerth and Tenschert made numerous changes to diminish the ideological favour shown to the Tribunes and the Plebeians in both Brecht's and the Ensemble's versions. By cutting lines, the Citizens become less politically savvy in 1971's Scene 12 (Coriolanus' bid for the Consulship) and, by replacing Shakespearean dialogue, the Citizens become more fickle in 1971's Scene 19 (when news of Coriolanus' planned invasion arrives). The sound recording suggests that the People were occasionally dangerous and fickle: they chanted frighteningly in celebration of Coriolanus' victorious return (Scene 10) as they had in the Ensemble production, but, unlike their brave counterparts in 1965, Derek Woodward's scared Third Citizen appeared to deserve the scolding from John Moffatt's Menenius when the former gave voice to the terror that Coriolanus' invasion had struck into the People's hearts (Scene 19). Still, the People were, in fact, rational and serious debaters in the production's opening uprising and when questioning Hopkins's irritable hero in the scar-showing ceremony (Scene 12). In the 1971 production, meanwhile, the Tribunes were deprived of their function as the People's honest, selfless representatives: they lost lines in which they give Martius credit for his usefulness as a warrior (Scenes 1 and 7); they did not question Coriolanus about his plan to distribute captured Volsce grain (Scene 13); and they did not form an alliance with Cominius on behalf of the People to resist Coriolanus (Scene 23). In performance, the Tribunes became increasingly self-serving and unappealing as the production unfolded. The sinister tone of their calculating dialogue at the end of Scenes 7 and 11 was mitigated by the demagogic threat embodied in the People's chanting for Coriolanus. Yet, by Scene 11, Bernard Gallagher's Brutus and Charles Kay's Sicinius sounded as if they relished their own plotting, their self-confidence was closer to officiousness when accusing Coriolanus just prior to banishing him (Scene 15) and, unlike the 1965 staging, the Tribunes were exposed to what seemed like a justified rebuke from Cummings's furious Volumnia right after Coriolanus' banishment (Scene 16). Finally, their unattractively smug condescension towards Menenius about the rightness of exiling Coriolanus turned into even less attractive desperate rage and disbelief upon hearing of the impending Volsce invasion (Scene 19).

One of the most significant changes Wekwerth and Tenschert made to the 1971 production was to delete the extra final Senate scene they had staged in 1965, in which the Tribunes assume executive power. As a consequence, Coriolanus' assassination became the climax of the 1971 staging, giving the production's narrative an endpoint that focuses attention on the hero's individual tragedy. Even if the battle sequences were part of a gestic use of military symbols to track the hero's development, the blatant war-lust that Hopkins's Martius displayed not only contributed to the visceral experience of the fight but grounded his heroism in the personal military glory that would be at stake in the final scene. When the noise of war began, he intoned 'O, they are at it' with quiet but profound satisfaction (Scene 4). Moments later, he returned from his lone battle within Corioles' walls; breathing heavily, Hopkins rallied the Roman soldiers with a rousing speech that ended with him shrieking, 'We'll beat 'em into bench holes. I have yet / Room for six gashes more' (Scene 4). The ecstasy with which Hopkins infused his vow of personal sacrifice was an apt prelude to the terrifying chanting ('Au-fi-di-us' and 'Cai-us Mar-tius'), which personalized the combat that immediately followed. Wekwerth and Tenschert made sure that Hopkins set himself apart from the common soldiers when they retreated in battle by playing a recording of the actor growling and shouting his way through Martius' 'All the contagion of the south light on you, / You shames of Rome!' speech (Scene 4). While Hopkins's disembodied voice might have been a distancing technique, there was little such distance in his conflicts with the People elsewhere in the production. In his first encounter with the People, Hopkins derided them with an often relaxed tone of contempt that was all the more contemptuous for his apparent refusal to expend much energy on them (Scene 1). Yet Hopkins revealed Coriolanus' neurosis when undergoing the scar ceremony, and made a show of controlling himself as his anger mounted, forcing himself to adopt a more charmingly humble disposition by the end of his calling repeatedly for the People's voices (Scene 12). He did not control himself, though, when assailing the Tribunes and the People at Coriolanus' banishment, making a dramatic exit by flinging down his leather cloak once he had delivered the 'There is a world elsewhere' speech with intense scorn (Scene 15). The directors replaced Sicinius' orders to vex Coriolanus as he leaves Rome's gate with the Tribunes' less petty-sounding instructions about the details of his banishment. Yet the scene ended with Moffatt's Menenius and Michael Turner's Cominius looking first to each other and then at the cloak on the ground, redirecting the audience's gaze to the sign of the hero's absence.

By moving directly from the women's embassy at the Volsce camp to the assassination, Wekwerth and Tenschert reinforced the importance of Volumnia and Aufidius as individual antagonists to the development of Coriolanus' identity. Cummings's Volumnia was not bloodthirsty but, like Weigel, she was calmly rational when talking to Carteret's Virgilia of Martius' valour (Scene 3) and spoke with restrained passion when anticipating Coriolanus' victory procession (Scene 10). Her subdued tone when reasoning with Hopkins's petulant Coriolanus to humble himself before the People finally gave way to guilt-inducing anger as she told him, 'Do as thou list. / Thy valiantness was mine, thou suck'dst it from me, / But owe thy pride thyself' (Scene 14). Their roles were reversed at Coriolanus' exile, however, where Hopkins had to console a mournful and quavering-voiced Cummings, who, moments later, unleashed her desperate rage on the Tribunes. She carried such emotions into her final scene. Here, the familial bond alone broke Coriolanus since, unlike the 1965 staging, this Volumnia did not tell her son that the Plebeians' resolve to fight had rendered him dispensable to Rome (Scene 24). The power of the familial bond registered early in the scene; when Carteret's tender-voiced Virgilia presented Michael Gould's Young Martius to Hopkins, the latter paused for a dramatic thirty seconds, caught up in the emotion of the moment. Cummings used Volumnia's two long (and now uncut) speeches to deliver a slow passionate burn. By the time she neared the end of her second long speech, her voice was trembling pitifully. She paused to great effect for twenty seconds between 'Down' and 'an end', concluding her plea with a combination of browbeating and lament (Scene 24). Hopkins then remained silent for another emotionally charged thirty seconds, before bursting out 'O mother, mother! / What have you done?' (Scene 24). Quilley's Aufidius used this mother-induced (rather than Plebeian-induced) emotional breakdown against Hopkins's Coriolanus in the final scene. This last scene was a flashpoint for Quilley; although he greeted Hopkins's exiled hero with intense passion, their exchange in battle was not exceptionally hate-filled, and Quilley played the Volsce mostly as a coldly reasoning schemer who could easily out-manoeuvre his enemy. Hopkins made the strain of Coriolanus' encounter with his mother show in the final scene, shouting his greetings to the Volsces in apparent desperation, though he had been carried in on the soldiers' shoulders. Quilley lashed out quickly, probing the familial wound that had been opened in the previous scene with tremendous derision on 'his nurse's tears' and 'thou boy of tears' (Scene 25). He clearly hit his mark, as Hopkins shrieked his defiance, and raged each of the three times he repeated, 'Boy' (Scene 25). Although the Volsce soldiers surrounded Hopkins while James Hayes and David Henry's two Conspirators killed this Coriolanus, the last moment echoed the hero's banishment scene while reiterating the personal agonistic nature of his defeat. Quilley's last words were not Shakespeare's 'Assist' but the loudly commanded and non-Shakespearean 'Give me his sword' and the weapon was passed to him along a line of soldiers (Scene 25). The soldiers then carried Quilley off stage on their shoulders as the 'Au-fi-di-us' chant began, leaving Hopkins prone on stage, just as he had discarded his cloak when banished from Rome. The image was a powerful refutation of Coriolanus' belief that he could find a world elsewhere allied to his rival, the rival who had won a key symbol of his military glory from Coriolanus.

As in 1965, critics framed their response in relation to an idealized Shakespearean characterization that involved creating powerful emotions and complex, outsized individual personalities. Reviewers admired the production for its 'emotional relationships' (Cushman 59) and 'The plausible but unexpected character development of the principal protagonists' which 'generates the excitement of a thriller' (*Sunday Telegraph* 9 May 1971). Critics went even further to single out Hopkins's performance than they had Schall's, perhaps because the English script allowed critics to place Hopkins's speaking of the role within a context that specifically rewards emotional realism in a way that they could not do with Schall's German dialogue. They valued Hopkins for his 'wide-ranging performance of power and authority' (*Daily Express* 7 May 1971), his 'warmth', 'his extraordinary transitions from repose to roaring danger' (Cushman 59) and the 'heroic scale' (*The Times* 7 May 1971) of his performance. The degree to which these reviewers depoliticized the production's Brechtian aspects is particularly evident in their eagerness to pronounce Hopkins a theatrical celebrity who 'is clearly being groomed as one of the stars of the National Theatre' (*Daily Express* 7 May 1971) and who was ready to join 'the ranks of the leading actors of his generation' (*Sunday Telegraph* 9 May 1971) with 'a performance which clinches his claim to be regarded as one of the most formidable talents to emerge since Nicol Williamson' (*The Observer* 9 May 1971). Such comments do not simply venerate 'bourgeois individualism' but, by elevating Hopkins to the level of a star, undermine Wekwerth and Tenschert's efforts to demonstrate Coriolanus' dispensability.

As they had in 1965, British critics once more simultaneously politicized the 1971 *Coriolanus*. They derided, for instance, the Brechtian elements of the production as too simplistic and thus ideologically incompatible with Shakespeare. Benedict Nightingale complained of the limits imposed on the production by Wekwerth and Tenschert, whose attempt 'to turn the stupid, brutal plebs into the oppressed and worthy heroes of an Eisenstein film' showed 'less respect for the name on the front of the programme [Shakespeare] than the one invoked inside it [Brecht]' (*New Statesman* 14 May 1971). Furthermore, reviewers repeated criticisms of the 1965 production's aesthetics as specifically foreign. Philip Hope-Wallace asserted that 'Rome looked as drab as Berlin in the Depression and rang with heavy rather un-English sounding declamation' (*The Guardian* 7 May 1971), while J.W. Lambert echoed his own earlier xenophobic comments: 'The English actors proved, one was almost thankful to note, quite unable to match, in the interminably extended battle scenes, the savage militaristic zest of their German opposite numbers' (28). Ronald Bryden, too, who responded very positively to the production, argued that, while it was the National Theatre's job to stage the classics innovatively, 'it should be able to run up its own, not buy them abroad off the peg ... It's an alien hand-me-down and it looks it' (*The Observer* 9 May 1971).

The direction in which Brechtian incarnations of *Coriolanus* moved, from the German director's work on a proposed production in the early 1950s to the National's 1971 staging, gives some credence to the charges that Brecht's plays were depoliticized over time, especially by British practitioners and reviewers. However, such critiques' implicit idealization of Brechtian theatre – the same idealization which supposedly animated work on *Coriolanus* – misses out on how the processes of adaptation, production and reception entailed complicated interactions between the ideal and real historical imperatives, between politicized and depoliticized theatre. It is precisely the complexity of such interactions that Günter Grass takes up in *The Plebeians Rehearse the Uprising*, and London audiences would get a chance to reflect upon the recent history of this interplay between the real and the ideal on their own stages when the RSC mounted Grass's play in 1970.

Rehearsing Brecht rehearsing Shakespeare: *The Plebeians Rehearse the Uprising*

The RSC opened *Plebeians* at the Aldwych Theatre in July 1970, four years after its German premiere in Berlin. The play dramatizes the 1953 East German workers' uprising from within the theatre housing a fictionalized Berliner Ensemble, overseen by a fictionalized Bertolt Brecht called the Boss. As the company rehearses something like Brecht's *Coriolanus*, the workers enter, seeking a statement of support from the Boss for their protest against increased production quotas. The Boss, in turn, wants to use the rebelling workers' experiences as material for his own aesthetic purposes in adapting Shakespeare. The play thus raises

[73]

questions about the nature of adaptation and theatrical rehearsal, about the politically committed artist forced to confront impossible historical circumstances and about Brecht's identity as a revolutionary playwright-director. The London production raised all these issues but it also demonstrated the durability of an aestheticized approach to Brechtian theatre in Britain, as well as the British theatre establishment's reluctance to contemplate fully the political implications of an institution like the RSC staging such an overtly political representation of the recent theatrical past.

Aspects of Grass's 1964 address to the Academy of Arts and Letters in Berlin, which is prefixed to the published version of *Plebeians*, leave the impression that the play is a personal attack on Brecht and his Marxist aesthetics. In this speech, Grass charges Brecht with, among other things, scripting 'a play of partisanship, in which Coriolan becomes an increasingly crude military specialist, the wise fool Menenius turns into a reactionary clown, and the two tribunes of the people are metamorphosed into class strugglers of the second if not the first water' (xx–xxi). At the end of the address, however, Grass offers an alternative to the *ad hominem* interpretation, opening his perspective outwards to consider the broader historical circumstances captured by the play that he eventually wrote: 'A public place in Rome and the Government Building on Leipziger Strasse ... History and its adaptation. Literary property and its owners. The national holiday and the Shakespeare Year: this play demands to be written' (xxxvi). In this comparative framework, Brecht's personal identity and his fictional behaviour serve as a pretext for exploring something more than personal animosity or the shortcomings of adaptations that are unfaithful to their originals. The collision of the Boss's theatre and the workers' uprising becomes, in Grass's drama, an opportunity to explore the role of the artist in mediating reality and how the demands of the present can be served by adapting the past.

Plebeians incorporates very little of Shakespeare's or Brecht's scripts directly. The Boss occasionally cites several of Coriolanus' lines, two actors speak about a dozen of the Tribunes' speeches, the actor-Plebeians rehearse their opening scene and some dialogue after they have elected Coriolanus Consul, Erwin the literary adviser/dramaturg quotes Menenius' 'Tale of the Belly' and the Volumnia character speaks a few of her name-

[74]

sake's lines. For the most part, though, the unfolding action depicts a series of implicit and explicit analogies between Shakespeare's Rome and the GDR of 1953 and, as the events in East Berlin take their course, the director comes increasingly to resemble the hero that Brecht wished to show was dispensable. Just as Shakespeare's Plebeians ultimately rely on Coriolanus for his military prowess, Grass's East German workers rely on the Boss to articulate their case eloquently to the GDR officials in a letter, and, just as Shakespeare's Coriolanus despises the Plebeians for their inconstancy and cowardice, the Boss mocks the workers' lack of preparedness for committed revolutionary action. Coriolanus must contend with the two Tribunes' enmity but the Boss must cope with two sets of Tribune figures: his actors playing Sicinius and Brutus who wish the company to join the workers' uprising; and Wiebe and Damasschke, two labour organizers who threaten the Boss but flee in terror once they learn of the Soviet tanks that have been deployed to crush the unrest. In a reworking of Coriolanus' and Menenius' confrontation with the Plebeians in Shakespeare's opening scene, the Boss and his dramatic adviser Erwin are nearly hanged by the angry workers. Similarly, while Coriolanus pits his valour against Aufidius and momentarily joins his antagonist, the Boss mocks fellow-writer Kozanka for being a second-rate government poet-lackey, and nearly agrees to sign Kozanka's condemnation of the uprising before devising his own equivocal statement.

The analogy between the Boss and Coriolanus is solidified by the former's relationship to the actress playing Volumnia, who stands in for Helene Weigel, and who was played by Peggy Ashcroft in 1970. Like Shakespeare's Roman matron, Grass's Volumnia first urges the Boss to support the uprising but then to withdraw his support (thus playing into Kozanka's hands) once the authorities declare martial law. However, Grass gives the analogy an ironic twist. The Boss quotes Coriolanus' complaint to Menenius, namely that he must 'Brag unto them [the Plebeians], thus I did, and thus ...' (47), but he does so by way of refusing Volumnia's initial request to support the uprising. Unlike Coriolanus, the Boss denies this Volumnia a second time; explicitly accusing her of trying to turn him into Coriolanus by embracing an Aufidius-like Kozanka, he declares that he will not play the assigned role. Grass's final ironic stroke occurs as the

Boss, alone on stage, delivers the play's closing speech, apparently to the defeated workers: 'Condemned to live forever with your voices in my ears. You. You. I'll tell you. Do you know what you are? You, you, you're a ... You poor babes in the woods! Bowed down with guilt, I accuse you!' (111). The last clause echoes the exiled Coriolanus' riposte to his Roman enemies, 'I banish you'. Yet, unlike Shakespeare's protagonist, who finally and ostentatiously embraces death after compromising himself twice at his mother's bidding, the Boss's tragedy is that, having twice refused his Volumnia, he must go on living. He finally plans to retreat from his political theatre to the privacy of self-imposed exile at his country villa where he will write poetry, and live with the guilt of his failure to help the workers.

Grass builds towards this shift from the political into the aesthetic from the start of the play by having the Boss constantly incorporate the 'real' offstage world of the GDR into the theatrical process. He listens to recordings of women at the market complaining about food shortages and encourages the workers to act out their experiences of the uprising, using their performances to clarify his own staging of *Coriolanus*. Similarly, he tape-records the workers' comments in his theatre, and plays back the Mason's insults, considering their theatrical value. When his actor-plebeians and the 'actual' workers start a real fist-fight (which sounds quite violent on the sound recording), the Boss comments, 'Now that I call the class struggle. A drunken wedding / Between plebs and proles' (37).[19] Emrys James delivered the line with the same sardonic tone that had characterized his speech from the beginning, his sarcasm signalling both the Boss's confident awareness of his own status as 'Boss' and an ironic distance from that superior role. James maintained this sarcasm, arguably a variation on orthodox Brechtian distancing techniques, when he quickly intervened to choreograph the battle, remarking with mock-admiration that he would like to cast them in bronze as a statue demonstrating how 'Socialism, scorning pain / And muscle cramp ... conquers!' (38). The Boss takes this choreography a step further, getting the workers to perform, acting out the uprising on stage alongside his own actor-Plebeians whom he transforms into rebelling East German workers.

Plebeians, in fact, shows a two-way movement between historical events and their aesthetic counterparts. When the workers grow tired of the Boss turning their uprising into art and actually prepare to hang him and Erwin 'in the middle of their phony Rome' (75), Erwin saves them by paraphrasing Menenius' 'Tale of the Belly'. The workers in the 1971 production were convincingly angry, especially Michael Gambon's ruthless Tribune-substitute Wiebe. Nicholas Selby's Erwin delivered his version of the 'Tale of the Belly' emphatically, becoming increasingly confident and persuasively chastising as the parable unfolded. The ironies of such an emotionally committed performance were palpable. The actor Selby was playing the fictional Berliner Ensemble dramaturg, who was quoting a role, a standard Brechtian distancing technique. Yet such commitment to a fable that the Boss considered patently trite and insufficient to convince real workers did actually sway the present workers in a fashion that Brecht's alienation effects were meant to combat. Meanwhile, Selby's powerful emotionalism made plausible the notion that Erwin could save the fictitious Brecht with beguiling artifice. Moreover, Grass depicts the relationship between the offstage reality of the uprising and its aesthetic double to be a kind of feedback loop, in which the aesthetic plays into and converts offstage reality which, in turn, intrudes upon the theatrical. For instance, as the uprising begins outside the theatre, Volumnia encourages the Boss to support the protesters but, when she describes the workers, he mocks her for borrowing quotations from him; her understanding of the real uprising has been shaped by his theatre and her 'Every word's rehearsed' (20). However, the Boss subsequently loses his sarcastic detachment and becomes caught up in his own feedback loop. Fascinated by the sight of the injured Mason, shot in an offstage skirmish, the Boss is nearly convinced to join the uprising by the Hairdresser who helps recount the events. Like Grass's Volumnia, her call for actual revolution in the streets of East Berlin is shaped by the Boss's theatre. She tells him that, four years earlier, she watched his self-sacrificial character Katrin 'drumming on the roof. / As now I scream. The tanks are coming! / Come on, Boss. Come, and crawl out of that shell: / And we'll put on a play for the whole world, / Enacted in the street, on barricades' (92). Lisa Harrow delivered these lines with a compelling, almost bloodthirsty (almost Volumnia-like) romanticism for street-fighting, giving credence to James's Boss being momentarily persuaded by a woman who draws inspiration for real battle from Brecht's *Mother Courage*. In the same way that the Hairdresser imagines the real battle as a play, the Boss imagines the poetry of real political action. In performance, Harrow and James fed off each other's mounting emotional intensity, until James's Boss became enraptured, lyrically declaring that, 'As in [his] youth, under a sky swept clean', 'Alone for the time of a poem', he would speak on the radio to 'Conjure up chaos, rivers' (92, 93).

Yet, in the same way that the play links the Boss's retreat into poetry with his failure to help the uprising, Grass ultimately emphasizes the limitations of this aestheticization in the face of historical and political realities. Volumnia and the Mason repeatedly accuse the Boss of shirking his responsibility to the uprising by merely playing at politics in his theatre, and his assistant, Podulla, having witnessed the Soviets battling the workers, derides the effort to theatricalize the uprising, bitterly wondering how they might get a tank on stage. While Grass lets the Boss defend his extended rehearsal of real political struggle by arguing that the 'indoctrinated tribunes' in his adapted *Coriolanus* 'will show the plebeians how you make a revolution and how you don't' (13), Grass halts the feedback between reality and theatre by ironically evoking Volumnia's theatrical and historically real identities to force the Boss to face real political consequences. Early in the play, when urging the Boss to support the workers, Ashcroft's Volumnia became carried away with the romanticism of the uprising, or at least she made a fine show of putting on her revolutionary idealism, which James's Boss found laughable. Later, Volumnia stops her husband, his actors and the workers from leaving with the Hairdresser by showing them the city commandant's order to institute martial law. When warning the Boss to 'calm down, and start thinking up the answers' (93), the hard-edged pragmatism of Ashcroft's delivery shed a sceptical light on her previous idealism. Grass's irony is that Volumnia's insistence on the political reality of the authorities' military power is itself strongly reminiscent of both Shakespeare's Volumnia and Brecht's Mother Courage (historically played by Weigel in the 1949 Berlin production that inspires the Hairdresser) who survive Coriolanus and Katrin respectively through their superior guile and recognition of political necessity. The further irony, of course, is that Ashcroft was apparently turning this Volumnia into a version of the historical Weigel, whose instincts for appeasing **GDR** authorities were crucial to the Ensemble's survival and success.

There are good reasons, then, to understand why Grass later insisted that the play is as much about a politically engaged artist like himself as it is about Brecht (Preece 103). Grass allows the Boss a convincing defence of his aesthetic principles against the short-sightedness of the workers and the self-interest of Volumnia and Kozanka, the Boss's theatricalization of the uprising makes his stage a revolutionary one and the Boss abandons his Brechtian rehearsal techniques only in the face of overwhelming social and military forces. It is thus not unreasonable to regard all the members of *Plebeians'* fictional Berliner Ensemble as figures comparable to Grass, who worked for Willy Brandt's West German Social Democratic Party and commented actively on German politics. Viewing the play in this light, Grass appears to be negotiating with the past not simply to criticize Brecht's personal artistic judgement nor to single out the failings of ideologically motivated adaptation. Rather, he adapts recent history in order to meditate on the limits facing those who try to influence a political reality by theatrical means.

Plainly, such a work cuts to the heart of the issues that were raised by the production and reception of Brechtian Shakespeare in the 1960s, and staging *Plebeians* in 1970 allowed the RSC and its audiences to reflect upon the company's identity in its first decade *as* the Royal Shakespeare Company. It gave the company, which was dedicated to performing both classical and modern drama, the opportunity implicitly to comment upon more than a decade of Britain's incorporation of Brecht, an incorporation that had been most visibly undertaken by the RSC's principal rival, the National Theatre, when they hosted the 1965 Ensemble tour. Of course, the RSC had itself been greatly influenced by Brecht, a fact made clear in design choices during the 1960s and in projects like John Barton's adaptation of the *Henry VI* plays, *The Wars of the Roses* (Loehlin; Hampton-Reeves and Rutter 54–79). Even more significantly, when Peter Hall took over the Artistic Directorship of the Shakespeare Memorial Theatre in 1959, his most obvious change (besides altering the name) was to seek to create a permanent, government-subsidized company modelled on the Berliner Ensemble. Finally, the dilemma that the Boss faces, torn as he is between real political action and an ethically questionable aesthetic retreat, is analogous to tensions within the RSC. Stuart Hampton-Reeves and Carol Chillington Rutter have a point when they write that, in the early 1960s, 'Hall did not need to move very far left of the right-aligned status quo to be called revolutionary' (57), and the radicalism of the first decade of the RSC's institutional and theatrical agendas did not rest on anything like Brecht's Marxist-theatrical ideology. Instead, as I will discuss further in the next chapter, critics have argued that the RSC embodied what Alan Sinfield famously labelled 'Shakespeare-plus-relevance': a focus on the individual and a belief in the need to produce 'relevant' theatre which simultaneously reinscribed the traditional literary authority of the dramatist's play-text (183). In other words, claims of political progressiveness existed alongside an ostensibly depoliticized – if updated – bourgeois aesthetics.

Plebeians' director David Jones expressed a keen awareness of such tensions in the company's identity, and understood that he had to negotiate British audiences' resistance to political theatre. Indeed, if Grass wrote *Plebeians* as an examination of 'the problems of the artist ... working in a pluralist society' (Hollington 115), Jones was eager to convey these problems to RSC theatregoers. Although he feared that English indifference to foreign history would hinder the production's appreciation in London, he began rehearsals not with a reading of the play-text but with workshops, lectures and discussion to ensure that his cast was fully informed about the specific historical circumstances leading to the 1953 uprising (Jones 20). Jones also wished to use the production to comment on the current state of English performance by connecting the Boss's disillusioned retreat into the aesthetic to what he regarded as contemporary British theatre's preoccupation with undermining established artistic forms at the expense of social engagement (21).

Jones's attitude may have represented the 'radical' heritage of the RSC but the *Plebeians'* programme reveals an instinct to take the edge off any such radicalism. The programme, for instance, suggests an aversion to identifiable political stances by insisting that Grass is 'dedicated with single-minded fanaticism to the cause of moderation' and proves it by quoting him: '"I have no ideology ... no Weltanschauung. The last one I had fell apart when I was seventeen years old [i.e. the collapse of National Socialism and his capture as a German soldier by American forces]'". Furthermore, despite a 'Sightlines' assertion that the situation within the play can be read into other historical situations, the programme seems to limit comparisons to those between ancient Rome and East Berlin. That is, it outlines the historical-political realities that served as the basis for Shakespeare's *Coriolanus* and Grass's *Plebeians*, but offers no explicit commentary on the production's own relationship (or even its relevance) to then-current British political and historical situations. Nor does it have anything to say about how the production was positioning the company in relation to its Brechtian inheritance except to reiterate that the play is not a personal attack on Brecht or his actions during the 1953 uprising.

A similar tension existed in Jones's staging, which conflated a realistic scenography and what might be regarded as Brechtian staging techniques. The set was a tidy, sparsely furnished theatre in which the Boss watched his performers rehearse on a raised platform upstage from his armchair on a slightly lower downstage platform.[20] On one side of the Boss's platform stood a work-table and stool; on the other were a table and chair where the Boss could operate his tape-recorder. Several stage lights and a bar of the lighting grid hung visibly over a large white circle painted on the upper platform, at the back of which stood an eight-foot tower-like structure on wheels. The circle and tower evoked, respectively, the revolve and the reversing archway used in the Berliner Ensemble *Coriolanus*, even if Brecht himself never rehearsed the production in this configuration. Other details of the staging reinforced this appearance of historical verisimilitude, which, unlike the common Brechtian juxtaposition of realistic and anti-illusionistic elements, arguably helped to contain the action behind the fourth wall of a supposedly accurate historical past. The workers, who appeared to drink real beer and carried real sledge-hammers, and whose disputes were played back in real time by the functioning tape-recorder, were plausible mid-twentieth-century East German labourers dressed in worn work-boots, frumpy trousers and jackets and battered cloth caps. Similarly, Nicholas Selby's goateed Erwin, in a turtle neck and badly cut checked sports coat (with pens thrust into the breast pocket) was a reasonable facsimile of a down-at-heels Continental intellectual. Meanwhile, Ashcroft's Volumnia – with her compact frame covered by a drab skirt and coat-like blouse, and her brown hair pulled back high off her broad forehead under a scarf – looked quite similar to Helene Weigel. Jones completed the illusion by dressing Emrys James as the historical Brecht appears in so many photographs, wearing pseudo-proletarian shabby trousers and a lapel-free collared jacket.

However, Jones complicated any such containment of the action within the fictionalized recent past of an Eastern Bloc country through a series of visual and spatial analogies that functioned like the relationships within Grass's narrative between the dramatis personae and their historical counterparts. Ashcroft's Volumnia did not simply look like Weigel but, more specifically, like Weigel's head-scarfed Mother Courage as she had appeared in the ground-breaking Berlin production. What is more, as spectators familiar with recent theatre history witnessed Ashcroft's Volumnia, they may well have been aware of the similarities between the English actress and Weigel: the latter was East Germany's best-known actress, whose turn as Mother Courage had helped make the Ensemble's reputation; the former was among the finest classical actresses in England, and her commitment to the RSC and its founder Peter Hall, including a historic turn as Margaret of Anjou in 1963's *The Wars of the Roses*, had helped make the company's name. James's Boss, too, appeared to be a combination of Brecht and Grass. Production photos may show him grinning sardonically and chomping a cigar like so many images of Brecht while his full dark moustache and (somewhat thinning) hair are strikingly similar to the photograph of Grass in *Plebeians'* programme. Jones added another layer of analogy when the Boss's assistant placed a large portrait of Stalin on the edge of the tower; facing the audience, seated downstage right of the portrait, James's lush moustaches made him look like the dictator himself. Such visual cues obviously help confound the levels of reality and fictitiousness being evoked in the production, as the audience watched James's Grass-like Boss ventriloquize Brecht, Coriolanus and even Stalin. These cues may also have been, for those who recognized them, an invitation further to identify with the workers, especially the Hairdresser, who realizes that she is encountering these theatrical figures who inspire her to act out in reality the heroism she had previously witnessed on stage.

The visual analogies were enhanced by the metatheatricality of placing the fictional Berlin performance space within the actual Aldwych Theatre. This metatheatricality was itself enhanced by the fact that the Aldwych's proscenium arrangement put many in the audience in a similar spatial relationship to the action that James's Boss had on his platform within the play, suggesting at least a partial connection between those who witness the action and one who both watched and actually affected that action. At the production's conclusion Jones purposely and definitively broke the realistic barrier that may yet have contained the display of Brechtian staging techniques, and overtly invited his London spectators to make the comparison between the onstage action and themselves explicit. After James's Boss wistfully recalled a time when he could write easily, before he had become 'Taciturn' and was left 'With fewer and fewer certitudes', his Electrician (Peter Messaline) returned him to the mundane practicalities of the theatre, reminding him of upcoming holidays and newly installed equipment (110–111).[21] Then, alone on stage, James peered at the tape-recorder, part of the feedback loop between onstage and offstage realities. Addressing the machine stage left, he said, 'Condemned to live forever with your voices in my ears' in a slow, quietly serious voice (111). Then, turning to face the stage right exit, he shouted, 'You. You. I'll tell you. Do you know what you are? You, you, you're a ...' (111). Finally, he turned to the audience and addressed them directly in a tone of self-reflection and sympathy, 'You poor babes in the woods! Bowed down with guilt, I accuse you!' (111).

Written response to *Plebeians* did not necessarily depoliticize the play's action but it did contribute to the insulation of British theatre from the political implications of Brecht's theories. Reviewers encouraged an *ad hominem* interpretation of the production, demonstrating an almost urgent need specifically to cite and then refute a programme note that warned audiences against closely identifying Brecht with the Boss. While some critics regarded the Boss as emblematic of artists everywhere who must face impossible political circumstances, almost all framed the role in terms of a vivid depiction of Brecht the historical individual, who was personally responsible for the decisions he made in an isolated past. In the same way that reviewers had, ironically, singled out Schall and Hopkins as stars of productions that sought to undermine Martius' indispensability to Rome, critics emphasized the *ad hominem* interpretation by expressing an admiration for James's performance of individual personality that was described as 'almost beyond praise' (*Stage & Television* 30 July 1970), and 'a genuine creation: unexaggerated, absolutely controlled and real' (*Sunday Times* 26 July 1970). This focus on James's creation of the Boss as an individual artist (and, to a lesser extent, Ashcroft's performance of Volumnia) coincided with a total lack of discussion about Grass's documentation of Brecht's aesthetic practice in relation to the latter's political theory beyond labelling him a Marxist writer-director.

Like the British response that repoliticized the 1965 and 1971 productions at the National by deeming them to be too German, critics depicted *Plebeians* as decidedly foreign and understood the performance almost entirely in terms of German politics and culture. Kenneth Hurren, for instance, lamented the 'glum' and 'idealistic portrayal of workers ... in Continental plays' (*What's On* 31 July 1970) and Harold Hobson repeated the programme notes' remarks about Grass fighting for the German army, doubting whether these were 'the best credentials in the world for lecturing us on political morality' (*Sunday Times* 26 July 1970). Even the critic for the *Glasgow Herald*, who admired Grass's dense political dialogue, observed, 'It is, by our standards, very intellectual theatre' (23 July 1970). Except for Ron Bryden (*The Observer* 26 July 1970) and Irving Wardle (*The Times* 22 July 1970), who both wondered if left-wing German anger at Grass for assailing Brecht had kept the play off the stage in Britain until 1970, no critics had anything substantial to say about the context of this London production; none mentioned the 1965 Ensemble tour, and none considered Brecht's current stature in Britain or how *Plebeians* affected that stature. Certainly no reviewer drew any explicit connection between the political role of the fictitious Berliner Ensemble in the fictitious GDR of *Plebeians* and the role that the RSC was then playing in relation to Britain.

Thus, despite Grass's locating the process of theatrical adaptation within highly charged political circumstances, and despite James's final words, which turned the fictitious world of the stage back on to the 'reality' beyond the stage's fourth wall, the RSC's *Plebeians* did not measurably alter Brecht's British public identity. Considerable praise notwithstanding, the critical community was not particularly inspired to extend Grass's feedback loop between the theatre and their own political reality by reading the production as a spur to political action or even serious political interpretation of theatre. Nor, for that matter, did reviewers take up Grass's positioning of Shakespeare in relation to multiple historical contexts. They had little to say about the play's depiction of Brecht's adaptation methods, other than noting the basic connection between Coriolanus and the Boss. For them, explicitly political theatre is something done elsewhere; it does not affect their own artistic institutions, nor does it touch the National Poet. Admittedly, Grass himself forecloses the radical political possibilities of adapting Shakespeare and of theatre generally in the Boss's guilty retreat into poetry but this foreclosure reflects a scepticism about political theatre that appears to have been especially welcome in the British theatre in 1970.

CHAPTER IV

Brechtian vestiges and Shakespeare-plus-relevance – The RSC's *Coriolanus* 1972–73

In April 1972 the Royal Shakespeare Company (RSC) opened its Stratford season entitled *The Romans* with *Coriolanus*. The 1972 *Coriolanus*, and its 1973 transfer to London's Aldwych Theatre, represent a culmination of the forces that shaped Brechtian *Coriolanus*-related productions in England between 1965 and 1971, and arguably bear out critical remarks about the depoliti-cized, merely formal application of Brechtian techniques in British theatre. The 1972 staging certainly appeared to evoke the Berliner Ensemble's scenography. Trevor Nunn redesigned the Royal Shakespeare Theatre's (RST) stage, thrusting it far out into the audience and building into it a sophisticated hydraulic system that allowed the platform and walls to turn and tilt into numerous configurations. As in the Berliner Ensemble's staging, the stark white playing space remained bare throughout. The only scenery was a fire pit in the forestage that emitted real flames; props such as chairs, weapons, banners and a massive she-wolf statue were employed as needed. Like Wekwerth and Tenschert, Nunn deployed these elements to spectacular effect: *Coriolanus* was full of seething crowds, formal processions and noisy battles, and was rounded out by the athletic lead perform-ance of Ian Hogg. Yet, although the play's dramatization of class warfare must have had considerable resonance for a country that had recently experienced the divisiveness of labour unrest, including a disruptive national miners' strike two months prior to the Stratford opening, the impetus for the ambitious *Romans* season was politically vague.[1] The company would explore the rise and fall of civilizations through Shakespeare's four Roman tragedies (all directed by Nunn, with assistance from Buzz

Goodbody and, in 1973, Euan Smith) which, staged in historical order, ostensibly traced a line from the birth of the Republic to the decline of Rome's Empire (*Coriolanus* Basic Programme 1972). *Coriolanus* played its part in this exploration by combining spectacle with reverence for a view of Shakespeare's intentions that was grounded in a fundamentally non-Brechtian focus on characters' (especially the hero's) individual psychologies and which purported to find timeless political lessons in the text. This privileging of the operation of immutable human nature, rather than changeable social-political forces, on the characters' individual psyches became even more pronounced in the 1973 transfer, when Nunn replaced Hogg with Nicol Williamson, who delivered the heroic star turn that reviewers felt was missing from his predecessor's performance.

The RSC's *Coriolanus* reveals even more about the company's institutional identity in the early 1970s than Jones's *The Plebeians Rehearse the Uprising* does. The whole *Romans* project might be understood as a departure from the Brecht-inspired ensemble philosophy that was so central to the RSC's conception and character because, despite a highly successful 1971 Aldwych season, the London company was disbanded so that the *Romans* performers could be transferred to the Aldwych once the Stratford run of the four-play cycle ended (Beauman 314–315).[2] The sense that the company was retreating from its ensemble philosophy was partly confirmed when Nunn replaced Ian Hogg with Nicol Williamson, a move that edged the company back towards a star-centred system that Nunn's predecessor Peter Hall had set out to abolish when the RSC was established in 1960 (Addenbrooke 161). To be fair, though, until the 1972 *Coriolanus*, Nunn did consciously attempt to maintain certain basic consistencies with the company that Hall had shaped during his directorship.[3] Furthermore, there was a 'cold administrative logic' behind the huge company needed for *The Romans*, and there was an artistic logic because, as Nunn remarked, '[e]xploring the plays as a group might turn up other connections, shed cross-lights between them and over an oddly neglected area of Shakespeare's work and imagination' (Nunn and Jones 55). Of course, *The Romans* is the kind of ambitious, complicated project that could only be undertaken at a large-scale publicly subsidized theatre organization such as Hall had worked so hard to establish. Some critics even suggested that Nunn's true efforts at institutional consistency are to be found in the director's desire to leave his mark on the company in a way that Hall and John Barton had done a decade earlier with a redesigned auditorium and the grand political and theatrical gesture of the *Wars of the Roses*.[4] The perception of continuity between Hall's and Nunn's directorships has, more persuasively, been attributed to their shared artistic philosophy, commonly labelled 'Shakespeare-plus-relevance', or 'the combination of traditional authority and urgent contemporaneity' (Sinfield 183). If the RSC of the 1960s and 1970s has come to be seen as a liberal institution characterized by its members' commitment to a vaguely left-wing ideology, this perception is at least partly the result of Hall's and Nunn's persistent efforts to strike a balance between a 'radical' approach to classical theatre and a traditional deference to Shakespeare's cultural authority.[5]

Such liberalism appears most overtly in *Coriolanus* as Nunn's approach to the Tribunes, at least in the way that he rhetorically framed their parts in the play. Like Brecht, Nunn combined his belief that it is necessary for Coriolanus 'to be thrown out before there is any kind of political development' in Roman society (Nunn and Morley 26) with textual alterations that improved Gerald James's Brutus and Raymond Westwell's Sicinius. Specifically, he cut lines of cynical political manoeuvring in which the two characters discuss the likelihood of Coriolanus' election as Consul (2.1), speeches in which they encourage the Plebeians to turn against Coriolanus (2.3) and he reduced dialogue in which they scheme to incite the hero's anger and exile him (3.3).[6] Also like Brecht and the Ensemble directors, Nunn regarded the Tribunes as important intermediaries, arguing that the play 'presents the case of the liberal politician or tribune who tries to make a bridge between the plebeian world and that rigid, ruthless aristocratic group determined on the preservation of their own type. And the poor tribunes end up being reviled both by the patricians and the plebeians' (Nunn and Morley 26). However, the Tribunes' function in the 1972 production was quite different from that of the Ensemble's *Coriolanus*, largely because the two companies were the products of two fundamentally different political contexts. Brecht and his successors at the Berliner Ensemble elevated Brutus and Sicinius arguably to reflect the directors' own view of themselves as committed Marxist Tribune-artists who could successfully represent the People's interests in the face of a dictatorial communist leadership. By contrast, Nunn's *Coriolanus* emerged from within a social democracy, where the supposedly benevolent government intervention in the lives of its citizens that had characterized postwar British society was beginning to be undermined, especially by industrial action such as the national miners' strike of January and February 1972.

The strike, which overlapped with rehearsals of *Coriolanus*, may not have marked the end of Britain's postwar consensus, but it did represent both a powerful challenge to Britain's statist system of government and a rich opportunity for the RSC to point out Shakespeare's ongoing political relevance. The work stoppage, the first national miners' strike since 1926, exposed resentments that had been building in recent years within Britain's mixed-economy state and quickly had a dramatic impact on the country's ability to function properly.[7] The miners' flying pickets effectively reduced supplies to generating stations, which led to electricity cuts and to more than a million workers being laid off in other industries when businesses could not power their factories (Taylor, *The NUM* 67). On 5 February, less than a month into the strike, Edward Heath's government declared a state of emergency, when, as Carol Chillington Rutter points out, 'the complete technical refit of the RSC stage got further and further behind schedule' (Taylor, *The NUM* 67; Rutter 78).[8] The generous settlement that the miners won after the strike proved the effectiveness of their tactics but their power to impede the nation's infrastructure left both sides uncertain about the future of those compromises necessary to maintain the equilibrium of Britain's social democracy: the government was convinced that the strikers had flouted the rule of law with impunity; moderate union leaders feared that the tensions caused by the strike would damage their long-term bargaining positions (Taylor, *The NUM* 72–84). The compromises that characterized Britain's social democracy were also fundamental to the existence of subsidized arts organizations like the RSC, and the RSC chose to avoid any strident political stand; Rutter persuasively argues that 'Nunn's Roman season seemed evasive of politics' and that neither British labour disruptions, nor the country's racial tensions, nor the violence in Northern Ireland, nor America's ongoing war in Vietnam registered on stage in *The Romans*' productions (75).[9] Indeed, rather than Nunn making any direct connection between the strikers and the Plebeians, the 1972 commemorative *Coriolanus* programme stresses the company's commitment to the established order in Britain, and emphasizes the Tribunes' role as liberal defenders of this political system. In the programme, Shakespeare's timeless relevance is persistently conveyed by numerous juxtapositions of historically disparate quotations, including assertions that Shakespeare intended the worlds of his Roman plays to be read as analogues for early modern England. These juxtaposed excerpts reveal, in turn, a preoccupation with political equilibrium. For instance, a long passage from Friedrich Nietzsche about the dangers of a viciously enforced and imbalanced aristocratic rule appeared shortly after an essay devoted to the early modern English horror of rebellion; both are directly preceded by a copy of John Case's 1588 *'Sphaera Civitatis'* engraving of Elizabeth I, which implicitly equates immutable natural hierarchies with political ones.[10] Within the programme's network of citations are three which give the production topical force by asserting a vision of 'liberal' Tribune-politicians who uphold the established order. The first, which appears above an essay describing the careful social calibration of 'Republican Rome', is Menenius' exhortation to Brutus: 'Be that you seem, truly your country's friend, / And temp'rately proceed to what you would / Thus violently redress'. Below this are two quotations, one from Edward Heath, the other from *The Sunday Times*; they date from mid-February 1972, and both exhort union leaders to compromise for the sake of the nation. In other words, these citations align the production with a social establishment built on compromise by rejecting the perceived radicalism of the representatives of contemporary Britain's unionized labour force in favour of a Conservative government whose statist policies helped underwrite the RSC.

For all the effort made in the programme to signal the production's political allegiances, and despite Nunn's apparently favourable treatment of the Tribunes, the two characters were hardly the focal point of the production. Nunn's changes to their dialogue, for instance, should be considered in relation to the director's other textual alterations, which are far less extensive but more politically equivocal than the changes made by either Brecht or Wekwerth and Tenschert. Cuts to the Plebeians' speeches in 1.1 and 2.3 reduced their quarrelling amongst themselves and reassigning numerous speeches uttered in unison to individual Citizens made them less of an amorphous mob. Yet Martius became more sympathetic by losing much of his disdainful speech in 1.1 and 3.1. Mark Dignam's Menenius, too, was made more dignified by cuts to some of the extravagant language in his 'Tale of the Belly' (1.1) and in his boastful remarks to the Volsce guards (5.2). Cuts that 'improved' characters on both sides of the Patrician–Plebeian divide could be regarded as a feature of Nunn's desire for political equilibrium but were most probably simply part of his efforts to speed the action and provide a more exciting spectacle, which can be discerned in other deletions. Cuts to the dialogue between the battles of the first act rendered those short scenes even shorter and more hectically paced. Eliminating many of the Tribunes' instructions to the Plebeians at the end of 2.3, and heavily cutting dialogue (especially Coriolanus' long diatribes) in 3.1 also sped the shift from the protagonist's election as Consul to Brutus' and Sicinius' mobilization of the Plebeians against Coriolanus. Nunn employed the same strategy in the final scene, where removal of much of the Conspirators' and Volsce Lords' speech hastened Coriolanus' entry, singled out Coriolanus' and Aufidius' final harsh verbal battle (by getting to it faster and leaving it largely intact) and decreased the time it took for the incited Volscian Citizens to call for Coriolanus' death and help kill him.

Nunn's approach to the actual staging, too, was politically equivocal in the sense that, while he was interested in the alienating features of *Coriolanus'* spectacle, neither he nor his cast and crew understood the spectacle in Brecht's Marxist terms, nor even in the vaguer socialist terms employed by the Berliner Ensemble. Like the designer Christopher Morley, who hoped that the redesigned stage would break the 'illusion' of the RST's 'Victorian ... picture-frame', Nunn emphasized that they 'lit the whole play bright, unchanging and hard' in order to draw attention to the stage as an actual stage (Nunn and Morley 26). However, the director was more concerned with eliminating the division between the stage and spectators which, he explained, was a principal goal of redesigning the playing space (Nunn and Morley 26). He further hoped that *Coriolanus* would not 'be remote, something that is happening romantically at a distance' and even expressed the quasi-Artaudian wish that 'the sweat,

[91]

blood, clash of swords' would 'be a very real, tactile experience in the auditorium' (Nunn and Morley 26). Nunn and Hogg portrayed the actor's job within this semi-alienating scenography not in the idealistically activist and liberating terms of Brechtian performance, where the actor stands apart from or 'quotes' his or her role, but as a passive act of surrender to the playwright. The director approvingly recalled the voice coach Kristen Linklater's insistence to '"Let it [the Shakespearean word] use you"' (Nunn and Jones 56), and, even a decade after his performance, Hogg insisted that Shakespeare 'takes the actor by the hand and leads him into the circle of a test which ... will bring him face to face with the physical, mental and spiritual centres of his being' (240). The two men's articulation of the production's politics, meanwhile, was restricted to the kind of analogy that pervaded the programme. Nunn explained that in rehearsal the cast performed 'exercises based on parallel modern instances of political violence' (Nunn and Jones 56), while Hogg recalled that he strove to 'become a man ... who is a mix of Tarzan of the Apes and Richard Nixon' and that, for him, the Republican Rome of the production was somehow simultaneously 'the USA of 1968 during the Chicago riots' and 'Poland faced by the shadowy eminence of the USSR' (250).

Despite Nunn's and Hogg's avowal of orthodox 'Shakespeare-plus-relevance' principles, spectators who did not have recourse to the commemorative programme might well have had difficulty apprehending such specific comparisons in the visual details of *Coriolanus'* violent action. Only the production's costumes and props served to situate the action since, besides a rudimentary forum represented by some clotheslines and make-shift stalls in 2.3, the stage lacked even the basic stockade-gate scenery of the Berliner Ensemble's set. However, these costumes did not suggest any locale other than a generalized ancient Rome. The Patrician men and women wore togas during peace time and the men put on vaguely Roman armour with striking feathered helmets and calf-length sandals during the battle scenes. The Plebeians, meanwhile, wore tunics and ragged cloth coverings. Still, Nunn and Morley did use costuming to distinguish the Romans from the apparently more barbaric Volsces. Unlike the Roman men's clean white togas and carefully groomed beards and hair, the barefooted Volsces had long wispy moustaches, kept their long black hair shaggy and were virtually naked. In battle, they sported long feathered headdresses like their Roman counterparts, but otherwise they wore only black leather arm-bands, ankle-bands and jockstraps 'veiled' with chainmail in front.

As in the Berliner Ensemble's production, Nunn employed his large cast to create plenty of carefully choreographed and visually impressive spectacle, though with a quite different purpose than Wekwerth and Tenschert had in mind. In the extra-textual opening procession, which emblematically re-enacted the 'Birth of Rome', fifteen Patricians, split in two columns, with Clement McCallin's Cominius at the head, marched from upstage of the proscenium down to the forestage, carrying the she-wolf (by long poles attached to its feet) and two children. The prompt-book specifies that, on the fifteenth bar of music, Cominius lifted up his hands, and the Patricians did likewise in response before they raised the children to the animal's teats, as though they were staging a ritualistic version of the legend in which Rome's supposed founders, Remus and Romulus, were suckled by a wolf. On the twenty-fifth bar of music, the group all lowered their hands, the wolf was turned stage right, and the members of the procession crossed back upstage. Similarly, for the victory procession in 2.1, the director devised an impressive and formal stage picture by marching nearly fifty actors on stage, arranging them symmetrically in a 'V' formation, branching out stage left and right. He glorified Hogg as Rome's saviour by making him the group's visual focal point upstage centre at the point of the 'V', directly in front of the she-wolf. He created a similar effect for the procession of 5.5, where Margaret Tyzack's Volumnia, Rosemary McHale's Virgilia, Edwina Ford's Valeria and nine Patricians entered led by musicians, and crossed the forestage where twenty-one Plebeians were massed left and right before exiting in procession upstage. Yet Nunn disrupted the stateliness of these celebrations of Roman civilization by revealing their underlying violence. Cominius, for instance, broke the sober tone of the opening procession by crossing downstage left to kick a Plebeian before following the others upstage. The formality of Coriolanus' victory procession, too, gave way to the collective, dangerous energy of the Plebeians who mocked and intimidated the shackled Volsce captives as they exited. To a lesser degree, the same occurred at the end of the Roman matrons' procession when the Plebeians broke into an exuberant dance. The implication of such disorganized violence is, significantly, the opposite of Brecht's political optimism; it echoed the Nietzschean pessimism (cited in the programme and alluded to by Nunn in interview) that an immutable, vicious will to dominate lies behind all forms of social organization.

Although Hogg was absent from the opening she-wolf tableau, his Coriolanus – and especially his virtually naked body – provided an index for the production's representation of the latent barbarism supposedly inherent to all social milieux. The battle scenes leading up to Martius' lone entry into Corioli's gates duplicated the rhythms of the processions by fluctuating repeatedly between highly structured set pieces in which the two armies fight as unified groups (almost like two *corps de ballet*) and disorganized violent skirmishes. As the battle progressed, however, Hogg – alone among the Romans – lost much of his armour and began to resemble his Volscian enemies; stripped down to a black loincloth, he revealed a torso covered in scars, those outward signs of his military sacrifices that bring him so much esteem in Rome. Hogg wore Roman clothing for Acts 2 and 3 but the visual transformation into his homeland's more overtly barbaric enemy began again in 3.3 when he removed his toga in response to the Plebeians intoning 'It shall be so' (119) shortly before going into exile. He completed this transformation after he joined forces with Patrick Stewart's Aufidius by 'growing out' his hair and beard to an unruly length and by wearing the Volsces' revealing uniform. During the fifth-act embassies to the Volscian camp, his appearance strongly suggested a contrast between what Coriolanus had become and the Roman women and Menenius, whose careful grooming and covered bodies seemed to mark them out as more civilized.

Hogg's visual metamorphosis into Rome's overtly barbaric neighbour anticipated the violence of his experiences among the Volsces. This violence began with the riotous slapstick that initiated his desertion to the Volsces in 4.5. Here, he attacked Aufidius' Servingmen, mashing a loaf of bread in one's face, slamming a basket on another's head and brutally pinching the nose of the third before knocking them all down like dominoes. No such comedy remained in the final scene's brutality. After Stewart and Hogg circled the forestage's hydraulically raised central block, Hogg's Coriolanus first singled himself out by mounting the block, but then descended, leaping into a crowd of his assailants. Thus metaphorically absorbed into the Volsce collective, he died when Stewart stabbed him. Nunn then made Coriolanus the victim of the Volsces' communal savagery a second time: as flames rose from the pit, they lowered Coriolanus' body onto the fire before unleashing a 'death cry' in unison. In one sense, the way that Nunn makes a spectacular sacrifice of Coriolanus here is reminiscent of Coriolanus' incineration at the end of Edwin Forrest's production, though without any of the hopeful, melodramatic mysticism about a phoenix-like spiritual rebirth. Indeed, it seems that, during one phase of the production, Hogg appeared to be repeatedly lowered into the flames and then raised back up to show the audience what looked like scarred tissue, until his Coriolanus succumbed to the ordeal.[11] In another sense, Nunn's visual tracking of the violence done to Hogg's stripped, wounded and scorched body is reminiscent of Wekwerth and Tenschert's tracking of Coriolanus' character through gestic military symbols. The crucial difference between the 1972 *Coriolanus* and the Berliner Ensemble and National Theatre productions is that Hogg's Coriolanus yielded to an explicit Volscian barbarism that Nunn depicted as relatively concealed by Roman ceremoniousness. The gist of this scenography, then, was not simply that society must rid itself of a military hero who has become no longer useful as a result of political changes at a particular historical juncture but that, no matter how societies may represses their violent or radical tendencies, they will always come out; collective human violence is ubiquitous and thus timelessly relevant.

The mixed published reaction to *Coriolanus* reveals that the critical community shared many of Nunn's assumptions about the goals of performance but also that they abided in their distaste for 'radical' political elements in Shakespearean theatre. By and large, reviewers limited discussion of the play's contemporary political relevance to analogies between the Tribunes and trade union leaders, and, despite Nunn's vision of the Tribunes as a conciliatory force within the play, the Tribunes seem to have been the source of significant critical disagreement, possibly as a consequence of the divisive political atmosphere created by the miners' strike; certainly no reviewers mentioned trade unions when writing about the 1965 or 1971 productions at the National Theatre or about the RSC's *Plebeians* in 1970. However, critics' apparent difference of opinion about the Tribunes conceals a deeper political agreement. On the one hand reviewers believed they conformed to Nunn's image of 'an eminently respect-worthy pair' (*The Times* 13 April 1972), of 'reasonable politicians' (Cox 36) and 'moderate representatives of the people' (*Punch* 20 April 1972). On the other hand, like the passages from Heath and the *Sunday Times* printed in the programme, critics implicitly chastised current 'radical' trade unionists through the Tribunes who were 'a fine ugly pair of trade union' officials (*Oxford Mail* 13 April 1972) and 'rabble-rousing shop stewards' (*Leicester Mercury* 12 April 1972) who generated 'the finest moments of political confrontation' by acting 'like Marxist opportunists' (Thomson, 'No Rome' 144).

Critics were far less concerned with *Coriolanus'* politics than they were with their perception of the production's failure to live up to Nunn's own professed ideals about Shakespearean theatre. Although Hogg received some praise for his performance, nearly two-thirds of the reviewers disliked it, typically citing its perceived lack of heroic grandeur that the playwright supposedly demanded. They criticized Hogg for relying on 'gentle irony where there should be patrician pride' (*Stage & Television* 20 April 1972), and for being 'hotheaded rather than noble' (*Saturday Telegraph* 15 April 1972), and 'a shifty petulant hippy instead of an insufferably arrogant patrician' (*Daily Mail* 12 April 1972). They located Hogg's failure to make the imaginative leap into the heroic character that Shakespeare requires in the actor's actual body that Nunn had made so central to the scenography. He was merely 'an athletic puppet' (*Oxford Mail* 13 April 1972) who 'concede[d] ... to the purely muscular aspect of the part' (*Listener* 20 April 1972). These criticisms were part of a larger distaste for the way Nunn's alienating spectacle interfered with the illusion of Shakespeare's fictional world. What stood behind comments like 'the visual pattern [was] too often at odds with the poetic pattern' is the same concern that animates John Barber's criticism that 'Hogg's small wiry Coriolanus' failed to 'dominate the restless effects' (*Daily Telegraph* 12 April 1972), namely the fear that the RSC has forgotten that 'the life of the theatre is in the actor, not the edifice, nor the lighting, nor the costumes and property' (Thomson, 'No Rome' 139). The concern was that, by placing 'its trust not in men and women, not in passion, wit, or ideas, but in machinery' (*Sunday Times* 16 April 1972), the company was becoming a '"director's theatre"' where actors lacked the freedom to discover their roles in Shakespeare's text because they had to submit to the director's vision (Thomson, 'No Rome' 140). In other words, if Nunn showed Coriolanus succumbing to a primitive and inexorable brutality, reviewers lamented the lost illusion of a grand romantic hero succumbing to an abstract concept that Nunn had devised in accruing too much creative agency to himself. Such comments are significant not merely for what they reveal about the widely shared attitudes of those journalists who helped frame *Coriolanus*' public image but also because their criticisms anticipate the changes Nunn made to the production for its transfer the following year.

When *Coriolanus*, along with the other *Romans* plays, moved to London for the 1973 season, it changed in a number of ways. At the Aldwych Theatre, instead of the hydraulics and the fire pit of Stratford's redesigned stage, the audience was presented with a proscenium frame that opened on to a playing space the walls and platform of which did not heave or blaze. In London, furthermore, the four *Romans* plays could more easily be seen as a group, and thus the thinking behind playing them together could be observed in a way that the Stratford performance schedule did not so readily permit. Finally, by replacing Ian Hogg with the 'star' Nicol Williamson, the RSC strengthened its emphasis on the title-character for the Aldwych production, though Sally Beauman's contention that the transfer represents 'a change from a[n ensemble] Sixties approach to a [star-centred] Fifties one' and that the 'production's previous emphasis on the upheaval of a tribal society changed to a Bradleian emphasis on the personal tragedy of the hero' (317) somewhat overstates the differences between the 1972 and 1973 stagings.

The transfer demonstrated, to be sure, strong consistencies with the 1972 Stratford production. The company maintained the Stratford commemorative programme, the costumes and the symbolism of the she-wolf tableaux, even adding the wolf statue to Coriolanus' entrance in 2.2. The 1973 prompt-book, furthermore, indicates that Nunn's textual alterations resulted in a script of approximately the same length, and that he mostly extended the strategies of the cuts to the 1972 script. A few more lines of Citizens' dialogue were explicitly individualized, one more of Sicinius' cynical speeches in 2.3 was expunged, and

Nunn sped up the action by removing blocks of text from the Volsce Servingmen's conversation (4.5), Menenius' exchange with Sicinius and Brutus (4.6) and dialogue between Aufidius and the Third Conspirator (5.6). Furthermore, Williamson understood his role in the same analogical and vaguely psychological terms that had guided Hogg's performance. Considering his character 'as a case history' he suggested that Coriolanus 'would always have been the author of his own downfall' (Williamson 23) and he regarded the hero's attempts at the Consulship as 'rather like trying to make a Prime Minister out of Bernard Montgomery: a man who was a total soldier, and a very good soldier, but would have been a disaster as a head of state' (23). Like Hogg, he insisted upon the actor's submission to Shakespeare, though he was even more insistent than his predecessor, suggesting that, because '[a]cting is not an art – it's a craft', actors must remember that '[t]he character has to be built up in the way it was written and was meant to be played' (20). He claimed, furthermore, to have gone to great lengths to ensure this scrupulous obedience to Shakespeare: 'I'm paying somebody at the Aldwych to stay behind and rehearse me, after the other rehearsals every night. I want that guy to tell me for at least two hours, if I have uttered so much as one word wrong' (23).

Despite such consistencies with the 1972 staging, there was a heightened sense of Williamson's place at the centre of the London production as a star performer whose persona would not easily disappear, whatever his professed obedience to Shakespeare's intentions. The actor came to the production with a reputation for (occasionally violent) confrontations with theatrical management, and was himself conscious of his status as an *enfant terrible*, parachuted into the role: 'When I walked into the first rehearsal I felt them all giving me the eyeball. Who the hell is this guy? they were asking themselves. And I thought, Oh Christ, are they going to give me a hard time?' (Oakes).[12] Although Williamson acknowledged the strength of the troupe the RSC had assembled, his conviction that it was his 'job to get up there and make the play work' tended towards hyperbole: 'People come to first nights to see the leading actor have a heart attack' (Oakes). The textual alterations that Nunn made to the lead's dialogue in the 1973 script only added to the image of Williamson's Martius as a belligerent self-justifying hero; most of the more than three dozen lines that the director restored to the protagonist's speeches were passages of self-assertive anti-Plebeian invective that he had cut from Act 3 of the Stratford script. Whereas Williamson's Martius was mostly sarcastically dismissive of the Plebeians in 1.1, the production's sound recording reveals that, in Act 3, he seized the opportunity to unleash Coriolanus' hatred of the People in great flourishes of contempt.[13] In responding to John Nettleton's Sicinius, who insisted that Coriolanus 'Shall remain a poison where [he] is' (3.1.87), Williamson paused a dramatic fifteen seconds, before scornfully rolling his 'r's on 'Shall remain! / Hear you this Triton of the minnows?' (3.1.88–89). Yet, in the first part of the scene, he was fairly restrained and rational, dismissing Nettleton with a calmly spoken 'Hence, old goat' (3.3176), though, once the People re-entered, his tone did change to match the often loudly violent chaos that ensued. Similarly, in 3.3, his early conciliatory tone quickly gave way to angry contempt, and, when accused of treason, Williamson viciously snarled, 'How, traitor?' (67). The scene's tension built up to provide Williamson with a thrillingly defiant exit. The People shouted 'It shall be so!' (119) with verve, but they cut the chanting dead, apparently when Williamson tore off Coriolanus' Consul's necklace, the outward sign of his office. Williamson then paused for ten seconds to ratchet up the suspense for his 'You common cry of curs' speech, which he spoke with a more-or-less even-tempered tone throughout (120–134), so that when he almost shouted, 'There is a world elsewhere' (135), the effect was powerfully jarring.

Nunn's changes to the scenography at the Aldwych clarify the director's renewed emphasis on his lead actor. Unlike the 1972 staging, which excluded Martius from the initial she-wolf procession, the 1973 production established the hero's centrality from the start. The action began with a loud rhythmic blend of rattles, metallic clanging sounds and pounding drums as Williamson knelt downstage of the wolf-statue being armed for battle. While this pantomime might have reminded audiences of Constance Cummings's Volumnia dressing Anthony Hopkins's Martius for battle at the National two years earlier, the irony of Wekwerth and Tenschert's borrowing from Cleopatra's arming of Antony is missing in the 1973 opening tableau. Instead, Nunn here explicitly substituted Martius' individual military heroism for the more broadly social significance of the birth of Rome that the procession had signalled in the Stratford production: once the hero stood up, fully armed, the wolf was raised; Patricians passed under the statue with children on their shoulders, and then circled the wolf; Martius subsequently turned upstage, exiting under the statue, followed by the rest of the Patricians. Admittedly, the 1973 opening procession placed Martius' individual heroism at the centre of an overtly Roman context (he literally exited between two sets of Roman nobles), but Nunn used the next procession to juxtapose assertions of Coriolanus' individual will with outbursts of powerful communal feeling. The Herald sat atop the she-wolf to deliver his speech welcoming Coriolanus home in the procession of 2.1 but Williamson's conquering hero refused to be lifted by the crowd on to the wolf as 'All' shouted 'Welcome to Rome, renowned Coriolanus!' (160) to the accompaniment of trumpets and drums.

Nunn similarly reshaped much of the production's violence in order to single out his hero's individual plight. In particular, Williamson's Martius engaged in more individual combat than Hogg did. In a skirmish not included in the Stratford production, Williamson appeared in an upper level and fought with three Volsces in succession as the Romans looked on below. Also new to the Aldwych staging was the blocking of the individual fight between Martius and Aufidius in the first act. Here, Oscar James's Aufidius opened the scene by shouting for Martius as the Volsce soldiers lined the outer edge of the playing space on three sides to watch the fight. While the two men battled, the Volsces gave the scene a ritualistic quality by loudly chanting first 'Caius Martius!' and then 'Kill!' repeatedly. Like the opening tableau, with its ritualistic percussion, this combat placed the hero within a violent and specifically social undertaking (i.e. his individual fighting is witnessed by an 'audience' of his homeland's enemies) but Nunn also carefully singled him out and placed him at the centre of this undertaking. Even though the director seems to have made the somewhat dubious decision to heighten the differences between the appearance of Roman civilization and Volscian barbarism by casting many of the Volsce roles with black actors, including James as Aufidius, the changes he made to the death scene in 1973 indicate Nunn's attempt to turn Coriolanus' last battle into a one-to-one fight rather than a violent submission to a group. For the Aldwych production, Nunn deleted several communal utterances that he had kept in the

Stratford staging: the People's 'Tear him to pieces! – Do it presently!' (121); the Conspirators' 'Kill, kill, kill, kill him!' (131); the Lords' lines 'Hold, hold, hold, hold!' (132); and the additional collective 'Death Cry' that the Volsces released at the very close in Stratford. As Hogg had done in the 1972 production, Williamson did fight with a group of Volsces who circled him before being stabbed by James. Yet, besides the fact that the Volsces did not collectively grill Coriolanus at the Aldwych, the two actors clearly conveyed the individual loathing that animated their final combat. James's Aufidius alternated between shouted rage and quiet intensity as he denounced Coriolanus, and Williamson replied in kind, switching from a quaking voice on lines like 'False hound' (113) to a bellowed 'Alone I did it boy!' (117). Williamson delivered his final lines, 'O that I had him / With six Aufidiuses or more – his tribe, / To use my lawful sword!' in an even but powerfully raised voice. Consequently, the ensuing forty seconds of silence, during which James dispatched Coriolanus, underscored the futility of the hero's final verbal challenge to his enemy. The personal nature of this struggle was further stressed by two key pieces of business that did not occur in 1972: echoing Williamson's act of removing his own Consul's necklace in 3.3, James's Aufidius removed a necklace from around Coriolanus' neck, and then put his foot on the dead body in a sign of individual victory.[14]

The hero's individual plight was especially pronounced in his relationship with Volumnia and, as the sound recording reveals, Williamson and Tyzack created a close emotional connection between parent and child. When Tyzack imagined her son's battle wounds in 1.3 and 2.1, she did not speak with bloodthirstiness or cold disregard for his life, but with genuine maternal pride and love. Likewise, when Tyzack chided her son in 3.2 in convincing him to humble himself before the People, her voice conveyed real concern for her son's fate. The performers amplified this emotional bond between Coriolanus and his mother in 4.1: Tyzack wept loudly and spoke with fear about her son's future; Williamson replied tenderly, trying to console her. However, Nunn's actors saved their most intense emotional display for the confrontation between Coriolanus and Volumnia during the Roman women's embassy of 5.3. From the moment the women entered, Williamson clearly signalled that this scene would be about the psychological unraveling of the hero as he struggled between a resolve not to betray the Volsces and an inexorable loyalty to his mother. In his first speech immediately following the women's entrance, Williamson's Coriolanus tried to dispel his love of family, urging himself, 'out affection! / All bond and privilege of nature, break!' (24–25). But he shortly acknowledged with quiet resignation, 'I melt, and am not / Of stronger earth than others' (28–29). During Volumnia's long imploring speeches to her son, meanwhile, Tyzack demonstrated a remarkable vocal range, alternating between a desperate gasping whisper on lines like 'Should we be silent and not speak' (94), and emphatic warning as she imagined 'The son, the husband, and the father tearing / His country's bowels out' (102–103). As Tyzack worked her way through Volumnia's second long speech, she played expertly on her son's loyalties, by turns imploring and angry. In her last six lines of the scene, Tyzack slowly built up a fierce, guilt-inducing tone, pausing dramatically for ten seconds after 'His wife is in Corioles, and his child / Like him by chance' (179–180) before continuing in the same voice on 'Yet give us our dispatch' (180). However, it was Williamson's response that gave the confrontation its tremendous impact: taking Tyzack's hand, he remained silent for nearly one full minute before shouting forlornly, 'O, mother, mother! What have you done?' (183). In his speech to Volumnia that followed this bravura silence, Williamson's voice trembled with feeling, revealing the devastation that her appeal to their relationship had worked on him. Williamson's performance here was not merely a flagrant *coup-de-théâtre* that conveys its emotional power even decades later on a sound recording, but is a continuation of the performance tradition that depicts the hero's destruction as the result of the mother–son bond, the tradition from which Brecht has departed in rewriting this scene with explicitly political implications.

Critical reaction to the 1973 production mirrors the changes that Nunn implemented. Reviewers made far fewer political comments than they had previously and had little to say about the contemporary relevance of the performance. The Tribunes received hardly any attention, and the previous year's strike seemed virtually to have vanished from the critics' memories.[15] The change in response might be attributed in part to scheduling; because all four plays were performed in one day for the reviewers at the Aldwych, and because the productions were more frequently rotated in the repertoire at the London theatre than at Stratford, over half of the extant *Coriolanus* reviews treat the *Romans* framework in its entirety. Considering the efforts made to place a heroic Coriolanus who resists the pull of Roman collective identity at the centre of the 1973 production, it is ironic that Hogg received more detailed critical attention than Williamson did because the latter's star turn was subsumed in the grand historical sweep of the cycle's depiction of Roman history. Nevertheless, the great majority of reviewers were very enthusiastic about Williamson's performance, which won him a London Theatre Critics' Award for best performance by an actor. In fact, reviewers perceived in Williamson precisely what many found wanting in Hogg: a larger-than-life protagonist whose psychologically 'real', complex and consistent heroism reflected their idealized notion of fidelity to Shakespeare's intentions. Williamson was 'the great commanding figure that Shakespeare drew from Plutarch, a man whose voice, whose expression even, could cow an enemy' (*Financial Times* 23 October 1973); he had 'assumed the title role playing [Coriolanus] for what he is: a military Junker, hating both patricians and plebs and suffering badly from arrested development' (*Guardian* 23 October 1973); he had 'create[d] a hero instead of the usual shouting oaf ... His courtesy, his tenderness for his son, his zest for a brave deed and the constancy of his temper all speak of a noble mind and so make his fall tragic' (*Daily Telegraph* 23 October 1973).

Three-quarters of the reviewers seized upon Williamson's performance in the pleading scene with Volumnia, turning it into the production's centre-piece and the hallmark of the actor's success. If critics at Stratford located Hogg's failure to portray an appropriately Shakespearean hero in a debased, even mechanical, physicality that was lost in the spectacular scenography, at the Aldwych they located Williamson's achievement in his appropriate physicality. This appropriate physicality was not discovered in his general physique; rather, critics focused on the great control with which Williamson manipulated his facial expressions during the long 'electrifying' (*Mitcham News & Mercury* 2 November 1973) silence of 'paralysing impact' (*New Statesman* 2 November 1973) that preceded his 'Oh, mother, mother!' speech. They read in the minutiae of the actor's bodily movements the anguish that Coriolanus felt: as Williamson's face 'turn[ed] visibly to pulp' (*The Times* 23 October 1973) and 'slowly crumpl[ed] and dissolve[ed] into tears' (*Guardian* 23 October 1973), 'his lust for revenge f[ought] a losing battle with his sense of filial duty and native patriotism' (*Daily Express* 23 October 1973); when 'every inch of his face [spoke] his part' (*Stage and Television Today* 1 November 1973), 'the house [was] hushed as it can only be when a master talent is at work' (*Daily Express* 23 October 1973). These comments function like cinematic close-ups, revealing not simply Williamson's performance but what the reviewers desired in Shakespearean tragic theatre. That is, to the extent that critics narrowed down their response to *Coriolanus* to an analysis of a single heroic performance, they also narrowed that performance down to the body part that most intensely registered the hero's profound emotional turmoil.

The implicit rejection of Brechtian politics that Williamson's performance represents is, arguably, simply the logical conclusion of the trajectory of Brecht-influenced *Coriolanus* productions on the British stage. His acting in the pleading scene, which signals a return to Olivier's heroic model of performance, certainly seems to follow Wekwerth and Tenschert's gradual reduction of Brecht's explicitly political adaptation of the encounter between Coriolanus and Volumnia. Of course, the acclaim that Williamson received from reviewers undoubtedly echoes earlier critics, who consistently agitated against Brecht's political rewriting of the play, even as they expressed their admiration for the Berliner Ensemble and Anthony Hopkins. Still, the 1973 Aldwych staging does not represent a decisive turning point in *Coriolanus*' stage history. While the transfer's reliance on Williamson's star turn may have caused the RSC to stray from the ensemble philosophy that Hall and Nunn had adopted from the Berliner Ensemble, the production did not unravel this system. Furthermore, while the transfer's singular emphasis on the hero's individual psychology may have distracted audiences from the suggestions about the Stratford staging's political relevance, in no way did it mean the end of politically charged *Coriolanus*es. To a considerable degree, Brecht's Marxism did become submerged in eight years of British *Coriolanus* production, but the tensions between political imperatives and star actors, inherent even in Brecht's desire to have Ernst Busch play the hero, would continue to animate productions for the next four decades.

CHAPTER V

Alan Howard on stage and screen

The RSC's *Coriolanus* (1977–79)

In one of the more widely circulated images from the stage life of *Coriolanus*, Alan Howard's black-leather-clad Martius appears in a shaft of light as he stands on a spear held horizontally aloft by four soldiers, grasping two upright spears for balance; his face is stretched into an expression of triumphant ecstasy as he supposedly says 'O, me alone! Make you a sword of me' (1.7.76).[1] The image reveals the director Terry Hands's ability to produce astonishing stage pictures by contrasting the stark white light with the bare stage and the harsh militarism of the monochromatic battle costumes. It also suggests the triumph that the production itself became: Howard won the 1978 London Theatre critics award for Best Actor, starred in successful *Coriolanus* remounts at Nottingham and London in 1978 and led a 1979 European tour.[2] But this image of the spotlit Howard, framed by the spears, points more specifically to the production's emphasis on the individual, and the metaphorical elevation of Coriolanus by the other characters in the production as the unquestioned heroic centre of the play. Moreover, Howard's blissful face, reflecting the glaring stage light, is almost mysterious, something approaching an apotheosis or an ascension to another realm, an embodiment of the actor's conception of the hero as an alien creature, the 'angel of death' who 'is in touch with some other state or sphere' (Howard, qtd in Daniell 165).

While the production shares with Trevor Nunn's 1973 RSC transfer a reverence for Shakespeare's textual authority and a tight focus on the hero, it was also, following *Henry V* (1975) and the three parts of *Henry VI* (1977), Hands's third major success for the company in as many years. Like the *Henry* plays, furthermore, it arguably represents a new company style that prevailed at the RSC as the 1970s progressed, though, with so many of his own productions on RSC stages between 1975 and 1978, Hands was largely responsible for this style at the time. Sally Beauman remarks that during the company's second decade there was a shift from the company's ostensibly political 'epic style of the Sixties' to an emphasis on 'the complexity of personal and family relationships' (329). In contrast to the 'balance, weight, [and] rationality' of the company's earlier performances, the new style's 'characteristics were unpredictability, the permitting of inconsistency, the relish of ambiguity' (342). As Carol Chillington Rutter argues of Hands's *Henry VI* productions, the director was less interested in depicting 'men as political machines' than he was 'investigat[ing] the human heart ... by thinking through the flesh' (Hampton-Reeves and Rutter 80–81). She connects this attitude to a decentralization and personalization of British politics in 1977 but she also notes that 1977 was the year of Queen Elizabeth II's silver jubilee, when 'the idea of England, framed in the national symbolism of the monarchy, was most on people's minds' (Hampton-Reeves and Rutter 82). This tension between the personal and the political registered in elements of Hands's *Coriolanus*. The programme, for instance, reprinted quotations from Aristotle, *Coriolanus*, Benito Mussolini and the British fascist Oswald Mosley, vaguely implying the tragedy's timeless political relevance. Yet during an interview, Hands disavowed any overtly political approach to *Coriolanus*. Instead, he wished to 'reveal the human being underneath' the extremes of 'saviour' and 'monster' that Coriolanus is perceived to be, and believed that, by casting Howard, 'an actor known for his humanity on stage', he would 'find the man in the middle' (qtd in Higgins). Yet, while *Coriolanus* toured Europe in the spring of 1979, Britain elected Margaret Thatcher's Conservative government, which was committed to reducing arts subsidies. A note of alarm that officially sanctioned national politics would once again matter intensely enters David Daniell's account of the RSC tour: 'as I add this note a few months later [i.e. after the tour], the RSC is facing permanent damage. The combination of unchecked inflation, punitive VAT on tickets, and the cuts imposed on the Arts Council grant, is already deadly' (4).[3]

The production itself, however, was devised well before the Thatcher government's assault on the British welfare state, and the staging clearly embodied Hands's preoccupation with unearthing the personal aspects of the tragedy. While he was careful to downplay his directorial control and to stress his reliance on allowing actors to find their way through Shakespeare's (very lightly cut) text, the production's powerful and inventive visuals are also characteristic of Hands's scenography, which he had developed over time in collaboration with RSC designer Farah.[4] In Rutter's words, Hands does not attempt to create 'a "whole" world' that 'approximates "reality"' (Hampton-Reeves and Rutter 86). Rather, '[h]is signature is austerity, and his most stunning visual effects are achieved almost architecturally, by locating bodies in space and writing physical compositions', effects he achieves by 'design[ing] in light' rather than '"stuff"' (Hampton-Reeves and Rutter 86). Hands's focus on a magnificent, highly emotional hero driven by personal relationships relied not just on the austerity of the bare black stage space and striking light effects that allowed him to build up a series of intertextually allusive images but also on Howard's remarkably physical performance and wide-ranging vocalization.

In the first act Hands employed his characteristic 'spatial intertextuality' (Hampton-Reeves and Rutter 86), punctuating the battle scenes with dramatic stage pictures and episodes to single out Martius. As 1.4 began, two huge black walls faced in shining metal and located stage left and stage right were brightly lit to show them closing, shutting off the upstage third of the platform, which became Corioli. The sound recording of the production captures the pounding timpani and brass instruments blasts that accompanied the Romans (dressed in black capes, tunics, trousers, boots and rounded helmets) as they entered downstage to parley with the Volscians.[5] The monumental gates subsequently opened, again to the sound of horns and drums, to release the Volscian soldiers, and, after a pair of clashes centre stage, the Romans were beaten back. These clashes were a pretext to demonstrate the prowess of Howard's Martius, who had broken through from behind his own troops to pursue the enemy beyond the closing gates. As the exhausted soldiers rested downstage, one called out 'Look sir' (63), and, accompanied by even louder martial music, a spotlight picked out the bloodied Howard, smoke billowing around him, standing high inside the now slightly parted gates (on a pedestal), encouraging his comrades to victory. Two scenes later, in 1.6, Hands paralleled and reinforced Howard's heroic elevation: still bloodied, he appeared atop the lower downstage gates, bellowing 'Come I too late?' (27), and then jumped from a considerable height to the platform to embrace Cominius. The next visual effect relied on Howard's powerful vocalization: building his 'Those are they / That are most willing' (66–75) speech in a climbing rhythm, each line more intense than the last, he shouted 'And follow Martius!' (75). Between bursts of trumpet and drums, the soldiers echoed 'Martius!' (75) three times, lowering their spears on the first, allowing Howard to step on one horizontally held shaft on the second cry, and heaving him upwards on the third cry, to create the image described at the top of the chapter. Standing in the spotlight, Howard capped this carefully choreographed heroic ascension by stretching out the vowels rapturously on 'Ooooooh, meeee alooooone! Make you a swooooord of meeee?!' (76).

If such images and moments reflected Howard's conviction that Shakespeare uses a series of short 'epic *physical* events' to reveal 'what a hero *is*' (Mulryne 324, emphasis original), Hands used ironic visual parallelism to reveal in Julian Glover's Aufidius what a hero is *not*. The individual fight of 1.8 was a thrilling display of two great warriors. It consisted of dozens of individual moves swiftly performed, both men wielding two swords, their cries and blows intercut with more trumpet and drum bursts. The fight was lit from above by follow-spots that flashed when they hit the blades and metal on the men's black leather armour. But it was also a display of Aufidius' inferiority: after Glover lost one sword, Howard threw aside his extra blade, and they fought clutching one another's wrists; when Glover lost the second sword, he switched to a trident, but he still had to be rescued by four comrades, despite his bitter protests. Hands visually clarified the contrast with Howard by recalling 1.4 and 1.6: the Volsces' assistance was not an elevation by comrades who collectively underpin the hero's glory but an ignoble rescue that contributes to Aufidius' downward spiral of shame. Hands repeated the contrast in the final two scenes. In 1.9, the Roman soldiers, holding spears, knelt in a wedge formation with Howard at its point downstage, while the whole army chanted 'Caius Martius Coriolanus!' (66), and the scene ended with a triumphant drum volley. The drums petered out at the top of 1.10, which found Glover surrounded by four soldiers holding spears. Admitting that he could not match his enemy in a fair fight, he knelt on 'Mine emulation hath not that honour in't' (12–13), his body emulating the baseness of his plan to defeat Martius with 'craft'. He slowly hoisted himself up, holding on to the other soldiers for support as he declared, 'My valour's poisoned / With only suffering stain by him' (17–18), an obvious physical and moral inversion of the honourable rise that Howard's Martius achieved in battle. Hands brought down the lights for the first interval at the end of the scene, appearing to draw a line under the first movement of the hero's rise and his antagonist's decline.

The visual parallelism of the soldiers' spears also recalled the Plebeians' opening revolt. The production began with seven Citizens, carrying wooden staves and dressed in black trousers, caps and leather coats, crossing in a tight group downstage in the dark. When Barrie Rutter's First Citizen banged his staff on the stage there was a burst of light and he addressed his powerful opening lines to the house. This dramatic tension continued as individual Citizens spoke their lines with urgency, and the group delivered speeches in strict unison, emphasizing their shared resentment by thumping their staves on platform. Graham Crowden's Menenius then entered, blocking their exit to the Capitol and defused their dangerous energy. Although the tall Crowden looked the part of the patrician nobleman (with his decorative sash, hand fan and shooting stick), the People were relaxed by his graciousness, laughing at his belch that punctuated the 'Tale of the Belly'. Howard was unperturbed by the Citizens, speaking to them contemptuously, his voice oozing derision. When he sneered 'I'd make a quarry / With thousands of these quartered slaves as high / As I could pick my lance' (196–198), they converged on him, their staves pointed at him threateningly. But this Martius had nothing to fear from them, and he merely waved his hand, scoffing. Howard understood his character to be 'the battle-ground' for all Rome's conflicts, and believed that in his next major encounter with the Citizens, the vote-seeking scene, Coriolanus was 'giving himself up' to Rome (Daniell 164). He also wished to give his portrayal psychological complexity by showing the embarrassment that the sacrificial vote-seeking would cost Coriolanus. Yet Howard's speech deflated the threat that the Plebeians represented. He bellowed 'Kindly, sir, I pray let me ha't' (2.374), giving the line an awkward irony, apparently driven by his embarrassed frustration. With characteristic vocal modulation Howard quietly and self-consciously continued 'I have wounds to show you' (2.374–375), and this comment, like his terse 'Hang 'em' (2.355), drew laughter from the audience, which flattened out the emotion in his voice. Furthermore, by following Hands's suggestion that he offer himself up as though he were 'a street vendor' (Daniell 164), Howard undermined the seriousness of his sacrifice, as he stretched out 'voices' (spoken seven times in twenty lines), into 'voiee-ces!' in a mocking sing-song tone.

Hands then reversed this comedy in order, once again, to elevate the hero. The rebellious spirit that the Plebeians and Tribunes generated at the end of 2.3 carried over into 3.1, which Hands staged with real violence: Howard shook Tim Wylton's Sicinius and hurled him to the ground as he shouted 'Hence, rotten thing!' (178); the Citizens and nobles lined up diagonally across the bare stage, recalling the battle formations of 1.4; Howard throttled the Aedile who tried to arrest him and then lunged at the Citizens, scattering them out several exits. In the last encounter between Coriolanus and the Tribunes in 3.3, Wylton and Oliver Ford-Davies's Brutus sat behind a large table stage left, Ford-Davies banging a gavel to call everyone to order. Standing before the two men like a prisoner being arraigned, and singled out in a patch of light, Howard powerfully conveyed Coriolanus' effort to restrain his anger by holding a thirty-second pause before replying 'I am content' (47) to Wylton's insistence that he should endure the People's 'censure for such faults / As shall be proved upon you' (46–47). But he could not restrain himself when called a 'traitor' (66), and Howard unleashed a steady flow of invective, sailing through Coriolanus' 'The fires i'th'lowest hell fold in the people!' speech (68–74). This conflict culminated in another of Hands's intertextually allusive stage images. With the Citizens' chants of 'It shall be so' (105) ringing in his ears, Howard strode stage right to the large table, lifted it above his head, backed up to centre stage, scattering all onlookers who froze, gaping in silence at him. Then, with the table still aloft, he spoke the first four lines of his 'You common cry of curs' (120–123) speech, ending it with tremendous emphasis on and a lengthy pause between each word of 'I banish you' before crashing the table to the stage. Although the hurtling table physically duplicated Coriolanus' own downfall in Rome, the thrillingly athletic feat of choler dramatically elevated him as much as the first-act scenes of literal ascent which it negatively mirrored.

Hands concluded the portrayal of Coriolanus' relationship with his family in a comparable visual parallel. The women's return from their embassy (5.5) began with the Romans gathered stage right and stage left as triumphant drums and horns signalled the women's victory. Fleur Chandler's Virgilia entered with Yvonne Coulette's Valeria ahead of Crowden, who was followed by Maxine Audley's Volumnia and young Martius (Jamie Glover / Vincent Macauley / Adam Rhodes). Part-way through the procession, Audley's Volumnia removed the boy's cloak – like the one Coriolanus wore into exile – to reveal him dressed in leather and clutching a sword before him, a miniature version of his father in Act 1 when Howard stood before the Roman army, his swords crossed in front of him. The wandering exile had, metaphorically, returned home, and was discovered to be the warrior-saviour through whom Volumnia would extend her domination of the Martian clan and continue to exercise her power in Rome. But Hands's physical separation of Virgilia from young Martius-the-warrior-saviour was also an extension of the family dynamics established in 1.3, where Virgilia was depicted as the loving, dutiful wife, and Volumnia the hardened, ambitious mother. While Chandler sat quietly sewing, Audley remained standing, facing the audience as she recounted Martius' past glory. Although Chandler spoke defiantly when she stood to say 'give me leave to retire myself' (28), Audley promptly shoved her back into her seat. Audley then returned to fantasizing of Martius' battles, stamping loudly as she declared 'stamps thus' (33), clutching her own breasts as she imagined Hecuba's to have 'looked not lovelier / Than Hector's forehead when it spit forth blood' (42–43), the phrase shouted at the audience. Coriolanus' relationship to the women became clearer still when he returned from battle (2.1). Although Howard eventually took both Audley's and Chandler's hands just before they exited, he kissed and embraced only the latter; Audley merely touched his oaken garland, the sign of his military glory, when she ordered him to rise from kneeling to her. Both women wept at his exile from Rome (4.1), but it was Chandler, at the start of the scene, who turned away in distress from Howard when he spoke 'The beast / With many heads butts me away' (1–2), and it was she who, after he exited upstage through the gates which closed on him, pressed herself against the doors, her arms outstretched in mourning for her lost husband.[6]

While Audley showed little of Chandler's tenderness, Hands devised Volumnia's two interventions with her son (3.2 and 5.3) to reveal that the terrible emotional bond between them was as inexorable as it was lethal to Coriolanus. Scene 3.2 began ominously, with a single white beam piercing the darkness, illuminating the black back wall; Howard emerged from a central upstage door and cast a shadow against the wall that grew menacingly as he crossed downstage into the light. He stood downstage, facing the audience to deliver his lines while Audley entered, and he spoke of her as though she lived so vividly in his mind that he saw her without actually laying eyes upon her (Daniell 160). When instructing Howard's Coriolanus how to behave in front of the People, Audley finally made sustained physical contact with him, starting by holding his hand. Yet these were no gestures of love but actual manipulation: telling him to stretch out his hand 'this far' (74), she stretched it out for him; telling him to kneel, she touched his knee; telling him to wave his head, she touched his head; finally, she simply dropped his hand, done with her puppet-son's lesson. Shocked at this performance, Howard demanded, 'Must I / With my base tongue give to my noble heart / A lie that it must bear?' (99–101), stretching out the vowels with disgust in 'liiiiyeeeee?' and pausing dramatically before conceding, 'Well, I will do't' (101). When he tersely conceded again, 'Well, I must do't' (110), Howard paused a full thirty seconds, generating tremendous emotional tension before quietly and slowly intoning 'Away my disposition' (111). He then released the tension, speaking 'into a pipe / Small as an eunuch or the virgin voice' (113–114) with a mocking squeak but then wound himself into a rage, screaming 'I will not do't!' (120). Howard addressed his final words of concession to Audley in a frighteningly slow and portentous delivery, and, as he exited, he threw aside his sword, unmanning himself in filial obedience, thereby reinforcing the sense of dread with which he spoke those words.

The women's embassy in 5.3 specifically recalled 3.2, and Audley's Volumnia was now determined to finish what she began in the earlier scene. Once more, Howard's Coriolanus stood downstage facing the audience as he described his family's entrance, so powerfully did they occupy his imagination.

Although the women now wore their hair down in disarray, and put on looser, more informal robes than they had previously, Chandler and Audley still played their by now well-established roles. When Howard asserted he would act as though he 'were author of himself / And knew no other kin' (36–37), Chandler insisted upon their marriage bond: rising from her kneeling position, she removed her hood and said demurely, 'My lord and husband!' (37); ten lines later, they kissed, the rekindled love between them humanizing and breaking this hardened Coriolanus, thus making him susceptible to Audley's Volumnia. After shaming her son by bringing his young boy and showing him to Howard, Audley raked the grown man over the emotional coals. Audley demonstrated a vocal range no less impressive than Howard's, shouting 'O, no more, no more!' (86), asserting with quiet but deep feeling that he was 'tearing / His country's bowels out' (102–103), amplifying her fury when she declared that he was 'tread[ing] ... on [his] mother's womb' (123–124), and sniffling with self-pity when calling herself a 'poor hen' (162). As in 3.2, Howard revealed that his political decision turned upon the intensity of their emotional connection by dramatically sustaining a silence that lasted more than thirty seconds, though he now clasped her hand to his chest, a child desperate for maternal contact. But the encounter had also apparently broken Audley's Volumnia; as Howard ominously and quietly spoke 'But for your son – believe it, O, believe it – / Most dangerously have you with him prevailed, / If not most mortal to him' (188–190), she wept, and for the first time Coriolanus had to console the bloody-minded matron by embracing her. The double psychological breakdown not only sealed the priority of the personal over the political in Hands's conception, but it must have coloured perceptions of Volumnia's triumph in 5.5, though it is hard to know whether spectators saw Audley in that procession as a pitiable figure or as a ruthless hypocrite (or both) willing to destroy her family to fulfil her ambitions.

If Hands designed 5.3 and 5.5 to emphasize the triumph of Volumnia's emotional sway over her son, the director was determined to return the production to the depiction of Coriolanus' singularity, *his* heroism and *his* victory in death. Hands underplayed Aufidius' plotting at the top of the final scene (5.6) by cutting half of his dialogue with the Conspirators, allowing Coriolanus to get on stage more quickly. Once more, Hands's scenography purposely invoked earlier moments in the production. Howard's entrance was spectacular: accompanied by loud trumpets and drums and lit heroically by follow-spots, he crossed downstage through both sets of doors as though 'between two black cliffs' (Daniell 40), which closed behind him. The entrance recalled his heroic storming of Corioli in 1.4, though now the audience had a view from the 'inside', amongst the Volsces. Not only had the perspective of the first-act battle changed, but Hands quickly signalled Coriolanus' defeat. Howard halted stage left of Glover just as the music stopped, and he lay down his sword, recalling his symbolic 'unmanning' in 3.2, when he tossed aside his weapon after capitulating to Audley's Volumnia. As in 3.2, Howard put on an intensely emotional display in response to specifically personal slights, though his only emotion now was rage. After Glover taunted him with labels of 'traitor' (85) and 'boy' (101), Howard shrieked and drew out the vowels on 'measureless liar' (103), 'boy' (104, 113, 117) and 'my lawful sword!' (130). Hands kept the focus on Howard by having him join the chorus of Volsces screaming 'kill!' (131) before throwing himself on his own sword, which Glover had picked up. In Howard's mind, this suicide was an aspect of Coriolanus' 'angel of death' otherworldliness, and showed his readiness to return 'to the strange people he came from' (Daniell 167). Of course, by 'heroically' seizing control of his own death, he also denied Glover's Aufidius a fully 'honourable' triumph. This does not mean his demise was pretty: the spear-wielding Volsce soldiers descended on and trampled Howard's prone body, creating an image that reversed Martius' first-act ascent on the Roman spear. Nevertheless, Hands apparently believed that Coriolanus was ultimately victorious: the Romans actually joined the funeral procession as the Volsces carried out Howard; the director brought them on at the end because he wished to show that, while Coriolanus escaped in death, the bereaved Romans were undone in the end, wondering how they would continue without their hero (Mulryne 329, 332).

The 1977–79 *Coriolanus* might have reflected a change in the RSC's house style but reviewers had not altered their criteria of analysis. At any rate, the production was, arguably, more in line with what the critics had longed for and many found in Williamson's performance. Most of them appreciated the production for its uncut text, for the fact that it purportedly did not reveal a political slant, and for its grounding 'in the current dread of collectivism' (*The Times* 22 October 1977). Certain reviewers did complain that the relationship between mother and son was not satisfying (*Sunday Daily Advertiser* 13 June 1978), that '[t]heir encounters' lacked 'the crucial significance which Shakespeare allotted to them' (*Guardian Weekly* 18 June 1978), and that the encounter in 5.3 lacked sufficient emotion or psychological revelation (*The Times* 22 October 1977; *Observer* 23 October 1977). Others quibbled that Howard fell 'back too often on technique' (*Coventry Evening Telegraph* 21 October 1977) and that he 'often calculated his pauses and crescendos too obviously for conviction' (*Daily Telegraph* 22 October 1977). Despite these misgivings, critics revered the power of Howard's heroic performance, his 'trumpet voice which is the most thrilling sound at present to be heard on the English stage' (*The Times* 22 October, 1977), his 'outsize demonstrations' and 'subtle strength' (*Sunday Telegraph* 23 October 1977), and his combination of 'war machine' and 'rhetoric machine' Coriolanus, whose 'clangorous tones' are 'thrilling, ingenious and appropriate' (*Observer* 23 October 1977). It was this remarkable performance that, four years after the RSC's European tour, made Howard the obvious choice for the BBC television production (Fenwick 22). While the television programme was emotionally and visually toned down compared to the RSC production and lacked both the sustained flair that Hands created with lighting effects and some of Howard's wilder vocal fluctuations, it was nevertheless grounded in the same focus on the individual at the expense of the political that had made the RSC's staging such a popular success.

The BBC Television *Coriolanus* (1983–84)

The final moments of the 1.6 battle scene in the BBC's *Coriolanus* encapsulate director Elijah Moshinsky's depiction of Martius as singularly heroic.[7] Encouraging his comrades back to battle, Alan Howard is literally above the other eight or ten soldiers visible on the screen. The camera captures him on horseback, near the centre of the frame in the darkness of the background, a spotlight picking him out in his bloodied, white, Jacobean-ish shirt. Unlike Howard, who faces the lens, the soldiers are anonymous because we can only see the backs of their heads and the shoulders of their black uniforms. When Howard holds out his sword on the line 'And follow Martius' (75), the camera dollies to the right, past the silhouettes of the soldiers' raised blades, which briefly and partly obscure Howard's grimly smiling face. The camera then pulls in for a close-up on him as he lifts his sword a second time and speaks 'O, me alone! Make you a sword of me?' (76) with an understated intensity that turns the question into a command. The camera pauses for a few seconds on Howard striking a pose that seems to echo the same moment in the 1977–79 RSC production. On the soundtrack, several ethereal soprano voices sing 'O-o-o-o' at an increasingly higher pitch as Howard stares into the distance above the top edge of the screen, apparently lost in rapture at the thought of war, his mouth pulled down into a crooked half-smile. The television version might lack the athleticism and acrobatic daring of Howard's ascent on the spears in Hands's staging of this scene, yet Moshinsky here reveals his command of the camera as a device for selecting what the viewers see in order to exclude that which was peripheral to his vision of the play. The shift of the visual field from the group of soldiers to the lone hero is typical of Moshinsky's technique of concentrating on Martius (and his relationships with his family and Aufidius) to the relative exclusion of Plebeians, servants and crowds in general.

Recorded in April 1983 and broadcast one year later in Britain and the United States (on PBS, the Public Broadcasting Service), *Coriolanus* was created during the third phase of the BBC-Time/Life series, under the producer Shaun Sutton (producer 1982–85). The series relied upon British talent but was conceived in partnership with American financial backers who insisted that the programmes should be set in Shakespeare's time (or the time represented in the plays), that they should not last longer than two and a half hours, and that they should be acceptable to a very broad viewership (Willis 11). These constraints were most fully embraced by the series' first producer, Cedric Messina (producer 1978–80), though the quasi-naturalistic 'House Style' (Bulman) he instituted was relaxed under Jonathan Miller's tenure (producer 1980–81), while Sutton gave his directors even more creative leeway. If critics found many productions '[b]land, dull, pedestrian, [and] worthy' (Terris 219), and if there was 'an enervative, sanitised feel' to programmes recorded under each producer (Terris 225), the series has also served as a testing ground for academic arguments about the BBC's identity as 'an oppressive agency of cultural hegemony' (Holderness 181), the struggle between textual fidelity and the exigencies of television conventions, and the differences amongst television, cinema and the theatre (Holderness; Jones, 'Nahum Tate'; Willems; Willis). For instance, Michèle Willems argues that in the 'realistic' form of television Shakespeare, the purportedly aural medium of verse drama and the visual medium of the small screen 'often vie for the spectator's attention without supporting each other', and, in the desire for clarity that motivates 'realistic' television, the play is often reduced 'to its story-line and to a number of characters delivering speeches which are received as too long and pointlessly verbose' (75–76). While this argument hardly describes the full potential of performing verse drama on television, it does begin to describe Moshinsky's attitude to the filming of *Coriolanus*.

Coriolanus was Moshinsky's fourth programme for the BBC series in three years, and the director saw himself shifting from his earlier 'pictorialism' or 'painterly' touch to a concern with '*content, debate*' (qtd in Fenwick 18, emphasis original). This concern is unsurprising, given that Britain's debate with itself had only intensified since Daniell sounded his alarm over Thatcherite arts policy in 1979. Besides following up the 1981 national miners' strike by taking the country to war in the Falkland Islands in 1982, the Conservative government had continued to undermine funding for the arts, 'turn[ing] the Arts Council from Mr. Pickwick into Scrooge' (Sinclair 250). This last policy directly affected Moshinsky, who worked frequently in the opera, including productions at nationally subsidized British companies, during the early to mid-1980s. Yet the debate he envisioned was not political. He did not believe that a politically 'fair' production could be exciting, nor did he even think that 'political debates are really capturable on television because you have the debate *with* the audience' (qtd in Fenwick 21, emphasis original). Whether or not he based this decision primarily on personal artistic preference or on the strictures imposed by the American educational videotape market that the BBC was ultimately seeking for the series is unclear. What Moshinsky did make clear is that the debate he wanted to have with the audience resulted from pursuing a single 'very passionate' theme, that of the 'doubt-ridden hero who travelled through the political and military world and through his own society and made himself an outcast and finally a suicide' (qtd in Fenwick 21).

Textual alterations were meant to focus on the doubt-ridden hero story-line, to launch into scenes rapidly and to emphasize Martius' transformation into Coriolanus 'as quickly as possible' (Fenwick 20–21). They were also designed to provide the narrative with 'two peaks': Coriolanus' winning and losing of the Consulship and his confrontation with Volumnia in 5.3 (Fenwick 20–21). Although the script editor David Snoddin insists that the removal of servants was not the result of any 'élitist preference' but was meant to maintain 'the pure thrust of the story', alterations to the script narrowed the political world that Coriolanus moved through (qtd in Fenwick 21). In getting to Martius' naming as Coriolanus near the end of the first act, Moshinsky and Snoddin removed more than 240 lines of dialogue, mostly from discussions between the Citizens and Menenius, and expository dialogue from the battle scenes (though they did insert the first 90 lines of discussion from 2.1 between Menenius and the Tribunes just before Martius is named Coriolanus in 1.9). To expedite progress to the first narrative 'peak', they excised more than 300 lines, much of it from the deletion of the officers' speech in 2.2, the Tribunes' plotting dialogue with the Citizens at the end of 2.3, the argument that duplicates the physical struggle to arrest Coriolanus in 3.1, and the Plebeians echoing the Tribunes when they accuse and sentence Coriolanus in 3.3. The same is true of the 340 lines cut between 4.1 and 5.3: Aufidius' servants disappear from 4.5, the Citizens appear only at the very end of 4.6, and the Volsce guards who mock Menenius are absent from 5.2.

Many of the scenes left largely intact are those between or among small groups of speakers, so that the content of the remaining debate circulates among relatively few characters, rendering the action private, though not without 'political' import. Moshinsky achieves this effect in part by dividing the scenes into smaller episodes. Once Howard finishes haranguing the Plebeians in 1.1, the camera cuts away from the street to the Roman Senate chamber where the nobles discuss the Volsces' war preparations. Moshinsky repeats the effect in 1.9 by cutting from the battlefield to the interior of a tent when Howard's Coriolanus, alone with Patrick Godfrey's Cominius and Peter Sands's

Titus, begs to save the unnamed old man's life. He repeats it again in 2.1 by relocating the initial conversation between Joss Ackland's Menenius and John Burgess's Sicinius and Anthony Pedley's Brutus to the Senate chamber, and transposing the scene to appear directly after the battle of 1.8. Not only is the action in these scenes explicitly separated from the People and the soldiers but the enclosed space of the interiors adds to the privacy of the debates that occur therein. The private moments between Burgess and Pedley, meanwhile, lend a conspiratorial edge to their relationship that colours their apparently upright and genuine anger with Coriolanus in Act 3: at the end of 1.1, Moshinsky cuts to the Tribunes standing in a gloomy alley, a faint light partly revealing their heads and shoulders; the director concludes 2.1 by cutting to a room in the Senate where a lone candle illuminates the men sitting at a table, Pedley weighing something on a scale and Burgess making notes in a book. In both cases, with their faces imperfectly lit in the enveloping darkness, their knowing fear of Coriolanus' increasing power acquires a particularly sinister and cunning tone. Moshinsky encourages the sense that an ignoble cabal is operating against Coriolanus in the play by establishing through the private scenes parallels between the Tribunes and the relationship that Mike Gwilym's Aufidius has with Valentine Dyall's Adrian, who replaces Aufidius' lieutenant (4.7) and the Conspirators (5.6). The men's conversation in 4.7 echoes the Tribunes' discussion in 2.1; they sit facing one another in a partly lit chamber and the camera slowly zooms in on them as Gwilym leans forward into the darker lower half of the screen, intensifying the secretive quality of his intentions for Coriolanus, which he elucidates for Dyall. The gloom of 5.6, meanwhile, is markedly hellish: wearing long, crimson robes, the men stand like a pair of fiends against a background of blood-red ruins. Again, the camera pulls in on the men's half-lit faces as their conversation becomes more intense. Moshinsky then visually narrows the cause of Coriolanus' impending death to the singular hatred of his enemy by zooming in slowly for a close-up of Gwilym, who delivers Aufidius' speech that concludes 'And I'll renew me in his fall' (49) with restrained passion.

Although the Plebeian scenes carry much of the production's political content, Moshinsky directs the People in such a way that their collective power rarely becomes a vital political force in Rome. The Plebeians of the opening scene are a sedate lot, and, rather than vigorously rebelling, these fifteen or so linger in front of a dilapidated beige wall. While Moshinsky provides a sense of the People's mass power by occasionally filming this group as a whole, much of the debate takes place solely between the serious but subdued First and Second Citizens (Paul Jesson and Ray Roberts), who are singled out in close-ups and two-shots. The People's reaction to Ackland's relaxed and self-assured Menenius is likewise subdued and lacking in tension. Most of the debate is a private, civil conversation between Ackland and Jesson, the camera picking them out through the group of Plebeians, each of whom is only partly seen. Ackland politely and seriously recounts the 'Tale of the Belly' (without belching) leaning carelessly against the wall as Jesson watches him impatiently before demanding 'Your belly's answer – what?' (112) grumpily but without menace. The tension increases palpably once Howard enters and scolds the People with a harsh, nasal delivery. Yet the tension is all on Howard's part, as the Plebeians are unmoved by his scorn; even when Howard venomously spits out 'Hang ye!' (179), Moshinsky's reaction shot shows six of the Plebeians standing perfectly still and glaring with mild resentment in Martius' direction. The Plebeians are yet more subdued in 2.3. Once again, they stand against the beige wall but now they seem to be on an extended work break, napping, eating, drinking and washing their faces. The debate amongst the People is earnest rather than comic, and, except for Jesson's sharp tone when he says, 'The price is to ask it kindly' (73), the People approach Howard humbly; they stand quietly listening to his speech and barely react when he protectively holds his hand to his gown, refusing to reveal his wounds. In 3.1, Moshinsky does, briefly, provide a sense of the Plebeians' collective power by having them break into the Senate chamber and surge directly at the camera. Yet, after a short struggle they become, once more, the sedate crowd of 1.1 and 2.3. They surge forward a second time when Burgess and Pedley call for Coriolanus' death, but they are reduced to mere muttering as soon as Ackland insists they 'temp'rately proceed' (219). When Howard then challenges them with his sword, the Citizens' blank stares caught in the reaction shot in fact make them appear nearly indifferent to the threat.

Furthermore, Moshinsky uses the Plebeians to highlight or

elevate Howard. In 1.1, he enters and remains on a horse, looking down upon the People whom he towers over in the crowd shots. In 2.3 he frequently stands posing on a ledge in front of a wall, raised above most of the Plebeians in the scene. Finally, Moshsinsky ends 3.3 not with the people's cheers at Coriolanus' banishment but, as many nineteenth-century actors had, with Coriolanus' final face-to-face denunciation of the People, which the director treats as another opportunity to 'pose' Howard (Willis 157). Although Howard does have to shout down the People who enthusiastically echo Pedley's 'It shall be so!' (120–121), once he begins his 'You common cry of curs' speech (122–137), the scene is all about Howard's Coriolanus. Moshinsky maintains a close-up on the actor until he says, 'thus I turn my back' (136), at which point the camera pulls back as Howard slowly walks away from it between two rows of Plebeians, most of whose faces are indistinguishable. The mass of largely anonymous People thus serves as a visual frame bracketing Howard's cloaked statuesque figure standing posed in the background for the scene's final line, 'There is a world elsewhere' (137), which the actor slowly intones with a quiet menace.

Moshinsky does create violent spectacle in the battle scenes, however, to depict the active and decisive involvement of the 'lower orders' in Roman politics, insofar as military conflict is an extension of the political. When Howard says 'Summon the town' (1.4.7), the camera cuts to the helmeted Roman fighting men in the eerie half-light lined up against a black wall. Moshinsky suggests the power of their collective will by tracking the camera along the row of soldiers who raise a terrible din by banging their shields and bellowing. When Sands's Titus says 'Ladders, ho!' (1.4.22), a soft drum beats and ominous strings sound as the camera shoots the soldiers from behind. A blinding white light then pours out of Corioli's opening gates, creating a menacing image of the massed ranks by illuminating a virtual forest of metal-plumed helmets and spears in silhouette. While the reaction shots of the men's uncertain faces undercuts their menace, the next scene re-establishes the common soldiers' violent power. Here, the men interlock shields above their heads to create the Roman 'tortoise' and advance, crouching, on the Volsces to the sound of a drum and chanting male voices. Moshinsky cuts from a shot above the shields to the men's perspective, revealing the fires burning within Corioli. He amplifies the sense of danger with close-up shots of advancing Roman siege engines; cutting to shots inside one of the engines, we once more get the soldiers' perspective as the engine's front wall opens and light floods in while the men file out, eager for battle among the flames and the smoke. Placing the camera in the thick of the fight, Moshinsky creates a brief montage of savage images: soldiers hacking each other; a close-up of a thickly muscled man, driving home his sword as he leaps towards an off-camera opponent; and another soldier in a close-up silhouette repeatedly slashing a foe.

While the power of the savage spectacle renders the common soldiers more politically significant than the common people in the production's peacetime scenes, Moshinsky is nevertheless careful to make Howard's Martius stand out from his comrades. After showing the Roman soldiers' initial hesitancy to fight, the camera cuts to Howard, on horseback, glaring scornfully at the fearful men. Positioned once more literally above the others, he curses them in voice-over rather than treating them as actual interlocutors, so that he is in a sense apart from them in overseeing their cowardice. Moshinsky also employs the battles as another pretext to pose Howard. When he re-enters from within Corioli just before the end of 1.4, the gates open to the sound of soprano voices singing several notes. Light and smoke precede Howard, who, in a blood-stained shirt, slowly advances and grandly leans one arm against the wall, peering meditatively at his gore-smeared sword. With a half-smile-half-sneer on his face, he then stares upwards to a point off-screen, lost in apparently bloody thought while the soprano voices swell, driving home the impression of Martius' singular military majesty. Besides the similar pose described at the start of this section of the chapter, Moshinsky carefully devises Martius' renaming to maintain a tight focus on the victorious hero. When Godfrey's Cominius tries to give Howard a disproportionate share of the spoils in 1.9, Moshinsky places the two actors and Sands's Titus in the background of the frame, filming them through two rows of soldiers whose faces are unseen. The three men stand directly in front of another group of soldiers, so that they are bracketed by their comrades on three sides. When Howard refuses the extra share of booty (his words accompanied by drums and a fanfare), the camera slowly zooms in on the trio of generals before cutting to a close-up of Howard angrily declaring that they praise him 'In acclamations hyperbolical' (1.9.51). Moshinsky repeats this technique when Godfrey crowns Howard with the garland and names him Coriolanus, moving the camera through the crowd of anonymous soldiers and ending on a close-up of Howard, who now resignedly remarks, 'I will go wash; / And when my face is fair you shall perceive / Whether I blush or no' (1.9.68–70). The double zooming-in aggrandizes the hero while establishing a visual sequence that Moshisky repeats in the banishment scene which, as noted above, poses Howard in the background when he is stripped of his honours.

Moshinsky further singles out the hero during the battle in one of the production's three 'duet' scenes (Willis 159) that Howard has with Gwilym, each of which the director crafts to underscore 'the *power* of the sexuality' that drives the men's mutual hatred (Moshinsky, qtd in Fenwick 24, emphasis original). This power is on full display in the programme's 1.8, which is filmed against an indistinct background in the half-light of the fires burning at Corioli. Both warriors are shirtless, and are shot mostly from the mid-torso or higher, thus showing off their lean, sweaty bodies. At the start, they battle with spears and shields, but, during the vicious fight, they switch to swords. Eventually, they repeatedly batter each other up against a dark wall, grunting with each blow, 'till the two are locked, nearly naked, in an almost loving, sado-masochistic conflict' (Fenwick 25). The scene does not end with Aufidius' unsolicited helpers but remains focused on the two combatants. Howard holds Gwilym by the throat against the wall and, with their faces nearly touching, they stare at each other with an anger that implies a deeply passionate connection. Their connection is more explicitly erotic in 4.5, which features only the two actors. In the low white light, the camera captures a close-up of the seated Howard, now with long bedraggled hair, staring away from Gwilym, who stands over him from behind. When Howard's Coriolanus reveals his identity, the camera dollies to the left, putting him in the lower right of the screen and Gwilym above him to the left, both facing the camera. From this perspective, we watch Howard present his throat to Gwilym, and the latter slowly, almost lovingly, eases his hand around the proffered windpipe. Speaking 'O Martius, Martius!' (101) like an aroused lover, he curls one hand around Howard's shoulder and thrusts the other beneath his shirt, slowly caressing his chest, before swinging around to gaze into his eyes. Taking Howard's head in both hands, he lovingly speaks, 'but that I see thee here, / Thou noble thing, more dances my rapt heart / Than when I first my wedded mistress saw / Bestride my threshold' (115–118). Moshinsky ends the scene with a close-up of the two men while Gwilym recalls, in an erotic tone, his dreams of their battles and makes his invitation to invade Rome.

They consummate this exclusive relationship in the final scene where, except for a Volsce Lord calling for order (124–128), only Gwilym and Howard speak after the former concludes his talk with Dyall's Adrian. The scene is shot almost entirely in close-ups of Howard and Gwilym. After Howard hands Gwilym his sword and the peace treaty, they trade accusation and rebuttal with understated anger. Unable to countenance the mock-sympathy with which Gwilym speaks 'boy of tears' (101), Howard's face twitches and he slurs loudly before hissing and sneering through his 'Measureless liar!' speech (103–117). This exchange was merely a kind of foreplay to their final bloody congress: after Howard says with a quavering voice, 'Alone I did it. "Boy"!' (117), the camera stays on them in close-up as they struggle. They stare knowingly at each other and Howard allows Gwilym to lift the blade to his breast and grimly instructs him to 'kill' before helping to pull the blade into himself. Howard repeats the command, his head jerking with each 'kill' he utters and each push of the blade, until a look of pained ecstasy spreads across his face. Then Gwilym, rapt by the violent and repeated thrusting, begins shrieking 'kill' as Howard slips from his enemy's embrace and sinks out of the frame. Gwilym stands over his now-unseen victim and appears ready to gratify himself with one final thrust, but he halts his sword in mid-air and slowly regains his composure. The scene remains an affair between the two men to the very end, as Moshinsky concludes the action with a tight close-up of Aufidius explaining his murder, but never calling for his comrades to 'assist' with the corpse.

The scenes of Coriolanus' family life serve explicitly to counterpoint to the hero's antagonistic relationship to the Plebeians and the fatally sexualized one he has with Aufidius. Howard shares a deep, loving bond with Joanna McCallum's Virgilia, who is from the start the epitome of chaste Roman womanhood. She and Irene Worth's Volumnia sit at a Jacobean table in a brightly lit room, demurely sewing. Although the scooped neckline of McCallum's dark dress is slightly more revealing than Worth's similar high-collared gown, McCallum speaks quietly, her eyes downcast. Moshinsky emphasizes her modesty in her relationship with Heather Canning's subdued Valeria. Throughout their interaction, he films the three in a tight shot of a seated McCallum at her sewing frame, and the other two standing behind her. While she stitches, she politely refuses Canning's invitation to socialize and studiously averts her gaze as though she were being pressed to commit adultery, just barely turning her head when Canning suggests the possibility of news from the wars. We witness the strength of the connection between husband and wife when, in a series of close-ups, Howard tenderly kisses an overtly passionate McCallum upon returning to Rome (2.1), at his exile (4.1) and when he greets the women's embassy (5.3). Furthermore, Moshinsky rearranges the action to play up the contrast between Coriolanus' home life and his public behaviour. Between Howard's exit into Corioli's gates and his emergence, blood-soaked, from those same gates (both in 1.4), Moshinsky briefly cuts back to McCallum and Worth at their stitchery, the contrast between the sinister half-lit battles and the sunny sewing room adding poignancy to this reminder of what the hero fights for. Moshinsky's splitting of the action in 2.1 has an analogous effect. Because the director transposed Menenius' conversation with the Tribunes (2.1.1–89) to appear between 1.8 and 1.9, the action cuts directly from Aufidius' bitter conversation with Adrian in 1.10 to Coriolanus' family rejoicing at his impending return and then to a happy reunion with the hero in a Roman street. Similarly, Moshinsky creates a brief domestic scene in the former sewing room where Howard's Coriolanus now proudly shows his son how to use a sword while the women admire father and son. For contrast, he cuts from this sunny scene to the half-lit conspiratorial conversation between Burgess and Pedley described above.

Volumnia may trigger her son's downfall at Aufidius' hands in Moshinsky's *Coriolanus*, but Worth is hardly a domineering matron. Instead, she embodies the director's belief that it is necessary 'to find the weakness in her character and play the weakness' (qtd in Fenwick 22), and the 'weakness' she plays is an over-fondness for her family. She speaks to McCallum with tenderness as the two stitch away in 1.3, and is actually saddened when she remarks that if Martius had died in battle 'Then his good report should have been [her] son' (20). Worth's Volumnia is conscientiously gentle with her daughter-in-law, speaking to her of Martius' military feats as though McCallum were an oft-indulged child being favoured with a bedtime tale. When McCallum is distressed by Worth's vision of 'Hector's forehead when it spit forth blood' (42), the older woman puts her arm around McCallum's shoulders and says consolingly, 'He'll beat Aufidius' head below his knee / And tread upon his neck' (46–47). Worth is more stern when convincing Howard's Coriolanus in 3.2 to humble himself before the Plebeians, gritting her teeth on 'At thy choice then' (123) and angrily speaking, 'Thy valiantness was mine, thou suck'dst it from me; / But owe thy pride thyself' (129–130), her dark eyes flashing rancour. Yet her valiantness fails her after Coriolanus fails to humble himself, and she is an emotional wreck when seeing him off to his exile in 4.1. In a close-up of mother and son, the parent–child relationship is fully reversed: Worth can only weep and snivel when Howard calmly asks her, 'Where is your ancient courage?' (3). Still in close-up, she peers, distraught, into Howard's eyes and desperately throws her arms around him as she sobbingly shrieks, 'My first son, / Whither wilt thou go?' (33–34).

Even in the embassy scene, Worth's Volumnia does not regain full maternal control, though the red tent in which the scene occurs was envisioned as her domain; Moshinsky related that he 'meant [the red interior] to be womblike' (qtd in Fenwick 19). Nevertheless, Howard succumbs to Worth's urgent emotional appeals, the variations of which the actress handles with great subtlety. In the first half of their encounter, she is imploring rather than commanding, which Moshinsky emphasizes by shooting much of her second long speech over Howard's shoulder to show Worth looking up beseechingly into his face. She does become angry and her dark eyes bore into her son when she tells the women, 'Down, ladies; let us shame him with our knees' (169). She looks defeated as she says, 'Down' (171), and the camera closes in on the kneeling women, who lower their heads even further towards the sandy ground. Worth's hard edge returns when she stands and delivers 'This fellow had a Volsce to his mother' (178) with disdainful brittleness. Yet she looks once more into Howard's eyes as she says resignedly, 'I am hush'd until our city be afire, / And then I'll speak a little' (181–182).

Now Moshinsky reveals the emotional toll that the embassy has taken on mother and son: the camera briefly stays in close-up on the two as they stare silently at each other before panning down to Howard's white hand framed against his black cloak; it slowly unfolds and clasps Worth's hand; the camera pans back up to their faces in close-up and Worth peers at Howard's face as he says, 'O my mother, mother!' (185) with quiet intensity. Tears come to Howard's eyes, but Worth is the more visibly distraught. Horror plays across her face when the actor remarks, 'Most dangerously you have with him [your son] prevail'd, / If not most mortal to him' (188–189), and she buries her head in his shoulder, sobbing audibly on his calmly spoken 'But let it come' (189). Aware that she has engendered her son's death in this 'womblike' tent, Worth's Volumnia is a broken woman, her face grimly pensive rather than victorious in the brief procession of 5.5.

Reaction to Moshinsky's *Coriolanus* was markedly similar to response to Hands's production. Although reviewers were not exceptionally concerned with the formal use of the visual medium, they did appreciate the way that Moshinsky 'fully exploited the possibilities of television by subdividing scenes into smaller units set in different locations' (Warren 336), its 'peaceful, pictorially composed interiors' (*TLS* 4 May 1984), and the 'sparing use of slow motion shots' (Pearce 98). Yet most critics were primarily concerned with how well the principal actors embodied Shakespeare's text. Either Moshinsky had found the perfect match in Howard and Gwilym to depict their 'love/hate obsession' (Warren 336) or this relationship 'never fully comes alive' (*TLS* 4 May 1984), because the excessive 'homosexual caresses' between them in Moshinsky's 4.5 'excessively motivates what is merely an undertone in the text' (Charney 5). Either Howard's 'harsh and strident voice was perfectly attuned to the metallic resonance of the blank verse' (Pearce 97), or he was 'seriously miscast as Coriolanus' because '[h]is extraordinarily affected diction could never be mistaken for [the] military roughness' required of him (*TLS* 4 May 1984). Either he 'scaled down the grandeur of his 1977 RSC performance ... without any loss of intensity' (Warren 336), or his 'too old for Shakespeare's Marcius' Martius 'disrupts the logic of the play', even if he is 'very energetic' and 'splendidly dismissive' (Charney 1). Critics also established the reverent tone of response to Worth's performance that would prevail in the reaction to her next two efforts in the role: 'her richly musical delivery brought out every nuance of the text' (Warren 337); her 'magnetic rendering' rested on a 'steely maternal dedication' (*TLS* 4 May 1984); and her 'long speeches of supplication in the final scenes are delivered with consummate artistry' (*New York Times* 26 March 1984). The critics were pleased by Moshinsky's apolitical take on the play: although, 'for democratic societies', it might be 'the most questionable of Shakespeare dramas', it does reveal that '[t]he genius of Shakespeare still takes many forms' (*New York Times* 26 March 1984), and 'the class war is heavily weighted against' the production's 'Marxist' Tribunes (Charney 1). The filming and reception of the BBC *Coriolanus* arguably represent a far point in the decade-long shift away from the explicitly political productions that appeared on British stages between 1965 and the early 1970s. This view of *Coriolanus'* political potential would, however, be put to the test eight months later when Peter Hall mounted the play with a highly topical, if star-driven, production at the National Theatre.

Coriolanus.

Act. 4. Scene. 5.

Published Oct. 10.1799. By Vernor & Hood, Poultry.

1 John Philip Kemble as Coriolanus in Act 4, Scene 5

2 Edwin Forrest as Coriolanus

3 Laurence Olivier as Coriolanus and Anthony Nicholls as Aufidius

4 Emrys James as The Boss and Peggy Ashcroft as Volumnia in
The Plebeians Rehearse the Uprising

5 Anthony Hopkins as Coriolanus and Constance Cummings
as Volumnia

6 Ian Hogg as Coriolanus and Margaret Tyzack as Volumnia

7 Alan Howard as Coriolanus

8 Ian McKellen as Coriolanus

9 Christopher Walken as Coriolanus, Irene Worth as Volumnia and Ashley Crow as Virgilia

10 Jonathan Cake as Coriolanus and Mo Sesay as Aufidius

11 Ralph Fiennes as Coriolanus and Gerard Butler as Aufidius

CHAPTER VI

Shakespeare and Thatcher's England – The 1984–85 NT *Coriolanus*

On 7 February 1985, less than two months into the run of the National Theatre's (NT) 1984–85 *Coriolanus*, the battle that had been waged privately between the theatre and the Arts Council erupted publicly in what came to be known as NT Artistic Director Peter Hall's 'Coffee Table Speech'.[1] At a press conference, Hall, who directed the 1984–85 *Coriolanus*, denounced what he described as an insufficient increase in the National's government subsidy, and accused the Arts Council of betraying the NT (Thorncroft) by abandoning its responsibilities as an arm's-length government agency: 'The Arts Council, instead of fighting for the arts, is becoming more a straight instrument of government policy' (qtd in Hewson). In the same speech, he announced cost-saving measures that included closing the NT's Cottesloe Theatre and dismissing one hundred (out of seven hundred) employees (Thorncroft). Although the 1984–85 *Coriolanus* embodies many of the ideological assumptions that animated the RSC's 1972–73 production, Hall's speech reflects how much more the 1985 staging was explicitly engaged with its immediate political context. The most obvious sign of Hall's desire to engage politically with 1980s Britain was literally to bring it into the action: a portion of the paying audience sat on stage on what looked like crumbling amphitheatre steps. From this vantage-point, the onstage audience witnessed the production's smoke-filled battles, featuring the bloodied and stripped bodies of Ian McKellen's Martius and Greg Hicks's Aufidius. The onstage audience also participated in the production's spectacular red-banner-hung processions and in Martius' violent confrontations with the Plebeians, which occurred in the large circular sand-pit placed in the centre of the Olivier Theatre's stage.[2] Despite the markedly political nature of the staging, Hall, his actors and reviewers all remained preoccupied with a reverence for Shakespeare's verse, his supposed universalism and an understanding of character which stressed the performance of coherent, psychologically plausible subjects. The 1984–85 *Coriolanus* reveals the Shakespeare-plus-relevance ideology under strain from the factious political climate of mid-1980s Britain, as the transformation of the nation's postwar consensus made itself felt in the traditional world of subsidized classical theatre production.

Hall's outburst was the not unlikely result of years of stagnant arts funding from Margaret Thatcher's Tory government. Hall's dispute with the Arts Council in the 1980s was by no means the first battle he had fought since taking over as the NT's Artistic Director from Laurence Olivier in 1973. Up to 1985 he had wrestled with delays and cost overruns in trying to open the theatre's South Bank building, experienced three strikes at the company (labour tensions provoked Hall to vote Tory in 1979), and in 1981 and 1982 the theatre was taken to court by the crusading Mary Whitehouse over its production of Howard Brenton's *The Romans in Britain*.[3] However, the funding crisis of the mid-1980s was among the theatre's most important struggles, and symbolizes the breakdown of the middle ground of British consensus politics.[4] Indeed, large, vaguely liberal subsidized performing-arts institutions like the National had arguably been on the defensive throughout the 1970s and 1980s, first from the far left and alternative-theatre communities, and second from the right-wing monetarists of Thatcher's Tories.[5] While Thatcher may have spoken out frequently against 'consensus', and replaced 'the discourse of post-war Conservatism, based on the maintenance of traditional institutions' with 'a radical discourse grounded on a Neo-liberal belief in individualism, competition and anti-statism' (Peacock 13), her government did not necessarily revolutionize the British welfare state overnight. Still, the Conservatives did work against what Richard Vinen calls the '"progressive consensus"' of the late 1960s and early 1970s, which he identifies with a significant curtailment of the free market's powers, and a perceived slackening of social order driven by the perpetuation of 'progressive' left-wing values in education (7, 27–31). Certainly, ever since Thatcher's party formed a government shortly after 1978–79's 'winter of discontent' that capped a decade of labour disputes, power outages and recession, the Conservatives had successfully assailed their opponents on the left. As Hall's comments suggest, the Tories employed the Arts Council – surreptitiously intervening in and eroding the body's ability to operate as an arm's-length organization as the decade progressed – to impose its market-oriented ideology on the nation's theatrical community, a policy that caused significant unrest within the Council.[6]

Although *Coriolanus* might be read in light of the 1982 Falkland Islands war, with Thatcher as a Volumnia figure, consolidating political power at home by exploiting others' military victory abroad, neither the production team nor reviewers said much about the war, and the more current and apt context was the miners' strike, which lasted from March 1984 to March 1985.[7] The Conservatives' response to this national strike provided a parallel to Hall's funding woes that suggested both were part of a momentous reversal in the country's politics. The Tories did not intend to be forced to make concessions to the National Union of Mineworkers (NUM), as governments had in the past; indeed, government members believed that the NUM 'had to be defeated if the Thatcherite revolution was to take root in British politics and society' (Taylor, *The NUM* 173–174). The sometimes violent strike, which remained in the headlines for its duration, split public opinion, set trade unions against each other and divided the miners against themselves, thus providing a highly visible context of intense political animosity against which the public could judge Hall's comments and against which theatregoers could assess the production's explicitly topical action. Both the NUM and the NT feared that their roles in British society – even their very existence – were being seriously threatened by a powerful political enemy. The parallel between the two national institutions was strengthened by the fact that, just as Hall had accused the government of attacking the arts community through the Arts Council, the Tories were employing the National Coal Board and police forces to confront striking miners.[8] Yet the parallel is also instructive for the contrast it provides: the subsidized arts community was far less of a concern for the Tories than the miners were; the Conservatives may not have funded the National to levels that Hall wanted but, unlike their response to picketing miners, the government never deployed riot police to silence the director's complaints.

The toxic political atmosphere represented by the miners' strike and by Arts Council funding cuts did not fundamentally alter Hall's or his actors' commitment to a version of the 'Shakespeare-plus-relevance' ideology, though the framing of the NT production's politics was more explicit than that seen in the previous decade at the RSC. Hall, McKellen and Hicks all insisted upon the primacy of Shakespeare's verse, and the two actors were concerned to 'obey' Shakespeare while rendering psychologically consistent characters that were unambiguously 'relatable' to a modern audience.[9] Yet, significantly, Hall began to shift from merely asserting the playwright's universal relevance to employing Shakespearean theatre as a means of aggressive political dissent. A month after his 'Coffee Table' speech, the director repeated his accusation that the Arts Council was no longer an arm's-length body in a lengthy *Sunday Times* opinion piece. He did not confine himself to the analogical relevance of his art, but declared that theatres 'have been told that reasoned argument will get us further than noisy protest. We know this is not true ... Any theatre that puts its case quietly can die quietly' ('We Will Mount'). Hall followed this up with impassioned commentary in *Plays and Players* in which he attacked the Arts Council for its betrayal of the National by specifically linking postwar subsidy to the political maturity of postwar English theatre. It is in the context of this tense political battle that he explained the attraction of *Coriolanus'* 'confrontation and extremism' ('J'accuse' 6), and it is in this context that he construed a markedly oppositional, rather than conciliatory, function for the National's production. The commemorative programme, too, suggests the NT's conscious transformation of the Shakespeare-plus-relevance ideology into a more oppositional one. The NT's programme prints numerous textual and visual juxtapositions from various historical eras to suggest the timelessness of the play's political violence. However, a message later inserted into two different sections of the programme gave the production a more pointedly political bent: 'The NT's Cottesloe Theatre, closed due to insufficient Arts Council subsidy, re-opens in the autumn thanks to a special GLC [Greater London Council] grant'. This message, which took Hall's campaign against the Arts Council directly to his audiences, drew the production explicitly into the ongoing battle between the Tories and the left-leaning GLC, thus clearly announcing the National's political affiliation and defiance, rather than a stance of conciliation and compromise.

Such a blend of universalist claims about timeless political relevance and topicality registered powerfully in the anachronism of the production's scenography, which extended the post-Brechtian tradition of minimalist settings. This vacant off-white space, where much of the action occurred, evoked the spirit of the RSC's 1972 Stratford staging, but the pit's circularity and the broad symbolism of its upstage double doors, with gold ones representing Rome and black ones for the Volscian scenes, more closely resembled the Berliner Ensemble set. What chiefly distinguished this stage architecture (designed by John Bury) from those earlier empty sets was the onstage audience seating placed on either side of the doors. These seats, which, as noted above, were made up to look like dilapidated classical amphitheatre benches, were nevertheless embedded in the pragmatic modern framework of twentieth-century scaffolding. Furthermore, on the upstage wall stage left of the gate were political posters, including one for the contemporary Italian communist party, 'Democrazia Proletaria' with a fist clenched before a hammer and sickle. The costumes, too, struck a contrast between the modern and the classical: Plebeians wore jeans and T-shirts; nobles draped togas over business suits; McKellen and Hicks battled each other in loincloths and were armed with classical helmets, swords and shields; and after their individual fight, Hicks put on a modern black leather trench coat. The exception to the historically identifiable dress was the costuming for the battle at Antium, where soldiers wore vaguely futuristic outfits.

The production's most evident anachronism was Hall's introduction of the onstage audience into the action. By having this portion of the audience leave their seats and participate on the platform in the most politically charged scenes (the opening riot, the voices scene of 2.3, the Tribunes' rejection of Coriolanus as Consul in 3.1, his exile in 3.3 and the concluding assassination), Hall emphasized the crowd of late twentieth-century spectators' specifically social function.[10] The non-performing audience was invited to contemplate their own roles in similar political encounters, though such identification could have coincided with a kind of alienation, for, while the performing audience reduced the aesthetic distance between stage and auditorium, it also held the potential to disrupt the fictional world of the play by bringing into it the 'real' world of 1980s Britain. At the same time, because the onstage audience members were not rehearsed in the same way as the actors playing the Citizens, they posed a constant threat of breaking character by acting awkwardly. They also risked obstructing planned blocking, especially as they were inserted into scenes that included carefully choreographed outbursts of violence. Indeed, the actors had difficulty orchestrating the performing audience in the violent action when the Tribunes first inform Coriolanus that he will not be Consul, and, by February of 1985, audience participation on the platform was limited to three scenes: 1.1, 3.3 and 5.6 (Bedford 337). Although it is difficult to gauge what kinds of identification or alienation the larger audience actually experienced, Hall attempted to use the onstage theatregoers to establish a parallel among the political situation in Rome of the play, Jacobean England and mid-1980s Britain even before the first line was spoken. He began the production with the onstage audience members (in their street clothes) mingling with the actors playing the Plebeians in the sand-pit. The paid actors distributed, as in a modern demonstration, leaflets that drew a relation between Rome and Shakespeare's England: 'Citizens of Rome: / Caius Martius is chief enemy to the people. / We want corn at our own price. We are hungry for bread. / The patricians' storehouses are crammed with grain. / LET US REVENGE THIS WITH OUR PIKES!' (Bedford 12). One actor extended this historical juxtaposition by employing a twentieth-century device – a spray-paint can – to spell out 'Corn at our own price' across the upstage gates, giving the symbolically vague doors a more specific signifying function. They underscored the link between republican Rome and contemporary Britain by wielding placards (reading 'Hunger For Bread' and 'Corn at Our Own Price') and by carrying a Union Jack on stage, thereby localizing the political significance of Shakespeare's Roman protest in the present directly outside the theatre.

Hall concluded the production with the same kind of politically charged historical juxtaposition in representing Coriolanus' death in 5.6. The actors brought the audience on to the platform when Coriolanus entered so that the larger audience watched this portion of the modern British public bear witness to the hero's last act, one that allowed McKellen and Hicks to unleash a final, resounding burst of mutual hatred. On the sound recording, Hicks slowly increased the intensity and anger in his first long speech (88–100) as he denounced Coriolanus' betrayal 'For certain drops of salt' (93).[11] He then scolded Coriolanus with a sneering emphasis on 'boy of tears' (101) but coolly dismissed McKellen's breathlessly exclaimed 'Ha?' (101) with a curt 'No more' (102). McKellen's Coriolanus was at first shaken, speaking 'Boy' (103) with a quiet intensity but he quickly wound himself up, taking off his gloves and hurling them away before screaming, 'Stain all your edges on me. "Boy!"' (113). He then dropped back to a powerfully understated delivery, until he asserted, apparently crying, 'Alone I did it. "Boy"!' (117). Hicks then retreated to the upstage seating while McKellen slurringly shouted, 'O that I had him, / With six Aufidiuses or more – his tribe, / To use my lawful sword!' (128–130). As McKellen began his last speech, he drew his sword and swept it around. Hicks, still on the seating, then unsheathed his sword, apparently to indicate the continuation of their first hand-to-hand battle. However, three Volscian Conspirators shot McKellen with modern firearms before any swordplay occurred, and Hicks rounded out this assassination by returning to the sand-pit from the seating to stand on his enemy's body in a sign of personally spiteful individual triumph. Hall wanted the scene to be quick and ruthless to undercut Coriolanus' heroic romanticism, and in rehearsal he saw 'the play's already well-established eclecticism' as a justification for the use of guns here for the first time in the production (Bedford 136). But the lead's death was not just about the timelessness of the lesson that Coriolanus dies because he cannot accommodate himself to political developments. Rather, by pitting the hero's ancient weapon against the Conspirators' modern ones, Hall undermined Aufidius' personal 'glory' by explicitly showing his individual victory to be the result of a craven pragmatism backed up by superior firepower. The assassination with modern weapons also suggested that Coriolanus was out of touch with and defenceless against the specifically contemporary, twentieth-century pragmatism that Hicks's Aufidius represented. Considering that Hall placed his fellow citizens directly into the action through the onstage audience, and given his repeated public charges that the government was using the Arts Council to attack the British theatre establishment, this assassination seems, in retrospect, to be an aptly topical (if unintentionally so) emblem for the director's attempt to preserve a passing way of artistic life against a cruel modern political reality.

While the onstage audience may have provided visual eclecticism and topicality, Hall also broke down the distance between the larger audience and the production's visually and aurally impressive scenography. The designer John Bury supplemented the Olivier Theatre's two alleys that led diagonally from the downstage left and right stairs of the round playing space to the front of house with downstage centre steps that led up a central alley normally blocked from the platform with several rows of seating. Consequently, the theatre's permanent curved amphitheatre seating area mirrored the diagonal alleys and upstage centre door of the set, and Hall blocked much of the most thrilling action so that it passed *through* the audience, rather than simply being delivered *at* them in a quasi-proscenium arrangement. For instance, at the top of 1.4, the Roman army took formation on the centre-stage stairs, mere inches away from the spectators. In 1.5, a bleeding Martius exited up the centre aisle steps towards the front of house, shouting, 'I will appear and fight' (20); in the following scene his voice echoed from within the bowels of the auditorium on 'Come I too late?' (27), and he repeated this cry seconds later when he entered from the stage-left alley, again directly in front of the audience in the theatre's regular seating. Similarly, for Coriolanus' victory procession in 2.1, two trumpets, one drummer and one standard-bearer entered from both the stage-left and stage-right alleys as McKellen, Basil Henson's Titus, John Savident's Cominius and two standard-bearers entered the centre alley from the front of house.

Hall's placement of theatregoers on stage to enhance the spectacle was a logical extension of such blocking. Besides swelling the crowd of Citizens in a number of violent encounters between sharply divided opponents, the onstage audience added to the aural vitality of the spectacular processions in Acts 2 and 5. Before Hall curtailed audience participation, he filled the platform in the first of these scenes (2.1) with both the onstage audience and some two dozen cast members. While vibrant red banners unfurled to the floor from the flies, and a carpet was rolled out from the upstage doors to welcome Coriolanus and his comrades entering from the centre steps, the audience applauded loudly and rhythmically, adding to the triumphant tone of the loud bass drums and rhythmic trumpet blasts. The audience similarly clapped Coriolanus off stage when McKellen led a long procession through the upstage gates towards the end of the scene, and they repeated this loud, rhythmic accompaniment to the more ominous drums and trumpets for Volumnia's triumphal procession in 5.5. Although the audience stood up from their seats only when Irene Worth marched through the gates, down the carpeted centre-stage area and back through the gates, these theatregoers descended to the platform area to applaud wildly when McKellen entered in 5.6, to the accompaniment of the same ominous drums and trumpets that sounded for Volumnia's procession.

Whatever the performing theatregoers contributed to the scenes in which they appeared, much of Hall's stunning spectacle employed rather general, emblematic staging to single out Martius' individual heroism. The thrilling battle scenes elevated McKellen through athletic displays of his half-stripped bloodied body and by tracking his centrality in the fighting through the use of various flags. The 1.4 battle began with trumpets and pounding drums and a choreographed fight between Volscian and Roman soldiers in formation. However, much of the fighting centred on McKellen, who made his parley with the Volscian Senators at Antium while holding the Roman flag. After the soldiers' formations dissolved, Martius pursued the fleeing Volscians, and the gates closed on him as a mysterious bass synthesizer chord sounded. Shortly after, the gates opened for a heroic discovery: a blood-stained McKellen appeared, shrouded in smoke and battling two Volsces; the actor then turned downstage and waved a ragged flag, enjoining the men to follow him. At the top of the next scene, McKellen was singled out when he appeared atop the ramparts and displayed first the Roman and then the captured Volscian flag to his comrades below. McKellen made yet another spectacular entrance in the next scene when, stripped to the waist and still smeared with blood, he entered from the downstage left alley and circled the centre of the sandpit, displaying himself to all sides of the audience. Shortly after, as a drum roll sounded, he stepped on to a soldier's shoulders with the bright red Roman flag in one hand and the other raised in a victoriously clenched fist. As he cried out, 'O me alone, make you a sword of me' (1.6.76), the other soldiers raised their fists in response and repeatedly shouted, 'Martius!' McKellen then leapt down, flag in hand, and charged off stage, heroically leading the army back into battle. The most sustained display of individual militaristic heroism occurred in the lengthy and gruelling 1.8 battle between Martius and Aufidius. Hall's extended demonstration of the combat's intense physicality suggested a kind of timelessness, a revelation of some fundamental human barbarity. He accomplished this depiction of humanity pared to its essentially savage nature by eliminating much of the scene's visual context. McKellen and Hicks began by pointing their flags at one another before handing them off to attendants, stripping down to loincloths and helmets, and arming themselves with swords and shields. Theatregoers thus witnessed a primal struggle between two virtually naked bodies set against a blank background of sand. Hall narrowed the focus on the actors' bloody flesh even further by dimming the lights on the house and the stage architecture, and illuminating only the circle of sand on which the fight occurred, thus reinstating the fourth-wall division between unseen audience and visible performers that he had eliminated from the very start.

Even in those scenes that included audience participation in the play's politics, McKellen's Martius shone as a marvellously singular and confrontational protagonist. After Frederick Treves's patient, didactic Menenius pleasantly cajoled the Citizens in 1.1, McKellen seemed to relish trying out a variety of tones in showing off Martius' personal distaste for the People. He ran through a list of the People's demands (204–207) with a dismissive sing-song rhythm, and threw away lines like 'Hang 'em!' (202) and 'Five tribunes to defend their vulgar wisdoms' (213) with a casual indifference, as though the Plebeians were beneath his notice. But he also spat out 'you curs' (166), 'Hang ye!' (179) and 'Get you home, you fragments' (220) with emphatic scorn. His encounter with the People in the scar ceremony of 2.3 was not as overtly confrontational. Although McKellen showed the strain of the ritual on Coriolanus in his sarcastic tone, and although Geoffrey Burridge's First Citizen was ostentatiously hostile to his candidacy for Consul, McKellen did banter comically with the People and eventually appeared to win them over unequivocally. The scene was more important for the way it solidified the Tribunes' identities as a foil to

McKellen's hero. David Ryall's Sicinius and James Hayes's Brutus had kept their cynical scheming subdued up to this scene; when they spoke of Martius' rise to power at the end of 1.1 and 2.1, they appeared motivated more by genuine fear of what he represented than by any base instinct for scheming. Yet in 2.3 they warmed to the task of berating the Plebeians, becoming increasingly manipulative and calculating as the scene unfolded. Having established their cunning and determination, the Tribunes became the individual figures who sparked Coriolanus' ire in a standoff in 3.1. If Hayes's and Ryall's unqualified confidence in speaking for the crowd of contemporary Britons who participated in the scene before February reminded the larger body of spectators of NUM leaders, the scene itself provided McKellen with yet another opportunity to stand out above his fellow performers by showing off his vocal and physical prowess. He easily bested the Tribunes' shrieked ire and he menaced his opponents, sending Hayes scurrying out of his way, knocking Citizens' heads together when 'They all bustle[d] about' him (184) and chasing them off stage with his drawn sword. In 3.3 McKellen restricted himself to verbal singularity. Again, the Tribunes stood out as his particular antagonists, speaking with conspiratorial urgency at the top of the scene, and maintaining their self-assurance throughout. McKellen responded by putting on a display of his impressive vocal range. He screeched Coriolanus' rage on 'What do you prate of service?' (84), though his raised voice started to break with feeling on 'Vagabond exile' (89), as he imagined his punishments. He devised his fifteen-line exit speech as a tour-de-force worthy of a star actor. His voice wavered on 'common cry of curs' (120) and he paused dramatically before he spoke 'I banish you' (123) with understated intensity. Circling the group of excited Plebeians, he continued to berate them, building his anger and pausing once more for effect on the verge of telling them with quiet hatred, 'Despising / For you the city, thus I turn my back' (133–134). McKellen chose to forgo the opportunity to stare down his enemies as he spoke his final lines in favour of an equally dramatic *cri de coeur*. He exited after his penultimate line and shouted 'There is a world elsewhere' (135) from off stage, so that his disembodied quavering voice resounded back into the playing space like the haunting memory of his staunchly personal defiance.

Hall emphasized the centrality of Coriolanus' individual

tragedy to the production by complementing his confrontational and militaristic singularity with a powerful domestic struggle between Volumnia and her son, which became the psychological mainspring of the hero's downfall. From the start, Worth's matron demonstrably revelled in her son's military prowess. She cried out eagerly when imagining Martius shouting to his comrades, '"Come on, you cowards!"' (1.3.34) and she exuded a steely certainty that her son would 'beat Aufidius' head below his knee' (1.3.47). Yet her maternal affection took the ecstatic edge off her hawkishness, and she did not relish her son's demise when she told Wendy Morgan's Virgilia that Martius' 'good report should have been [her] son' had he died in battle (1.3.20–21). Similarly, just before Worth had her first scene with McKellen, her voice choked with both pride and concern when she spoke, 'O, he is wounded, I thank the gods for't' (2.1.116), and when she actually greeted him, her voice conveyed these same mixed emotions as she told him, 'I have lived / To see inherited my very wishes / And the buildings of my fancy' (2.1.190–192). If Worth tempered Volumnia's militaristic 'fancy' with genuine affection, she was still a bullying force to be reckoned with. Worth and McKellen worked hard in rehearsals for 3.2, the first real confrontation between parent and child, to show Volumnia dominating her son with guilt when he tried to assert his independence from his mother, and to demonstrate his reversion to a childish dependence upon her (Bedford 84–89, 221–223, 254–256). In performance, McKellen behaved petulantly throughout the scene, twice pretending to storm off and later angrily hurling down his cloak in response to his mother's demands. On the production's sound recording, he asked Worth with exasperation, 'Why did you wish me milder?' (14) and he inserted a comically childish 'ohhhh' and 'uhhhnn' before peevishly demanding of Menenius, 'Well, what then?' (36). Worth replied with reasoned argument until McKellen's Coriolanus became overwhelmed with scorn at the idea of humbling himself to the Plebeians; pausing dramatically before he spoke, he defiantly asserted, 'I will not do't' (120) but the next moment his voice shook with fear as he declared, 'Lest I surcease to honour mine own truth' (121). Worth shifted her tone impressively, needling him with possessiveness and guilt as she told him, 'Thy valiantness was mine, thou suck'dst it from me, / But owe thy pride thyself' (129–130). She had hit her mark: all the resistance

[151]

went out of McKellen's hero, as he first comically humbled himself and then revealed the neurosis lurking in his earlier comedy, shouting desperately, 'Look, I am going' (133), anxious to prove his obedience to Volumnia.

The two actors repeated and deepened this personal battle in 5.3. McKellen's voice registered Coriolanus' painful inner struggle as he steeled himself against any tender feelings when watching his family enter, though this tenderness overcame him as he spoke to Morgan, 'O, a kiss / Long as my exile, sweet as my revenge!' (44–45). Worth's and McKellen's greeting was yet more emotional, with both their voices growing husky with feeling until McKellen's Coriolanus found his resolve, angrily telling her, 'Desire not / T'allay my rages and revenges with / Your cooler reasons' (84–86). Worth's two long speeches convincing Coriolanus not to attack Rome were remarkable displays of vocal modulation, combining a clear and metrically balanced delivery, understated anger and an emotional thickening and wavering of her voice. Working on her son's guilt over betraying the familial bond, Worth's voice seemed almost beyond her control when she told him that he would 'no sooner / March to assault' his 'country than to tread' on his 'mother's womb' which had 'brought' him 'to this world' (122–125), desultorily stretching the vowels in 'womb' and 'world'. By the end of her lengthy set piece, she conveyed this guilt by lashing out mercilessly at McKellen, speaking, 'This fellow had a Volscian to his mother; / His wife is in Corioles, and his child / Like him by chance' (178–180) with a harsh emphasis on 'Volscian', 'Corioles' and 'chance'. Worth capped off her display of rhetorical virtuosity by delivering her final line, 'And then I'll speak a little' (182), with quiet anger, at which point McKellen seized her hand and, like Nicol Williamson, maintained a lengthy silence (forty seconds) for an emotionally stirring effect. Unlike Williamson, however, McKellen spoke his first three lines with a calm intensity before breaking down into childlike sobbing on the line, 'O my mother, mother! O!' (186).

In fact, the director altered this scene's blocking two months into the run, at the height of his public battle with the Arts Council, to emphasize the archetypal quality of Coriolanus' personal, family tragedy, rather than the production's topicality. When Coriolanus first addressed his son, McKellen put the boy on his shoulders and young Martius saluted in a visual echo of his father's salute in Act 1. The prompt-book indicates that before March 1985 McKellen spoke the last several lines of the scene, then crossed from Worth to Hicks, and the two began exiting upstage centre together. McKellen's Coriolanus then turned back to face his family before they all exited through the upstage centre doors. A second set of directions indicates that after March McKellen crossed from his mother to Hicks, but brought his son with him.[12] Hicks took the boy's extended hand, and the three crossed to upstage centre together. As in the earlier blocking, McKellen faced the three women, but now he knelt to his child before the boy returned to Worth. Coriolanus then stood and all exited upstage centre as in the first directions. The new blocking suggested that Coriolanus was offering the 'boy' within himself as a sacrifice to Aufidius but that the hero's childish self also remained partly attached to his mother. However audiences read the scene, the alteration employed a strategy of visual parallelism that relied on the archetypal imagery of generational transfer from father to son and not on the politically explicit juxtaposition of historically specific objects such as the Union Jack, spray-paint and automatic pistols. The onstage audience's presence and applause may have politicized Volumnia's victory procession in 5.5 and Coriolanus' assassination, but Hall's conclusion to 5.3 was fundamental to all audience members understanding the exclusively personal motivation for the hero's self-destruction in the final scene. As Bedford remarks, in 5.6, McKellen's Coriolanus was supposed to recognize Aufidius' 'Boy of tears' as a taunting reminder of his surrender to Volumnia in 5.3, and this recognition was what 'prompt[ed] Coriolanus to plunge headlong into the enemy's trap' (135). Whatever else the altered blocking in 5.3 did, it was meant to help the spectators make the strictly psychological connection between the two scenes that the lead was himself silently making, and it serves as a reminder of just how important the individual hero's psychology remained for Hall, despite the topicality of much of his scenography.

The production was generally well-received, though the critics baulked at the staging's alienating elements. Reviewers unreservedly praised Worth as 'one of the finest actresses of our day' (*Sunday Express* 23 December 1984) 'who, with her skilful presentation of the proud matriarch must be elected as one of the leading classical actresses in the world today' (*What's On and*

Where to Go 3–9 January 1985). Response to McKellen's individual performance, which won him the 1984 *Evening Standard* Award for Best Actor, was more complicated. Critics typically picked out the lead's commanding technical, physical and emotional range, but certain reviewers found his distinctiveness distracting: McKellen's 'euphonious whinny' betrayed 'a style too often mannered, too precious, too exorbitant to defend in the obvious way, by pointing out that Coriolanus is actually a rather mannered, precious, exorbitant character' (*New Statesman* 20 February 1985). In other words, he had taken the tradition of powerfully individualist or star performances that critics had typically endorsed in his predecessors too far in exposing the theatrical celebrity beneath the hero. Any sense of alienation from the illusion of Shakespearean heroism that McKellen's delivery may have provoked paled in comparison to the disturbance that the onstage audience caused for reviewers. The main problem was that Hall had displaced Shakespeare's fictional world with the real world of twentieth-century Britain, and it was the specificity of this intrusion that reviewers so resented. Critics charged that 'Shakespeare's wild, shiftless, poverty-stricken rabble didn't seem ... ideally represented by a young lady with a Gucci handbag, a beaming professorial type in tweed, [or] a dapper City gent' (*New Statesman* 20 February 1985). Francis King brought the purse motif closer to the National's home: 'As we all know from the example of Mrs. Thatcher, no crisis can separate a woman from her handbag, with the result that, during all the clamour for corn, a number of Mary Whitehouse clones can be seen with handbags dangling from them' (*Sunday Telegraph* 23 December 1984).

As King's allusion to two of the National's most public opponents suggests, critics responded in kind to Hall causing them to confront Britain's political landscape. Alluding to Hall's past difficulty with labour unions in getting the South Bank complex built, Irving Wardle suggested that the play's depiction of class strife 'could almost be a revival of the National Theatre's own history' but that Hall 'is no longer a director to underline any crude topical parallels' (*The Times* 17 December 1984). By contrast, Christopher Edwards disdained 'the crude political confections of the programme notes', and believed that the 'embarrassing and cumbersome' onstage audience pointed to the fact that Hall was still 'carrying a deal of Sixties baggage'; 'those

[154]

critics who have dubbed all this "exciting" must themselves be reliving their own heady youths of some 20 years ago' (*The Spectator* 12 January 1985). Edwards's comments are reminiscent of the politicized response to the Berliner Ensemble's London *Coriolanus*, though they also reveal divisions within the British press missing from the reviews of the mid-1960s. These divisions are particularly noticeable in two 'reviews' of the NT *Coriolanus* that have little to say about the production itself. For instance, Giles Gordon writing in *The House Magazine* made almost no mention of Hall's production but he explicitly took the director's side against the government on the matter of funding: 'For decades now we have been "better" at the live theatre than at almost anything else we do and we are in grave danger of losing this distinction *entirely* as a result of irresponsible ... underfunding by the Arts Council' (22 March 1985). Gordon's relatively restrained advisory tone, meant to persuade *The House*'s Parliamentarian readership on arts policy, is absent from the right-leaning diatribes that appeared in more widely read publications. For instance, the sometime Thatcher speech-writer Paul Johnson followed his brief but admiring comments about Hall's direction with a lengthy consideration of the play's history that devolved into a vitriolic attack on the left wing 'Polytechnocracy, that middle-class hydra, half-educated and highly opinionated' which was burdened by 'the accumulated rubbish of decades of self-deception, propaganda, and sheer ignorance' (*The Daily Telegraph* 16 January 1985).

Like Hall's scenography, especially his use of the onstage audience, such reaction helped make the NT production the most overtly political *Coriolanus* on London stages since the Brecht-inspired versions of 1965–71. Although the 1984–85 *Coriolanus* was very different in its ideology from the Ensemble's 1965 production, both reveal the consequences of negotiating contentious political circumstances through Shakespearean performance. Hall's topicality and his public denouncements of the Arts Council may have informed Gordon's defence of arts funding, but it did not necessarily cause Johnson's polemic. Yet, in the same way that the 1965 *Coriolanus* reflected Cold War tensions, both theatrical topicality and journalistic polemic are indexes of the factiousness of British politics in the middle of the 1980s. The real lesson about the theatrical consequences of such political engagement, however, is that the Shakespeare-plus-relevance view of performance abides in spite of explicit political engagement. The National's *Coriolanus* attended to the stratification of British political discourse that Johnson's vituperation clearly express. Yet the two men's preoccupation with political context did not represent the majority opinion. However reviewers approved or disapproved of *Coriolanus*, their criticism focused on how the production embodied Shakespeare's purported intentions, and shared with Hall and his actors assumptions about Shakespeare's timelessness and the need to concentrate on the characters' psychologies, especially the hero's. In the National's *Coriolanus*, the heroic individual so cherished by Thatcherites is brought low and gunned down in a world governed by Aufidius' ruthless ambition. While this assassination might be seen as a parable for the hero in a society where, as Thatcher later said, 'there is no such thing as society', only 'individual men and women' (margaretthatcher.org), the fate of the individual hero remained central to Hall's vision. In other words, although the government's purposeful diminishment of the public sector may have led Hall to devise a highly topical production and caused him to become embroiled in a public battle with the Arts Council, it only strengthened his faith in the Bard's transhistorical lessons, the centrality of his text and the system of subsidized theatre that had evolved alongside the Shakespeare-plus-relevance ideology.

CHAPTER VII

Shakespeare and goulash communism – *Coriolanus* in Budapest in 1985

On 16 June 1989 hundreds of thousands converged on Budapest's Heroes' Square to witness the ceremonial reburial of Imre Nagy, the former Hungarian prime minister whom the Soviets had executed in 1958 for trying to withdraw from the Warsaw Pact during Hungary's failed 1956 revolution. Writing about the long-delayed official public recognition of Nagy's government, the British journalist Timothy Garton Ash could not resist a Shakespearean allusion when meditating on Nagy's successor, Janos Kádár: 'He is Macbeth, and Banquo's ghost lies in state on Heroes' Square'. It is an apt comparison because, just as Macbeth is explicitly labelled a tyrant, the tyranny of the soon-to-be-defeated communist government that Kádár had led between 1956 and 1988 could finally be explicitly and officially recognized. However, when Gábor Székely staged his *Coriolanus* at Budapest's Katona József Theatre four years earlier in September 1985, such explicit public recognition was restricted by the system of 'goulash communism' which then prevailed. Under this system, Hungarians enjoyed relative material wealth, but were unable to express overt political dissent freely.[1] The corollary in the theatre was the exchange of heavy government subsidy for a degree of acquiescence to communist rule.[2] Practitioners had to be cautious when alluding to daily life under a dictatorship and were not allowed to refer positively to such topics as the 1956 revolution. Yet they were able to enter into private 'conversations' with their audiences, encouraging theatregoers to read subtle implicit political commentary in the stage action. Székely's *Coriolanus* is a decided rejection of the optimism about positive change at the social level found in

Bertolt Brecht's 'Marxist' version of the play; the 1985 production embodies a melancholy recognition that the futility of participating in a degraded public sphere has a profoundly corrosive effect on anyone who attempts to do so.

The goulash communism that characterized mid-1980s Hungary was the result of a decades-long development of the private economic and personal spheres in the country. Although Kádár continued the forced nationalization of the Hungarian economy for a time, 'the steady growth of the standard of living became the cornerstone' of his government's policy (Valuch 625). To achieve this growth the government gradually encouraged a 'secondary economy' sustained by citizens who, in addition to or instead of their own state employment, worked for their individual private financial benefit, effecting what László Kontler calls 'the greatest period of *embourgeoisement* in Hungary' since the end of the nineteenth century (437). By 1985 nearly two-thirds of the population participated in this secondary economy, effectively agreeing to live under communist rule while increasingly turning away from the imposed political obedience of the earliest days of the dictatorship (Kontler 457). There emerged from within this privatized environment a younger generation of Hungarians who hastened the end of the Kádár regime. This group included political dissidents who developed their own private political and cultural networks, and reformist politicians and bureaucrats within the communist party.[3] Yet, although by the late 1980s increased political pluralism and participation helped shape Hungary's transition from a communist dictatorship to a capitalist democracy, goulash communism had arguably 'infantilised people, reduced them to vulgar consumers of material goods' (Molnár, *Concise* 332). Zoltán Márkus calls this compromise a 'Faustian deal' wherein people 'had become politically and socially passive' ('War' 264–265), and officially sanctioned participation in the social realm was widely recognized as duplicitous because, as Veronika Schandl remarks, 'The stability of public life relied on the double nature of pseudo-important issues pronounced openly and of real problems only vaguely hinted at' (24). The consequence of the 'continuous "doublespeak" of politics' was, she asserts, 'an entire society perfectly trained at "reading between the lines"' (24).

Reading hidden political messages became a conventional interpretative strategy for audiences of the state-controlled theatre, including audiences of Shakespeare. Like the Germans, Hungarians had embraced Shakespeare as a substitute national dramatist during the nineteenth century when near-religious admiration for him gradually became institutionalized.[4] Cultural authorities within Hungary's Soviet-backed regime recognized the weight of Shakespeare's traditional value and sought to redirect respect for his work by fostering a belief in the dramatist's progressiveness in order to make him a 'good Communist' (Márkus, 'Loyalty' 185). In practice, this meant repressing oppositional messages, including expressions of nationalist sentiment about Shakespeare's Hungarian past, in order to gain acceptance for an externally imposed communist present. Márkus argues that, in fact, the 'autocratic anxiety' to suppress this history 'is precisely what opens up possibilities for those "ironic" and Janus-faced discourses ... of writing and reading "between the lines"', especially after the failed revolution of 1956 ('Loyalty' 185).

On its face, Székely's *Coriolanus* seems to combine a traditional respect for Shakespeare's textually inscribed intentions with an untopical reading of the play that nevertheless encouraged a degree of 'reading-between-the-lines' politicizing response about its contemporary relevance. Although Székely cut nearly thirty per cent (975 lines) of Shakespeare's script, resulting in a performance that lasted two and a half hours, he did not make any identifiably Brechtian textual additions or extraordinary changes to the basic sequence of the original narrative.[5] Székely did cut Coriolanus' leave-taking before exile (4.1) and the meeting between Adrian and Nicanor (4.3), as well as a minor battle scene (1.8) and the Roman women's procession in 5.5, but most reductions were made by shortening individual speeches. Furthermore, as the video of the production reveals, there was nothing Brechtian or alienating about the acting: performers did not distance themselves from their characters by 'quoting' their roles; there were no interpolated songs; the battles were not stylized or heavily artificially choreographed.[6] The actors simply attempted to provide psychologically realistic performances and, as I argue below, were quite successful in delivering the kind of powerful emotion so often associated with 'authentic' Shakespeare. The scenography, meanwhile, evoked the world that Budapest audiences lived in. The set (designed by László Székely) evoked a dilapidated, central European urban-

[159]

industrial landscape of the late nineteenth to mid-twentieth century. The floor was 'paved' in what looked like large grey square flagstones, thin metal pillars stretched up to the ceiling and modern scaffolding stood abandoned against the upstage wall, which was an expanse of rusting riveted sheet-iron, with a massive door that could open upwards or left and right. Stage left was covered in once-handsome but now dingy wood panelling with a bench and a rigid awning in front of it, suggesting an abandoned railway station. Benches were brought on and struck, as were large flats of rough boards used to create a sort of three-sided corral during Coriolanus' vote-seeking scene. The costumes included dark modern business suits for the Tribunes, twentieth-century work clothes for the Citizens, modern evening gowns for the Roman women and a combination of modern trousers and tops, greatcoats, boots and toga-like robes for the male Patricians.

Within this apparently traditional approach to performing 'relevant' modern-dress Shakespeare, there was a strong current of disillusionment about participation in public life. The ennui attached to political involvement in the production was evident from the opening scene, where the Plebeian 'uprising' began with Zoltán Varga's First Citizen, a bespectacled intellectual or university student in a shabby grey suit quietly but firmly chiding the six Citizens, who stood slouching at various points on the stage and staring listlessly about them. This downbeat opening is striking for the way that Székely eschewed the opportunity to begin with a dramatic riot, and the way that he extended this almost depressingly slow pace well into the scene. When Varga failed to stir his comrades by throwing a stone off stage to smash a window, he raised his voice in anger at the People's suffering, but the debate he tried to engender never reached a serious pitch because the other Citizens, who had most of their rebellious lines cut, either seemed annoyed by his revolutionary zeal or merely laughed derisively at what they took to be his naivety. Ádám Rajhona's convivial Menenius, wearing a dark, cloak-like greatcoat and carrying a furled umbrella, also had to coax the apathetic Citizens back twice to listen to him as they began to shuffle off stage. Other than Varga, who hotly disputed Rajhona's appeasement, the Plebeians were mostly indifferent to his efforts at peacemaking and just whistled and laughed cynically at the gruff-voiced senator's jocular chastisement and humorous besting of the First Citizen. Only when György Cserhalmi entered as Coriolanus did the Citizens rouse themselves, yet even here they were in no way energetically terrified or rebelliously disappointed by Martius' presence; they simply melted away swiftly, wary of using the crude weapons (chains, clubs and metal bars) they carried in a public confrontation.

The gap between the First Citizen's activism and the utter lack of enthusiasm with which Székely infused his opening-scene 'rebellion' reflects the disaffection of those dissident intellectuals who came of age in the 1970s and 1980s. The government operated a system of enticements and punishments for artists: officials openly rewarded practitioners who staged politically acceptable productions while marginalizing 'politically less trustworthy artists' by moving them away from the cultural centre of Budapest to theatres in smaller provincial towns (Schandl 30). More insidiously, the government infiltrated oppositional artistic circles by forcing actors and directors to inform on their colleagues, turning the opposition against itself and thereby corrupting artists' efforts to dissent. Székely and Cserhalmi were, by 1985, young veterans of Hungary's state-controlled theatre; sometimes working together, the two men had been involved in landmark Shakespeare productions of the 1970s and 1980s that conveyed their generation's disillusionment with public life and especially the plight of artists under the Kádár regime.[7] Given Székely's and Cserhalmi's history of politically incisive Shakespeare productions, it would not be surprising to find suggestions that the 1985 *Coriolanus* responds to the work of an earlier generation of practitioners who helped create the world in which younger artists find themselves. One such suggestion appears in a programme note by Tamás Major, the prolific director-actor who was to have played Menenius in Székely's production until he fell ill. Major had staged the Brechtian *Coriolanus* in Budapest in 1965, and his 1985 programme note, with its critique of bourgeois aesthetics and praise of Shakespeare's focus on the social forces that drive his characters, established Major's socialist credentials. His expressed admiration for Shakespeare's topicality, meanwhile, reminded audiences that one reason he was known as 'The Master' to younger practitioners like Székely and Cserhalmi was that he helped lay the groundwork for politicized Hungarian

Shakespeare that subtly critiqued the state. Yet Major's prestigious career was also connected to his close friendships with high-ranking members of Kádár's regime and the fact that he rarely went too far in his political criticism (Schandl 171–173). He was, in a sense, a successful cultural safety valve, one embodiment of goulash communism's effect on Hungarian theatre (Schandl 192–193).

Was the appearance of Major's comments in the programme both a recognition of his politically suggestive productions and an acknowledgement that his Brechtian optimism belies a murkier, morally compromised and pessimistic reality? There is no clear answer to this because, while the 1985 *Coriolanus* has none of the socialist hope with which Brecht refashioned the play, Major's programme note is the only indication that Székely was 'writing back' to an older, more complicit generation. That is, the 1985 production depicted a Rome where there was little simplistic ascription of blame in any direction. The indifference that the Plebeians displayed in Székely's initial non-rebellion opened on to a world where all were tainted by the morally compromised state in which they existed. Any between-the-lines political content to be read in this melancholy world was to be found in the production's coding of public ceremony in resolutely anti-triumphalist terms; war, diplomacy and social ritual were all portrayed as unrewarding at best and sordidly self-destructive at worst.

Székely placed most of the burden of the production's anti-triumphalism upon his lead actor. The tall, lean Cserhalmi first appeared upstage; wearing a tan greatcoat that accentuated his broad shoulders, he crossed slowly and confidently downstage left to Menenius. His initial denunciation of the Plebeians was an impressive display of the actor's vocal skills. Cserhalmi began with a low angry voice, asking them, 'What would you have?' (165; 'Mi kell hát?' p. 8). He developed this half-whisper into a snarl on 'He that trusts to you, / Where he should find you lions finds you hares, / Where foxes, geese' (167–169; 'Aki bizik bennetek / Nyulat talál az oroszlán helyén, / S róka helyén libát' p. 8), and then into a clear, piercing baritone as he spoke, 'You are no surer, no, / Than is the coal of fire upon the ice, / Or hailstone in the sun' (169–171; 'olyan szilárdak / Vagytok, mint hómezőn parázs, napon a jégeső' p. 8). The authority with which Cserhalmi infused this chastening revealed the character's conviction that the Plebeians were doing real harm to Rome, not that he was driven by a self-aggrandizing contempt for the People. Similarly, while Cserhalmi fought the battle scenes with great energy, Székely repeatedly diminished Martius' opportunities for violent self-serving spectacle. Not only did the director cut the action in 1.7 where the Roman soldiers lift Martius and he cries, 'O, me alone! Make you a sword of me?' (77), but he made the battle between Károly Eperjes's Aufidius and Cserhalmi entirely private by removing Aufidius' rescuers. Unseen by any comrades, the two sweaty and exhausted men, wearing dark padding or armour that made them slightly hulking, fought with quiet, concentrated hatred. After twenty seconds of vigorous swordplay, Cserhalmi overcame Eperjes's Aufidius, using his removable metal-studded sleeve to strangle him slowly and quietly, before mercifully reviving the unconscious man with a bucket of water. With the playing space partly obscured by artificial smoke, the scene had nothing to do with Martius publicly vanquishing his enemy in front of other soldiers, or even the world suggested by the set; it merely sealed the two men's private knowledge of the Roman's superior individual prowess and nobility. Then, upon Coriolanus' return to Rome, Székely avoided any celebratory or majestic tone for the hero's victory procession. Instead, a dishevelled Cserhalmi, wearing a grey tunic and sleeveless robe, barged in from an upstage door, seized a chair and sat with his back to the audience, set off against a rusty sheet-metal panel as he clutched his dark blond head in pain at the sound of his deeds being enumerated. In the final scene, once Eperjes made his denunciation, Cserhalmi spoke his first several lines of reply softly, smiling bitterly with the understanding that he had been deceived. As he said, 'this cur ... wears my stripes ... to his grave' (5.6.108–110; 'Ez a kutya halálig hordja hátán / Korbácsom csíkjait' p. 133), Cserhalmi turned down his lips in scorn, lowered his voiced to a growl and seized Eperjes by the collars. Letting go, his eyes flashing with rage, he shouted the rest of the speech, expressing, again, not so much his arrogance but the angry realization that he was the victim of a dishonourable foe. In staging the lead's death, Székely once more refused to make a spectacle of Coriolanus; Cserhalmi was forced to retreat upstage through the imposing rusty door that banged shut upon him with an ominous clang before he was killed off stage, out of the audience's view.

Significantly, the one time that Székely drew out the hero's self-display was during the humiliating vote-seeking scene, which was less a socially beneficial ritual than a gruesome interrogation. The director calibrated every aspect of the action to belittle Coriolanus, to demonstrate that he was now fully in the power of the state, or in the power of the People the ceremony is meant to enfranchise. Cserhalmi entered bounding in skittishly, the grey wooden flats placed on stage in a 'U' formation, making him look like a penned animal at a livestock auction. He wore a truly humbling garment; made of two rough blankets sewn together at the shoulders, this 'gown of humility' frequently opened to reveal that the actor was naked except for a pair of white briefs. At first, the unseen Plebeians rushed loudly behind the walls, unsettling Cserhalmi's Coriolanus even further. Shortly, the First Citizen opened a door and stared defiantly as loud mocking laughter rang from off stage. Székely then built up and broke down his protagonist to amplify the grimness of the ceremony. Cserhalmi knelt in apparent humbleness, holding out a tin cup into which the Citizens were supposed to cast their coin-votes. One Plebeian sadistically feinted left and right before dropping his coin on the floor, and Cserhalmi grabbed at the vote like a desperate beggar. Having gained confidence from outlasting the experience, he rudely dismissed the Citizen with a terse extra-textual 'adieu!' ('agyő!'), only to have a second group enter and jeer as they threw their coins at him. He again knelt, though the false modesty of Cserhalmi's averted gaze, his fulsome cringing and the forced humility of his softened voice as he spoke 'Therefore, beseech you I may be consul' (2.3.99; 'engedd meg nekem, hogy konzul lehessek' p. 59) made it obvious that he was inwardly defiant and that he was forcing himself to follow the ritual's outward form. Finally, after he finished angrily recounting his deeds, two other Plebeians voted for him with genuine good will, and he was then acclaimed by offstage cheers. By now, however, this Coriolanus had felt the full weight of the ordeal; while Rajhona congratulated him, Cserhalmi grew still, and, with a reflective, pathetic look of self-betrayal in his eyes, he walked silently and slowly off stage, bowing his head in dejection.

In contrast to this vicious public sphere, Székely depicted Coriolanus' family life as a private haven by reducing the political function of Erzsi Máthé's Volumnia and Erika Bodnár's Virgilia and largely separating them from civic life in Rome. The director converted the public aspects of Coriolanus' return (2.1) and the women's embassy (5.3) by shifting most of the other actors on stage into the upstage darkness, away from the intensely emotional individual encounters between Coriolanus and his mother and wife. At the end of 2.1, Cserhalmi was left alone on stage with Bodnár, a demure figure whose kind smile and sad liquid eyes made her a particularly sympathetic character in this brutal Rome. After they slowly approached one another, she cried softly while holding his hands to her face and he told her gently, '[Virgilia, m]y gracious silence' (171; 'Virgilia, te édes némaságom' p. 45), before embracing her lovingly. Meanwhile, between Székely's cuts and Máthé's consistently caring maternal perform-ance, Volumnia became less bloodthirsty when imagining, in 1.3 and 2.1, the public honour that Coriolanus' mutilation will bring her. Máthé's Volumnia, a woman of true patrician bearing, with carefully moulded dark blond hair, an erect but not severe posture and a dignified low voice, was also more reasonable and kind than ruthless when convincing her son to dissemble himself to the People (3.2). Cserhalmi began the scene shrieking his determina-tion to remain true to himself and striding about the stage for a full minute while Máthé watched him with restrained disapproval. She did sternly counsel him to humble himself to the Plebeians but she spoke to her son and withstood his raging replies with a calm maternal protectiveness, and, once he had agreed to do her bidding, Máthé sat alone on stage with a faraway look of concern, rather than victory, in her eyes.

While Székely reduced Volumnia's angry speeches to her son in 5.3 by cutting nearly half of the lines she has in Shakespeare's script, Máthé adopted her earlier stern tone when reminding Coriolanus of his duty to his former life in Rome as she begged him to abandon his invasion of the city. Máthé, now wearing a sombre black cloak over the grey animal-print frock she wore throughout, intensified the emotionalism of their encounter by holding Cserhalmi's head and gazing into his eyes on 'Speak to me!' (149; 'Mondj már valamit!' p. 125). She then broke down, weeping piteously as she sobbed, 'There's no man in the world / More bound to's mother' (159–60; 'Nincs, aki anyjának többet köszönhet' p. 126). Máthé quickly composed herself and bitterly said, 'His [Coriolanus'] wife is in Corioles, and his child / Like him by chance' (180–181; 'Corioliban él a felesége, / S véletlen, hogy e gyermek rá hasonlít' p. 126), but, as she began to leave, the seated Cserhalmi pulled her on to his lap and wrapped his arms around her. Although Cserhalmi made 'O mother, mother! / What have you done?' (183–184; 'Ó, anyám! / Mit tettél?' p. 126) a poignant realization that Volumnia's antagonistic pleading will force him back into a fatally corrupting political environment, there was little sense that the audience was to read this exclamation as a straightforward ascription of guilt to the older generation for perpetuating such an environment. Rather, Cserhalmi spoke to Máthé gently, gazing at her affectionately and clinging to her as though their embrace were the last thing standing between him and his final self-betrayal. The director then further diminished the political qualities of the fifth-act embassy by cutting the women's procession of 5.5, which in Shakespeare's script codes Volumnia's pleading with her son in 5.3 as a victory both for herself and for Rome.

If Székely implicitly mirrored the *embourgeoisement* of Hungarian communist society in Coriolanus' relationship with his wife and mother, he altered this pattern in his representation of the Tribunes and their relationship with the People. Géza Balkay's Brutus and Zoltán Papp's Sicinius took little pleasure in wielding their power and were poorly rewarded for overcoming Coriolanus during the play's public encounters. These Tribunes clearly regarded the protagonist as a dangerous opponent, and both actors strived to create sympathy for their characters by showing the debilitating strain of their fear and anger in planning Coriolanus' downfall in 1.1, 2.1 and 2.3. Indeed, sitting alone after they harangued the People into gathering votes against Coriolanus at the end of 2.3, the two let down their guard and showed themselves to be out of breath and scared. Balkay's nervous Brutus sounded as though he were reassuring himself as much as he was Papp's worried Sicinius when he told him, 'This mutiny were better put in hazard / Than stay, past doubt, for greater' (252–253; 'Jobb megkockáztatni a lázadást, / Mert később sokkal szörnyübb törne ki' p. 65). Székely may not have allowed the Tribunes the slightest bit of idealism – or even any dissembled populism – about serving the People, but he did afford them some conscience: in 2.3, Balkay's Brutus felt the gravity of Coriolanus' ordeal, hanging his head and holding the door for Cserhalmi as he exited, and in 4.2 both Tribunes were visibly deeply ashamed by Volumnia's and Virgilia's chastisement. Although Papp was relieved that Coriolanus has turned back his invasion in 5.4, the actor was humbled rather than joyous when he told the messenger who reported the good news, 'First, the gods bless you for your tidings; next / Accept my thankfulness' (58–59; 'Áldjon meg az ég; hálás vagyok neked!' p. 129). When the messenger walked away in disgust, Papp sat on a bench, centre stage, clutching his hands and hunching his shoulders as he quietly spoke to himself 'We'll meet them, / And help the joy' (61–62; 'Menj eléjük, s örülj velük te is' p. 129). Papp then stared meaningfully into the distance of the darkened playing space, appearing to reflect on his complicity in Rome's near-destruction.

Székely prefigured what the Tribunes had become – two sombre political agents whose only motive was survival – in Varga's down-at-heels student-intellectual First Citizen. This young would-be revolutionary was consistently the most rebellious of the Plebeians, throwing water at Cserhalmi, speaking rudely to him and physically hindering another Citizen from casting his vote in 2.3. He subsequently attached himself to the Tribunes, taking over the lines of Shakespeare's Aedile at the start of 3.3 and 4.2, where he displayed an enthusiasm for conspiratorial action that Balkay and Papp did not reciprocate. By 4.6, when word of Coriolanus' invasion arrived, it was clear that the director has singled out the First Citizen to parallel the hero's experience of the cost of political engagement. At the scene's end, after the Third Citizen accusingly told Balkay and Papp that he had always said it was a mistake to banish Coriolanus, Varga's deflated First Citizen, in a line added by Székely, asked the men pathetically, 'Why, did I not say this?' ('Miért, én nem ezt mondtam?' p. 110), or, to follow the Hungarian word order more closely, 'Why, I did not say this?' It was a truly pathetic moment, as the student's thick-lensed glasses magnified his wide-eyed juvenile desperation, like a child questioning his parents about some newly discovered horrifying fact of life. Yet, as in the 5.3 exchange between Coriolanus and Volumnia that echoed this moment, Székely was careful not to let such disillusionment sound like a simplistic accusation against the older generation because Varga twice repeated his question as the statement 'I did not say this' ('én nem ezt mondtam') with quietly compelling horror, and thus transformed the phrase into a self-accusation. In so doing, the actor powerfully conveyed – however briefly – the young man's profound awareness of his own guilt in sustaining a corrupted 'revolutionary' impulse that almost ruined his nation.

Eperjes's Aufidius was the lone character in the production who thoroughly relished the political realm, and the only one who was not diminished by participating in it. The actor spoke with vindictive longing at the end of Act 1 and with self-satisfaction in Act 4 as he imagined outmanoeuvring Coriolanus. At the end of 5.3, when he mechanically told Coriolanus, 'I was moved withal' (195; 'Én is megilletődtem' p. 126) by Volumnia's appeal, a narrow band of spotlight picked out his dark brows framing his darkly sinister eyes. Eperjes glared steadily at Cserhalmi with a menacingly cold confidence that implied he knew that he had finally beaten his foe. In the closing scene, Aufidius derisively taunted Coriolanus with accusations of treachery and wore a smug grin while he explained himself to the Volsces. The brazen cynicism with which the sneering Eperjes spoke 'My lords, when you shall know – as in this rage / Provoked by him you cannot – the great danger / Which this man's life did owe you, you'll rejoice / That he is thus cut off' (136–139; 'Urak, ha majd / Átlájátok habár e zürzavarban, / Amit okozott, még lehetetlen, / Milyen veszélyt jelentett ránk, hogy él, / Még hálálkodni fogtok, hogy végeztünk / Vele' p. 134) made it clear that he was without remorse and would not humble himself before the Volsce authorities. Finally, alone on stage with the still-open-eyed Cserhalmi, whose Coriolanus had been brought back on after his offstage assassination and dumped sprawling in the shallow depression that served as a grave, it was not even worth this Aufidius' time to stand on his enemy's corpse in victory. With nobody to watch him, and nothing further to gain from Coriolanus, Eperjes disdainfully dropped the dead man's cloak to the floor and nudged it with his toe over Cserhalmi's face. There was no elegiac sentiment, no concluding funeral march to offer either man any ceremonial veneer of dignity. All that was left of the once-mighty warrior was this ignobly discarded figure, lying anonymous in the middle of the set's vaguely central European environment. Aufidius may have been the single character not to feel any qualms about employing his political agency but Székely obviously designed this conclusion to emphasize that only those who possess the Volsce's singularly devious malice can prevail in such a compromising environment because they have nothing left to compromise.

Published response to this gloomy presentation demonstrates marked similarities with Western journalistic criticism insofar as the categories that reviewers employed to describe the production had little to do with either state-imposed communism or overt Marxist analysis. Instead, reaction to Székely's *Coriolanus* suggests that critics participated in the larger *embourgoisement* of Hungarian society. To be sure, reviewers were mindful of characters' relationships to their fictional Roman social contexts, and many noted that in Brecht's *Coriolanus* subjectivity is the consequence of social forces. Yet they frequently portrayed Shakespeare's play as the struggle of an individual against an alienating social environment that violates the individual's private 'true' self: the real challenge that the play poses for directors is to represent 'Coriolanus' great human dignity and loneliness and his relationship to society' ('Coriolanus nagyszabású emberi meltósága, magánya és a társadalom kapcsolata', Róna); the hero, 'when he strives to become consul, which is so alien to his character and expertise, clearly executes violence against himself' ('[amikor] pályázik a karakterétől idegen és "szakterületétől" távoli konzulságra … nyilvánvaló, hogy önmagán tesz erőszakot', *Magyar Nemzet* 12 October 1985); he is an 'unbreakable personality' whose 'contempt for the world, however, turns … into self-contempt' when he agrees to solicit votes (Koltai 198).[8] Critics, in turn, highly valued what they regarded as performances of Shakespeare's complex personal, private emotion. They praised Székely 'for exploring the play's human relationships in their fullness' ('mert valamennyi emberi viszonylatnak végére járt', Tarján 1), and for his attention to the fleeting moments that capture 'the double nature of the human soul' ('az emberi lélek kettősségé[t]', Róna). They also admired both Cserhalmi's performance of full and varied emotions and what they perceived to be his traditionally heroic 'grandiose' ('nagyivú', *Népszava* 27 September 1985), figure of 'greatness' ('nagyságát', *Magyar Nemzet* 12 October 1985) who 'desires and strives for perfection' ('a teljességre vágyik, a teljességre tör', Róna).

The impression that such positive response to Székely's critique of public life reveals how Hungarian Shakespeare in the 1980s could operate as an arena marked out for the subtle private questioning of totalitarian government is only strengthened by reviewers' assertions of *Coriolanus'* contemporary relevance. Again, none of the clichés about Shakespeare's trans-historical relevance which these Hungarian critics employed would necessarily be out of place in Western journalistic reviews: Shakespeare's plays are 'brilliant' because 'they address every age, including ours' ('éppen ez a zseniális bennük! – szólnak minden korhoz, így a mi korunkhoz is', *Esti Hírlap* 30 September 1985); his characters 'transcend the boundaries of time' ('de túllepnek az idő ... határain', Róna); and *Coriolanus* is eternally relevant because 'each age found in it what it did not seek, that which disturbed it' ('minden kor megtalálta benne, amit nem keresett, ami zavarta', *Pesti Műsor* 25 September 1985). What sets such expressions of relevance apart, however, is the fact that the Hungarian critics never explicitly linked the play or the production to any identifiable situation or individual, a perhaps necessary rhetorical strategy, but one that only raises more questions. If *'we don't need to look for [contemporary] counterparts* to Coriolanus because *'we see the tragedy of the private-public human behaviour'* ('*egy magánemberi-közéleti magatartás tragédiáját látjuk'*, *Esti Hírlap* 30 September 1985, emphasis in original) then who experiences such tragedy? If Aufidius' statement that 'Our virtues / Lie in the interpretation of the time' explains 'the meaning and the political outlook of this production' ('az előadás mondanivalója, politikus látásmódja', Róna), which addresses the present 'functionally and timelessly' ('[f]unkcionálisan és időtlenül', Róna) then whom is Székely accusing of opportunism? If Cserhalmi's Coriolanus allows us to 'get closer to the reality of our everyday life' because he is like those 'excellent professional people' who 'are put into such leading positions where they become uncertain or even lose their own identity' ('kiváló szakembereket ... olyan vezető pozícióba állítanak ..., ahol elbizonytalanodnak, később esetleg elveszítik önnön arculatukat', *Magyar Nemzet* 12 October 1985), just who are these people in danger of losing their identity?

Those accustomed to reading between the lines would have understood that answers to such questions could not be explicitly articulated under the communist rule of the mid-1980s, and, of course, it is this specific political context which distinguishes Hungarian expressions of Shakespeare's eternal relevance and complex individual psychology from the use of those tropes elsewhere. It is also this specific political context which distinguishes the indictments of corrosive public life in Székely's production, indictments that appear directionless insofar as they emanated in all directions: against current and previous generations, against those who wield power and those disillusioned by trying to acquire it. Four years after Székely's *Coriolanus*, just three months prior to Imre Nagy's reburial, Cserhalmi captured the spirit of the political changes then unfolding by participating in a massive public demonstration in Budapest's Szabadság (Freedom) Square; reading, on the steps of the national television service building, the '12 Points' or demands calling for the end of communism, he was one of many speakers calling for freedom of expression in Hungary (Kiscsatári). This act echoed the explicit resistance of those Hungarian revolutionaries who publicly read out their twelve demands to their Hapsburg rulers on 15 March 1848, the same day that the National Theatre staged Katona József's patriotic drama, *Bánk Bán*. In 1985, however, Cserhalmi's Coriolanus, humiliated and destroyed by political engagement, captured the mid-1980s spirit of political inertia. Because the time had not yet come for explicit demands, *Coriolanus* at the Katona József Theatre asked Hungarians, busily engaged in their private pursuits, where one stands, how one acts in relation to such a corrupted political environment. The answer was given a few years later beyond the theatre's walls, but in 1985 Székely could only pose this urgent question subtly and eloquently, veiling it in the language of a very traditional, even bourgeois, approach to Shakespeare's most explicitly political tragedy.

CHAPTER VIII

Shakespeare meets the American public – The 1988–89 NYSF *Coriolanus*

When the New York Shakespeare Festival (NYSF) launched *Coriolanus* in November 1988 at the 275-seat Anspacher Theater, the director Steven Berkoff had a perfect opportunity to devise a production of political specificity. The United States public had spent the last two years following media coverage of its own military celebrity, Lieutenant-Colonel Oliver North, as a consequence of his involvement in the Iran-Contra scandal. This affair, in which money raised from weapons sold to Iran helped fund anti-communist Nicaraguan rebels, cast doubt on members of the executive branch of the US government, including Vice President George H.W. Bush, who won the Presidential election shortly before *Coriolanus* opened.[1] Berkoff, however, appeared to be uninterested in overt topicality. Rather, the NYSF *Coriolanus* was a theatrically radical presentation with a heavily cut script, markedly stylized performance techniques and a chorus or ensemble that played many of the minor roles, all precisely choreographed and synchronized to Larry Spivak's live musical score. The production, furthermore, reflected Berkoff's avowed collectivist political beliefs to the extent that the director reoriented the relationship of Christopher Walken's Coriolanus to this ensemble, and encouraged his actors to execute a body-centred (as opposed to script-centred) performance style that mixed European theatre traditions. Despite such eclectic Continental influences, the 1988–89 *Coriolanus* was framed as a phenomenon of contemporary American culture by both reviewers and the NYSF founding artistic director Joseph Papp. The production also worked against the director's purported collectivist ideals, partly because the ensemble actually elevated Coriolanus' status and partly because of Walken's powerful, charismatic performance. Furthermore, this overtly experimental production, which transferred so much responsibility to the director in his assault on both conventional performance and Shakespeare's textual authority, ran afoul of the critics' desire for characterizations based on the portrayals of psychologically profound and consistent individual personalities as they understood Shakespeare to have intended them.

Coriolanus was part of the NYSF's Shakespeare Marathon, a plan to produce all of Shakespeare's plays over six years (1988–93), which Papp depicted as an exercise in fostering and continuing a popular American Shakespeare performance tradition. From its beginnings, the NYSF had been devoted to making Shakespeare accessible to American audiences, particularly through free performances in Central Park and elsewhere.[2] Papp's assertion that the Marathon would deliver an authentic Shakespeare was an extension of his long-running battle against an American anxiety about performing elite Shakespeare, a personal battle that recuperated an old American tradition of embracing England's most revered playwright while rejecting the English.[3] When he described his intention to turn the Marathon's stage works into films and books, Papp claimed he 'vehemently objected' to the British Broadcasting Corporation's televised Shakespeare series, because its productions 'started in the studio', whereas those of the NYSF were more authentic because they would 'all start on the stage', just as, he noted, Shakespeare's works had (qtd in Gerard). The Festival's advertising for the Marathon reflects this desire to portray the cycle of performances as a deliberate Americanization and popularization of an English author of the classics that nevertheless retained its Shakespearean authenticity. The full-page advertisement for the Marathon that the NYSF placed in the *New York Times* on 8 November 1987 approximates the First Folio's page layout. The advertisement, which asks readers to subscribe to charter memberships in the scheme, is bordered in a broken black line, employs vaguely early modern fonts, and includes blocks of cherub and floral engraving. The title at the top in capital letters, however, announces Papp's Americanizing agenda: 'FOR THE FIRST TIME IN AMERICA, SEE *ALL* OF SHAKESPEARE!'; immediately below that it read, '*All* of William Shakespeare's 36 plays performed by *most* of America's finest actors!' (emphases original). The notice also makes exclamatory appeals to populist sentiment, offering members an '"I've seen it all!" tee shirt', and a 'diploma' at the end of the Marathon that 'may even earn you college credits!' The advertisement informs prospective patrons that member status 'is transferable, like season tickets to the [New York] Giants' football team, another New York institution of popular American culture (emphasis original).[4]

Casting Walken in the lead and Irene Worth as Volumnia was a fulfilment of the promises implicit in the patriotic and popularizing rhetoric with which the Festival 'sold' the Marathon's Shakespearean authenticity. Worth was undoubtedly one of America's most revered classical actresses, who had long worked on both sides of the Atlantic. In addition to creating an unforgettable Goneril in Peter Brook's stage and film versions of *King Lear*, she had turned in the two powerful performances of Volumnia described earlier in the book, and would have been recognized in the United States by those who had watched her in the BBC *Coriolanus* on America's Public Broadcasting Service. However, Walken was the real star of the NYSF production, and hiring him was part of Papp's long tradition of popularizing Shakespeare by placing American screen stars in leading Shakespearean roles. Walken was not necessarily the most famous actor to have worked at the NYSF but by 1988 he had made more than twenty films. With his penetrating gaze, he exuded a dangerous off-kilter charisma on screen, whether he was delivering a cameo as the comically suicidal Duane in Woody Allen's *Annie Hall* (1977) or his Academy-award-winning performance as Nick, a psychologically damaged and tragically suicidal Vietnam war veteran in *The Deer Hunter* (1978). Well known to twenty-first-century audiences for his bizarrely parodic on-screen personae who all share his pronounced Queens, NY, accent and famously halting speech patterns, Walken must have been one of the most strikingly unusual Coriolanuses in the play's stage career. Still, he was arguably well suited to Berkoff's eccentric and physically demanding production; besides his penchant for playing neurotics, he is a talented dancer, with decades of Broadway and off-Broadway experience, including a performance opposite Worth in Tennessee Williams's *The Sweet Bird of Youth* in 1975.

By contrast, Papp's decision to hire the avant-garde British director-playwright-actor Berkoff for the 1988–89 *Coriolanus* seems odd, to say the least. As Craig Rosen argues, 'Berkovian' performance 'alludes to an actor-centred, physical theatre that rejects contemporary realism' and that draws upon numerous experimental European theatre traditions, especially the ideas of Antonin Artaud and those Berkoff acquired during his training in the 1960s at the École Jacques Lecoq in Paris (iii).[5] Although this approach to production relies on Berkoff's strong directorial influence, it replaces the verbal text with the actor as the centre of performance, while ostensibly diminishing the importance of star actors by foregrounding ensemble or 'choral' performers. The resulting presentational style purportedly combines Brecht-ian distancing techniques with an Artaudian belief in the affective potential of theatre to draw the audience into a mysti-cal experience.[6] Yet such observations only begin to describe the Steven Berkoff phenomenon. Berkoff appears to thrive on productive confrontation. If his *Coriolanus* did not make extended reference to Ronald Reagan's conservative, anti-communist policies, he has not avoided explicit political statements in his own plays, such as the expletive-laden *Sink the Belgrano!* (1986), an aggressive verse-drama assault on Britain's prosecution of the 1982 Falklands War, in which he excoriates Reagan's British conservative fellow-traveller, Margaret Thatcher. Furthermore, a number of those who have worked with him have recalled what Robert Cross labels Berkoff's 'dicta-torial' rehearsal techniques, though Cross understatedly notes that these perspectives have 'been at odds' with Berkoff's own (99, 100), and, as I will demonstrate below, the director openly celebrates the art of the supposedly democratic ensemble. Berkoff has also cultivated an anti-establishment, occasionally proletarian, attitude, reflected in plays like *Sink the Belgrano!* and in his criticisms of mainstream theatre. However, Cross, once again, questions Berkoff's true aims, suggesting that 'he has projected an image of himself as an East End "hard man" or "villain" in order to create a highly saleable aura of danger around his celebrity' (47–48). Cross further argues that, in spite of his avowed anti-Thatcherism, he 'has displayed crypto-Thatcherite tendencies as an entrepreneurial producer of "Berkoff", his commodified "self"' (19).

Berkoff's characteristic traits were on full display before, during and after the NYSF *Coriolanus*, and the public record of these traits is scattered with traces of acrimony that was at once personal, institutional and national. Papp recalls that Berkoff clashed with various members of the production team, including Walken, who seemed ready at one point to resign (Cross 99). Yet it appears that Berkoff also ran afoul of Papp's individual sense of his mission as artistic director. Before his death in 1991, very little happened at the Festival that did not bear Papp's personal stamp, and, whether motivated primarily by Berkoff's self-assertions or journalistic criticisms of the Marathon, Papp worked to identify the outcome of the 1988–89 *Coriolanus* as the result of his own efforts. He claimed credit for hiring Berkoff, who, he claimed, originally 'had absolutely no outward passion for the play', and for personally saving *Coriolanus* from disaster when conflicts arose during rehearsal. While such a statement raises the question of why Papp would ever engage such a person to direct the play (Papp's answer was that, at first, he alone understood Berkoff's potential for directing it), Berkoff expressed few doubts about what he was doing. In fact, the director's public statements during the run of *Coriolanus* complicated the populist rhetoric of the company's advertising by provocatively touting the production as an almost personal assault on a text- and star-centred form of theatre, the adherents of which signal their respect for Shakespeare through psychologically 'realistic' performances. With characteristic bluntness, he claimed to be doing 'the audience a favor' by reducing Shakespeare's 'extraneous verbiage', he disdained the way that 'naturalism' 'filter[s] actors through the set' and he asserted that his use of the ensemble worked against the 'English [theatrical] colonial system' of 'having a star actor surrounded by little plebes' (qtd in Rothstein). Berkoff may have shared both Papp's desire to democratize Shakespeare and his aggressive approach to public relations, but his 'avant-garde' attack on the playwright hardly seems designed to excite positively exclamatory response from, say, Giants fans. After the production closed, he continued to influence the meaning of the NYSF staging in essays, he wrote an entire book about his 1991 German *Coriolanus* and he starred in the production that he directed in Leeds in 1995. Long after the New York production, Berkoff depicted the NYSF's 'textbound' actors as his own personal problem: 'I inherited the whole lousy, lazy, stultified system of bad acting and bad physical discipline and creativity' (*Free Association* 368).[7] He

[176]

subsequently noted that *he* led his cast out of the mire of incompetence and lassitude by getting them to forget the text and embrace his movement-based performance, inspired by Spivak's music (qtd in Rosen 236). Berkoff's self-portrayal as a tough-minded crusader righting the wrongs of the kind of theatre that had, incidentally, drawn so many spectators to the NYSF over the years was hardly unusual for him, and his rebarbative comments are also a variation on the anti-American European villains he portrayed in Hollywood films of the 1980s, including a turn as Adolf Hitler in the US television mini-series *War and Remembrance* (1988).[8] It might be too simplistic to draw a direct connection between Berkoff's screen villainy and his use of European theatre techniques to assail Anglo-American performance traditions, but, as *Coriolanus* got under way, Berkoff himself crassly turned such cinematic villainy into the theatrical virtue of his cherished iconoclasm: 'I empathized with Hitler's inability to deal with criticism. Those enemy countries, France, England, America, became to me The Sunday Times, The Guardian, the Observer' (qtd in Kroll).

The director certainly meant what he said about the staging and script. Loren Sherman's set was far from illusionistic: the only scenery in the playing space was a stepladder from which Coriolanus asked for the Plebeians' votes in 2.3 and a set of twelve black lacquered chairs that were usually located on the raised platform, upstage of the lower forestage or deck. Both forestage and the platform were black, interspersed with large rectangular blocks of white. The modern-dress costumes (designed by Martin Pakledinaz), almost entirely in black, were equally minimalist, and most of them did little more than distinguish Plebeians from Patricians: the Roman women had simple monochromatic full-length dresses and occasionally put on plain hats; the male nobles wore dark modern business suits; ensemble members wore simple black trousers and collared shirts, adding torn workmen's coats and soft cloth caps, in the style of the 1930s, when playing the Citizens.[9] With his short hair brushed up and back, Walken looked like a Hollywood version of a chic contemporary gangster in his full-length black leather coat over a black V-neck shirt and trousers. Keith David's black Aufidius wore a slightly more embellished African-American gangster-ish outfit, wearing a black jumpsuit with epaulettes, a Sam Browne belt, a brimless black leather cap and long silver-studded black leather wrist bands. Berkoff, moreover, reduced the importance of the verbal text by removing over a thousand lines of dialogue, thereby streamlining and speeding the action significantly. Some excisions resulted in narrative simplification by purging scenes and characters that parallel or reflect on the dramatization of Coriolanus' relationship with Rome and the Volsces. These cuts include the removal of Young Martius, the encounter between Adrian and Nicanor (4.3) and much of the Volsce Servingmen's conversation at the end of 4.5. Other deletions seem designed to remove difficult language and thus make the play more comprehensible to the modern American audience, a strategy consistent with the director's thorough emendation of archaic words and phrases in the text.[10] However, Berkoff also cut large and easily comprehensible blocks of dialogue; more than half his deletions were of passages of ten to twenty-five lines, suggesting his wholesale approach to excising the text to simplify the action. Together, the production's minimalist set and heavily cut text may reveal 'Berkoff's commitment to the actor as the most dynamic scenic element' (Sherman 234), but his treatment of those actors also reveals his avowedly democratic conception of the 'fringe' roles as a 'corps', and his desire to elevate this group's status (qtd in Rothstein). The programme divides the performers into a 'Cast' of major roles and an 'Ensemble' of minor ones, and Berkoff flattened out the differences between these two groups by cutting far more heavily from the dialogue of the former.[11] Brutus and Sicinius lost much of their sinister plotting speech from 2.3 and 3.1, and Berkoff greatly reduced Menenius' role, cutting the part by more than two hundred lines. Coriolanus' speech, in particular, became less singular, as he lost long passages of angry eloquence (in the first-act battle scenes and in his confrontation with the People in 3.1), half of his only soliloquy (4.4) and much of his belligerent conversation with the Volsce Servingmen (4.5). The Plebeians, meanwhile, lost only forty-two lines, mostly from 2.3, in which they joke about their own diversity.

While the absence of either a sound or video recording of the production makes it difficult to determine how actors delivered particular lines or precisely what was happening on stage at numerous points in the production, the prompt-book does indicate many of the effects that Berkoff attempted to achieve. For instance, it is clear that he underscored the chorus's collective identities by carefully synchronizing the actors' movements and behaviour. It is also clear that the chorus's unified behaviour was directed at specific individuals. In 1.1 the Plebeians were massed upstage right when Paul Hecht's Menenius entered and they collectively took one step towards him as he said 'Speak, I pray you' (57); as Hecht began Menenius' 'Tale of the Belly', they turned away from him in a tight group, intoning 'Aaahhh' in unified exasperation. The ensemble then shared the First Citizen's lines when interrupting the parable: each of seven actors spoke in turn, 'Your Belly's answer – What?'; 'The kingly crownèd head'; 'the vigilant eye'; 'The counselor heart'; 'the arm our soldier'; 'Our steed the leg'; 'the tongue our trumpeter' (115–118). As they did elsewhere, the chorus thus seemed to speak from a single mind, each aware of the overall list of hackneyed metaphors, and each contributing his own part to this ritualized litany.[12] Walken's Martius scattered the Citizens when he entered but they quickly reassembled on the platform, clutching their heads in unison and collectively speaking a horrified 'Ahhhh!' when the Messenger announced that the Volsces had armed themselves for war. Here the chorus's synchronized speech and movement intensified not just their own emotions but also the significance of individual characters. Their collective 'Ahhs!' amplified the force of Menenius' parable and exaggerated the contrast of Martius' response to the Messenger's news, 'I am glad on't' (226). As if to drive the point home, Berkoff repeated these effects in the following scene while building up David's Aufidius. There, the ensemble rushed on stage as the Volsce Senators and formed a semicircle of chairs around the centre of the lower deck, at which point they collectively sat on one drum-beat, and crossed their legs right over left on a second drum-beat. After David finished reciting the letter about Rome's political situation, the chorus collectively mimed lowering their eyeglasses, as if to question him. The ensemble's built-up group identity then underscored Aufidius' elevated, singular position amongst the Volsces when they stood and exclaimed in unison, 'The gods assist you!' (36).

Not surprisingly, the chorus directed its energy most often at Coriolanus. The ensemble's collective speech and movement as the Roman Senators in 2.2 tracked individual moments in Coriolanus' awkward success before the Senate: when they saw Walken enter, the Senators performed a 'stylized mumble' and sat in unison on their chairs arranged in a circle; they leaned back in their seats with a collective 'gasp' when André Braugher's Brutus suggested that Coriolanus could have been kinder to the People (60); and performed a 'scandalized buzz' when Walken's Coriolanus exited to avoid hearing his deeds pronounced. Yet, in an echo of 1.2, Berkoff used the ensemble's built-up group identity to elevate Coriolanus amongst the Romans; when Walken was called back on stage, they stood together to applaud him. The ensemble performed a similar function as the Citizens in 2.3. When they stood from their upstage chairs and crossed downstage as a group to inspect Walken's scars, Spivak began playing a 'Happy Cit[itzen]s piano' tune, which continued throughout most of the scar ceremony, and which added to the Citizens' simplified collective identity. Although Walken exchanged dialogue with individual Citizens, the rest of the ensemble responded to these exchanges as a group, suggesting the persistence of their herd mentality: when Walken said, 'Ay, but not mine own desire' (71), the Citizens all said, 'Whuh?'; they 'agree[d] and applaud[ed]' the First Citizen's 'You have not indeed loved the common people' (96–97); and, as a group, they 'groan[ed] in disappointment' when Walken's Coriolanus refused to show them his scars. Berkoff immediately subordinated the ensemble to Coriolanus even further by having them 'Freeze [and] look away' as Spivak stopped playing, thus placing them in a kind of suspended animation while Walken complained 'Better it is to die, better to starve, / Than crave the hire which first we do deserve' (118–119). Once Walken continued with the ceremony eight lines later, Spivak resumed the Citizens' music, the ensemble broke the freeze and collectively applauded Coriolanus, and finally exited as a group with a second round of applause.

Jon Foley Sherman has a point when he argues that many of the scenes which made the ensemble 'appear as a dramatic entity in relation to the protagonist' (234) actually 'coarsen[ed] the political argument of the play' (240). More precisely, aspects of the chorus's performance give credence to Sherman's assertion that, by 'thrusting one [group performed by the chorus, the soldiers] into synchronized and efficient killing and another [group performed by the chorus, the People] into synchronized and inefficient resistance, ... unquestioned obedience results in glory and thoughtful deliberation has been banished from the

[180]

citizens' (244). If the ensemble's collective behaviour in Berkoff's 2.3 demonstrated their 'inefficient resistance' to Coriolanus, then parts of the first-act battle scenes reveal the spirit of their disciplined military synchronization. At first, this spirit was cowardice: the ensemble refused to follow Martius into the gates at Corioli, fleeing downstage and freezing with arms raised in a tableau of panic. However, when Thomas Kopache's Titus entered to ask about Martius, the ensemble crossed back to centre stage, walked around in a full circle, placed their hands on their imaginary swords, and collectively snapped their heads sideways to face Titus. As one soldier pointed out Coriolanus within Corioles' walls, the ensemble turned their heads collectively and charged off stage energetically shouting 'Martiuuuuuuuuus!' in conjunction with Spivak's pounding timpani to conclude the scene. Berkoff has written admiringly of the ensemble actors' ability to generate such collective energy (*Free Association* 7), and his chorus of Roman soldiers certainly conveyed the 'glory' of 'unquestioned obedience' viscerally at different points in the battle scenes, collectively shouting 'Maaaaaartius!' to Spivak's drumming just before they ran off to battle a second time (1.6) and shouting his name again twice in 1.9, first to Spivak's drum-roll (40) and next accompanied by synthesized tuba and chimes (67).

Berkoff crafted other equally affective moments for the ensemble's performance of both the Roman and Volscian Citizens' rejection of Coriolanus when their resistance to him *was* efficient, though not entirely rational. Like the soldiers' rousing cheers, these quasi-Artaudian moments, which were evidently designed to work directly on the audience's senses in the intimate Anspacher Theater, glossed over the Roman People's individuality by simplifying their behaviour. It is unclear just what happened in the 'barroom brawl' that the prompt-book indicate broke out when the Tribunes tried to arrest Coriolanus in 3.1, though the violence was perhaps stylized since the additional directions call for the actors to 'spin' off stage during the fight. However, the People made clear their violent collective impulse by repeatedly shouting from within the vomitoria 'kill him', and were accompanied by a building drum-beat. Berkoff increased this sense of the People's unified will in 3.3, which began with the Citizens seated upstage in partial darkness, leaning left and right as a synthesizer 'buzz' built in volume for

Walken's entry, when the lights came up fully on him at centre stage. The ensemble leaned forward as a group to shout with one voice, 'To th'rock, to th'rock with him!' (74) and began 'raggedly chanting', 'It shall be so, it shall be so!' (106) when they first endorsed the Tribunes' indictment of Coriolanus. This ragged chant became a 'call and response', the second time they echoed the Tribunes, with one 'It shall be so' (119) answering another three times. The ensemble completed the effect with rhythmic bodily movement, stomping in unison to the chant. This percussive stomping not only accentuated the chant's rhythm, and thus turned the utterance towards a ritualized manifestation of frightening group violence, the rhythmic sound and movement also presented an aurally and visually exciting spectacle for the audience. After Walken spoke Coriolanus' parting diatribe to the ensemble and exited, the People cheered and froze with their hands in the air, concluding the scene with a final outburst of collective emotion.

Although the violence of the production's last scene (5.6) was channelled into an affective expression of the chorus' unified ethos, the confrontation leading up to Coriolanus' assassination began and ended with a focus on individual combatants. Walken entered with Kopache's Titus, who knelt to present the peace treaty to David. After Walken and David had circled one another while trading personal insults, the Volsce People's collective thirst for blood was unleashed on Coriolanus. The ensemble actors all stood from their chairs at the same time and moved downstage in a group, encircling Walken while chanting 'Kill, kill, kill, kill, kill' (131) accompanied by Spivak's 'bass synthesizer' and timbale drum-beat. David's Aufidius, who had retreated to the platform, crossed downstage to stab Walken with a mimed blade. Walken then turned to face the audience downstage, crying out as he fell to the floor, and the ensemble returned to the upstage platform, leaving the final act of violence to take place between the two men. David stepped forward, and, straddling Walken, pushed down on the imaginary blade three times before removing it and dropping it on the ground. The ensemble had thus once again acted collectively in relation to Coriolanus the individual, here explicitly elevating his *personal* enemy. Berkoff then pushed the individual nature of the conflict even further. Kopache knelt by Walken and spoke the Volsce Lord's lines instructing the others to remove the corpse. As several of the ensemble carried out Coriolanus, Kopache put the discarded peace treaty back in his case and snapped it shut, at which point the lights faded to black. Berkoff thus left the impression that the People's unified violence is merely something to be employed in the cause of political games played by individual Patricians.

Yet the ensemble's unified behaviour and identity should not be regarded only in terms of coarsening the play's politics, because the chorus was merely one (crucial) aspect, of the production's thoroughly self-conscious theatricality. In other words, although the frequent simplification of the Plebeians may have worked against Berkoff's purported elevation of the minor roles, the larger thrust of his scenography was a purposeful attack on those established performance traditions, which he 'loosely call[ed] naturalism' (qtd in Rothstein) and which are so frequently deployed in Shakespearean theatre. The ensemble's collective identity defied the realistic convention of associating a single actor with a single character, but Berkoff also flaunted the chorus' amorphous identity: not only did ensemble actors share single characters' lines, but the group openly switched from scene to scene among the roles of Lords, Senators and Citizens, both Roman and Volscian. The most remarkable transformations occurred in the final two scenes. At the conclusion of 5.5, the ensemble switched from enacting the rejoicing Roman Plebeians who welcomed Volumnia home to the Volsce Conspirators of 5.6 simply by crossing the platform and sitting as a group in the upstage chairs, under which they stowed their Citizens' caps. The ensemble further effaced individual characterization in the scene in several ways. One ensemble actor was given the First Lord's speech beginning 'And grieve to hear't' (63), and the rest of the group indicated they were then playing the Volsce Lords by answering in unison, 'We have' to Aufidius's question 'have you with heed perused / What I have written to you?' (62–63). They completed their transformation by becoming the general Volsce crowd when, as noted above, they surrounded Coriolanus and chanted 'Kill'.

As these descriptions of the ensemble's carefully choreographed movement suggest, the signature feature of *Coriolanus'* patently artificial theatricality was the explicit and pervasive physicalization of meaning. In Berkoff's hands, this meant the ostentatious transference of characterization and attitudes from the verbal text to the actors' movements and gestures. Coriolanus' encounter with his wife and mother when he returns from war in 2.1 is one of the only places in the prompt-book that yields evidence about Coriolanus' relationship with his family, precisely because the encounter itself is devoid of ostentatiously artificial bodily comportment; Walken knelt to Worth in a gesture of filial piety and Ashley Crow's Virgilia reached out both her hands to her husband in a gesture of love. These moments single out the significance of Coriolanus' familial bond by equating that bond with conventionally realistic performance. By contrast, the apparently straightforwardly touching family reunion was surrounded by overtly theatrical gestures. Berkoff crystallized emotions in exaggerated gestures and facial expressions by having Hecht perform a 'Freeze of joy' upon first seeing Volumnia, Virgilia and Valeria, and by having Worth's Volumnia perform a 'stylized strut' on the words 'then men die' (167) while bragging of her son's military prowess. The Tribunes received the same treatment, beginning the scene with Larry Bryggman's Sicinius and Braugher's Brutus meeting centre stage and then freezing 'in a tableau of distaste' when they saw Hecht enter from upstage. Although the Tribunes' cynical speech was cut from the script, Berkoff concluded the scene by underscoring their deviousness by replicating the gist of their scheming dialogue in their highly patterned blocking. As Bryggman and Braugher conspired to check Coriolanus' rise to power at the end of 2.1, the convolutions of their scheming speech were mirrored in their lock-step march, which described a couple of maze-like rectilinear counter-clockwise circuits across and around the stage. In case anyone missed the point, Spivak completed the effect by playing a 'Sinister Synth' while the two walked about the stage.

While such exaggerated freezing, strutting and blocking flaunted Berkoff's directorial displacement of Shakespeare's text by simplifying character and motive, he used similar techniques to distil the powerful emotional shift from the confrontation between Menenius and Sicinius (5.4) to the exaltation at Volumnia's success (5.5) in a richly dramatic tableau of non-illusionistic gesture. Berkoff cut the last ten lines of 5.4, in which Menenius praises Volumnia, and he cut all dialogue from 5.5, including the First Senator's cry at the sight of Volumnia, 'Behold our patroness, the life of Rome!' (1). On Menenius' 'This is good news' (5.4.53), the ensemble cried, 'News, news, news!' and the deep sound of a timpani beat began, signalling the solemnity of the women's return. As the ladies began crossing in a single-file line from upstage left to upstage right (Crow first, followed by Sharon Washington's Valeria and then Worth), Spivak cut the drum and switched to a fanfare and gong music, adding a celebratory tone to the stately procession. The chorus, meanwhile, turned upstage to focus all eyes on the women; when they entered, half the ensemble knelt in supplication, all of them took in a synchronized breath of anticipation while waving in slow motion, and then froze in these postures, giving the scene a lyrical and reverent, even worshipful feeling. By thus displacing the verbalized joy and submission on to the actors' bodies, while focusing the poetically complex speeches of triumphant veneration into an elegantly drawn-out image of non-illusionistic bodily comportment, Berkoff once again singled out Coriolanus' family in what seems to have been one of the production's rare non-violent, non-confrontational blocks of action.

However, much of *Coriolanus*' self-consciously theatrical action *was* confrontational and violent, and such violence was frequently conveyed through the sustained use of mime, which transferred the onus of signification from 'realistic' props to the actors' gestures. In fact, there were no actual weapons in the production, so that, while the soldiers' co-ordinated shouting and Spivak's pounding drums may have added excitement to the battles, they were also highly artificial. For instance, Martius' extra-textual 'battle solo', which occurred at the end of 1.5, apparently involved Walken miming his fight against a series of imaginary opponents within Corioles' walls, and Spivak made this fight more artificially theatrical by playing 'weird music' throughout. The individual fight between Martius and Aufidius was also mimed; it began with Walken delivering a 'baseball swing' at Aufidius, after which they 'clash[ed]' and 'br[oke] apart' four times. Berkoff increased the artificiality of this fight by having Spivak crash a cymbal each time the men clashed; each time they broke apart, a bass drum sounded. However, the most anti-illusionistic scene of the first act was a second group battle that Berkoff had devised immediately to precede Martius' individual fight with Aufidius. Rather than employing what might be considered realistic conventions of combat (the

[185]

appearance of the swift, spontaneous and jarring movement of two opposing forces) and death (prone, motionless bodies), Berkoff combined mime and artificial blocking to highlight the action's theatricality. The battle involved seven members of the chorus who performed recognizably martial gestures, including an 'overhand thrust', a 'stab ... in [the] belly', 'slashes across' throats etc. Berkoff rendered these gestures less realistic, however, by requiring the actors to perform them silently and in slow motion, and disrupted the illusion of their deaths by having the actors simply walk off stage once killed. The director increased the scene's artifice by carefully ordering the deaths of the actors in which they spelt each other off without making any attempt to distinguish Romans from Volsces: once one performer killed his opponent, another stepped forward to kill the killer, and the pattern was repeated until the stage was empty.

While this analysis of the production's scenography indicates the extent of Berkoff's challenge to psychologically 'naturalistic' and text-centred Shakespeare, what it cannot capture is the degree to which the NYSF *Coriolanus* was marked by the particular nature of its lead actor's celebrity and magnetism. Indeed, the production's reception reveals the enduring appetite for the star system, especially when it is sustained by an actor of Walken's power. Critics admired his 'command and charisma' (*The New Republic* 2 January 1989), his ability to use 'his gift for gestural burlesque to lampoon male narcissism' (Kramer 140), and the surprises that his bravura performance held in store: 'Walken shrugs off his big moments, slouches past his epic encounters – and a minute later their full power hits you; his diffidence, like Coriolanus's, is a veil for his ferocity' (*The Village Voice* 29 November 1988). Berkoff's own recollection of this performance suggests that, despite the elevation of the ensemble, Walken's stage presence and personal identity were critical features of this *Coriolanus*:

> The audience likes him ... he inputs 'street shtick' everywhere ... little eeehs! and aaahs! A hybrid Brando/Pacino/Walken ... the New York street-wise guy and anti-hero. The audience giggle at Chris and like that Shakespeare should be grabbed by the scruff and dragged down Delancey Street [in Manhattan's Lower East Side], the home of delis and street graft spawning the small-time punk who becomes a parody of himself singing his ultra-limited

[186]

vocabulary and body language and thus lionized and exalted in a thousand movies. (*Overview* 104–105)

The New York native Walken, then, was not simply charismatic, he was satirizing the specifically American 'street-wise' celebrity closely connected to Papp's populist image of the NYSF as a democratizing force for Shakespeare. This vignette of Walken's powerful star turn may have been conspicuously well suited to Berkoff's own image as an anti-establishment director with a sideline as a Hollywood character actor moderately well known in the 1980s for antagonizing Americans on screen, but other critics singled out Walken's performance for similar reasons. Despite Walken's personal charisma, those reviewers who disliked his performance portrayed it as a specifically *American* failure to embody Shakespearean greatness. Walken was accused of failing to convey 'Shakespeare's sense of Coriolanus as a loner, as a spiritual outcast' because he 'is merely a spoilt gangland brat who don't get no respect' (*New York Post* 23 November 1988); 'too often he lapse[d] into his [fictional American rock star] Kid Champion stance and odd swagger accompanied by sidelong grins' (*New York Daily News* 2 December 1988), and his speech patterns were 'not that of a noble Roman' but 'smart-ass, sometimes perilously akin to those you hear elsewhere in the Public Theater' (*New York Daily News* 23 November 1988).

Such comments reveal how New York reviewers attempted to shape *Coriolanus* into an American phenomenon, in a way *somewhat* similar to what Papp hoped to do with the Marathon project as a whole. Besides interpreting the production within a framework of specifically US popular and political cultures (comparisons to President-elect George H.W. Bush, Marlon Brando and the American action film franchise *Rambo* abounded), critics depicted this *Coriolanus* as a clashing of nationally distinct theatrical traditions and expectations. Mimi Kramer summarized this attitude by noting that Berkoff's directorial style posed a challenge not only to traditional American Shakespeare's indebtedness to 'the realism of Belasco and Stanislavsky' but also to the NYSF's vulgar popularization of Shakespeare, which is in part due to the fact that 'to Papp "concept" means something that promises a box office draw' (139, 140). Critics were generally impressed with the directorial discipline that Berkoff imposed on his actors, but, sounding like British reviewers responding to the 1965 Berliner Ensemble production, they judged his strict control over his concept to be a foreign challenge to Shakespeare's cherished intentions, and emphatically linked the director's otherness to his inability to match Shakespeare's supposed political complexity. This otherness was not, however, explicitly counterpointed to American Shakespeare, nor was it simply a matter of Berkoff's British-ness or European-ness; reviewers also defended Shakespeare from the supposed limitations of Berkoff's director's theatre by attributing those limitations to his rebellious political impulse and class. Thus, just as Brecht 'had his way' with Shakespeare's play, so Berkoff 'cut it down to his own size' (*New York Post* 23 November 1988). Berkoff was an 'anti-establishment movie star' whose identity as 'a street kid from the wrong side of London' made him 'likely to give us a *Coriolanus* ... so corrosive as to blow-torch us right out of our seats' (*New York Native* 5 December 1988). According to John Simon, 'It t[ook] remarkable perversity to entrust ... *Coriolanus* to Steven Berkoff, an English actor-author-director specializing in low-life stories and characters' (194). Worth, by contrast, was uniformly hailed as an authentically Shakespearean actor, whose performance, moreover, revealed the extent of Berkoff's un-Shakespearean production: her 'great nobility' seemed 'out of step with the tongue-in-cheek tone of the production' (*New York Daily News* 23 November 1988); her 'soaring Shakespearean style ... jolts the casual contemporariness of this "mod" production' (*The Forward* 6 January 1989); 'Worth is Shakespeare rather than Berkoff/Shakespeare, and the director was perhaps ill-advised to let us see so clearly the difference' (*New York Post* 23 November 1988).

Reaction to Keith David's Aufidius sheds further light on the conflicting forces at play in the NYSF *Coriolanus*. Critics admired David for his 'well-spoken, imperious, charismatic, and intelligent' portrayal (*New York Native* 5 December 1988), for his 'intensely human Aufidius' (*Chelsea Clinton News* 15 December 1988) 'whose nobility dwarfs that of Walken's mock-epic hero' (Kramer 140), and whose 'virility and spirit' in verse-speaking 'make his character seem the real hero of the play' (*New York Daily News* 23 November 1988). Yet, for all the apparently conventional Shakespearean virtues of his performance, David's jumpsuit, tight leather cap that resembled a kufi and studded bracelets made him a rather visually clichéd African-American political outlaw, and critics treated him as foreign and exotically cruel.[13] He was 'a Third World guerrilla leader' (*New York Post 23 November 1988*), 'a mature and commanding African dictator, his spine arched with military stiffness' (*The New Republic 2 January 1989*) whose 'style is early Idi Amin' (Simon 194). Was his appearance, like Walken's parody, too American – or African-American – and was David therefore rhetorically shunted aside with foreign analogies as Berkoff was? The evidence does not explicitly bear out this conclusion explicitly but critics' response suggests how the production's domestication to American sensibilities coincided with an anxiety about specifically national identity (American or British) disrupting an idealized Shakespeare. Papp may have hoped that 'the artistic impulse, not the accent, is what matters' because 'nobody has a corner on Shakespeare' (qtd in Epstein 93), but this hope ran up against the enduring and widespread rhetoric of the transhistorical Bard, that combination of strong individual or star performances and a 'naturalistic' approach to psychologically consistent and heroic characters. In a production like the 1988–89 *Coriolanus*, where Berkoff's artistic impulses collided and overlapped with both the NYSF's Americanizing populist impulses and the charismatic personalities of the producer, director and star, this rhetoric of the playwright's timelessness and placelessness was used to determine what accent Shakespeare is allowed to speak with and who does or does not have a corner on performing his drama.

CHAPTER IX

Québécois Shakespeare
goes global – Robert Lepage's
Coriolan

In October 1995, less than two years after Robert Lepage's
1992–94 *Cycle Shakespeare* tour ended in Québec City, Canada
narrowly avoided what seemed like national dissolution when
Québec voters, by a margin of only one per cent, turned down a
proposal to negotiate sovereignty from the country. The tour of
the *Cycle* – comprised of *Coriolan*, *Macbeth* and *La Tempête* –
overlapped with a series of highly charged political events of the
early 1990s in Canada, events that harkened back to Québec's
nationalist movement of the 1970s in their divisive effect on
Canadian federalism. In October 1992, shortly after the *Cycle*'s
Paris run, Canadians voted in a bitterly debated referendum,
rejecting the national government's attempt to enshrine in the
Constitution Québec's status as a distinct society within Canada.
The following autumn, at the mid-point between the Montréal
Cycle performances (May to June 1993) and those in Québec City
(January 1994), the Bloc Québécois party, newly formed to
defend Québec's interests, became the official opposition in
Parliament, sitting across the floor from Prime Minister Jean
Chrétien, a man disliked by many Québécois for his centralizing
approach to federalism. In September 1994 Québec's provincial
government promised the referendum on sovereignty that was
defeated the following year.[1] In light of these events, Lepage's
comments nine months before the *Cycle* performances in
Montréal seem, politically, quite moderate. He described the
tour stop in his home province as a response to the double colonization that Québec has historically experienced within
Canada.[2] Explaining that, in an effort to defend French culture,
Québécois theatres have traditionally staged Molière and Racine

more frequently than Shakespeare, Lepage remarked, 'Shakespeare, until now, has been reserved for Anglophone Canada. He has always been presented to us as a deluxe author who can be read but not staged' ('Shakespeare, jusqu'à present, était réservé au Canada anglophone. Il nous était toujours présenté comme un auteur de luxe que l'on pouvait lire mais pas monter', qtd in Prouvost).[3] As he would later relate, his solution to this situation, in which loyalty to one former colonial power compounds the inequalities caused by obedience to another, was to re-deploy Shakespeare as a product of transnational culture. He believed that, by including performances at Montréal's Festival de Théâtre des Amériques (FTA) in the *Cycle* tour, he was allowing 'the French-speaking public [to] discover a repertoire that it virtually never gets to see', and was thus bringing global culture to Québec *through* Shakespeare (*Robert Lepage* 117). At the same time, by touring the *Cycle* to numerous countries, he implicitly validated an outward-looking image of Québec while helping to ensure the viability of international Shakespeare theatre.

Given these circumstances, *Coriolan* offers an especially significant illustration of why intercultural Shakespeare has become a crucial site for investigating the relationship among global performance, local identities and the playwright's traditional literary authority.[4] The plays in the French-language *Cycle* were based on 'tradaptations' by the Québec poet Michel Garneau, who ostensibly rendered each of the three dramas in a different register of Québécois.[5] Although Garneau began tradapting Shakespeare in the 1970s to help establish a distinct national Québécois culture, Lepage's *Cycle* had a markedly global identity; with their international co-producers and touring schedule, the *Cycle* productions complicated efforts to establish for them a specifically Québécois identity.[6] Lepage's *Coriolan*, furthermore, did little to suggest specific associations between Shakespeare's cultural cachet and the political hegemony of Anglophone Canada. That is, while the director's combination of inventive blocking and his placement of a 'letter-box' black cloth frame around the playing space, which, Lepage noted, put '*everything* – including the fragmented body – into parentheses' may have challenged Shakespeare's textual authority with the director's own *scenic* authority, *Coriolan's* scenography, as I argue below, did not appear explicitly to comment on Québec's place within Canada (qtd in Salter,

[191]

'Borderlines' 76, emphasis original). However, printed reaction to *Coriolan* reveals that the production did generate very specific local meanings for those in Québec and Britain. *Coriolan* embodies the competing influences that help define Lepage's Shakespeare production. The complexity of these influences is neatly captured by a question that Margaret Jane Kidnie poses of *Elsinore*, Lepage's *Hamlet* adaptation: '[I]s the idea of "local" [identity] best represented by a set of relations that exceeds both Britain and Canada?' (133). In the case of Lepage's touring Shakespeare productions, I suggest the answer is 'yes': the relations that such touring perpetuates are not simply those existing between Québec and England or English Canada but result from interaction amongst local-national Québécois concerns, the traditional authority of Shakespeare and global theatrical performance. *Coriolan* not only reveals how local identity is shaped by international performance contexts and histories of colonial subservience but it also demonstrates how globalization can spur the reinvention of the local and that such reinvents operate in global theatrical events to sustain Shakespeare's cultural prestige.

Garneau's *Coriolan* was an appropriate script for Lepage's international *Cycle* tour. Unlike the pseudo-historical French in Garneau's 1978 *Macbeth*, a translation aligned to the goals of the Québec nationalist movement of the 1960s and 70s, the register of *Coriolan* makes it easy to be understood in different parts of the globe.[7] In addition to removing virtually all references to the classical world, Garneau simplified Shakespeare's complex figurative language, and employed something close to standard French rather than 'joual', a distinctly Québécois dialect.[8] Lepage's treatment of the script, meanwhile, reflects a general disregard for either Shakespeare's or Garneau's textual authority. As the video of the Montréal production makes clear, by cutting nearly a third of the published translation that resulted in a performance which ran to just over two hours, Lepage simplified the drama considerably; eliminating more than two dozen roles, he foregrounded Coriolan's struggle with Volumnia, Aufidius and the Tribunes.[9] Perhaps Lepage's most significant alteration was his virtual eradication of the Plebeians from the production; *some* of their dialogue was heard but they never appeared on stage. This omission greatly reduced the play's debate over the Citizens' political enfranchisement, a conflict that could easily be interpreted as an analogy for the historical relationships between Québec and Anglophone Canada. Removing the Plebeians from theatregoers' view might be understood as a metaphor for the production itself. Jacques-Henri Gagnon's Menenius still had an exchange with the People at the play's opening, though the first one hundred and twenty lines of Garneau's script were cut, and Menenius delivered the 'Tale of the Belly' (as though from a radio studio) to a few offstage characters who were merely heard and whose voices were far from riotous. Speaking from what was supposed to be a television studio, Jules Philip's Coriolan still asked for the People's votes in 2.3, but the Citizens were, again, represented by unseen offstage voices; when they 'acclaimed' him Consul, their voices were replaced by honking horns, making them even more anonymous. Similarly, when Nomand Bissonnette's Brutus and Éric Bernier's Sicinius questioned the Plebeians after Coriolan's election as Consul, they spoke to the Citizens on the telephone; their lines cut here, the People were not even heard. Nor did the People have any voice in Coriolan's banishment, which was staged as a roundtable radio debate between Coriolan and the Tribunes, with Macha Limonchik's Valeria acting as the producer and only Carol Cassistat's Cominius and Gagnon as moral support for Philip; no Citizens appeared, and their political concerns were expressed entirely by Bernier and Bissonnette's Tribunes, whom Lepage understood to 'hate the people as much as the elite [Patricians] do' (qtd in Salter, 'Borderlines' 73). In other words, just as the *Cycle* productions' local Québécois identity might have been jeopardized by touring extensively to elite international theatre venues, so the Plebeians in the production became disembodied and anonymous, and the danger they represented was contained, made symbolic and turned into a debate amongst elites, with the Patricians on one side, and the Tribunes (privileged political representatives) on the other.

In fact, *Coriolan* does not suggest that Lepage was necessarily interested in devising a specifically 'Québécois' production, as there was little in the scenography that would readily signal 'Québec' to that elite in the 'Western, Northern, and metropolitan' parts of the globe to which he primarily tours (Harvie and Hurley 307). Like the soundscape of sirens, car horns and alarm bells, the costuming and sets were derived from postwar Western culture. The women wore evening frocks, the Tribunes had business suits, and the other men alternated between military dress and formal evening attire (black trousers and tail-coats, white waistcoats and colourful shoulder sashes). Most scenes were staged in the cramped shallow playing space against a black curtained background, while others occurred in contemporary settings, including a bar and the aforementioned broadcast studios, which could be found virtually anywhere in the modern world. The vote-seeking scene exemplifies this aspect of Lepage's scenography. Wearing black tails and trousers, with a spray of medals on the left breast of his jacket, and his left arm in a sling, Philip sat stage right in a wooden chair against a black background, responding to the Plebeians' offstage voices as though he were doing a political chat-show studio-audience question-and-answer spot (without a host, though), the kind of programme common across the Western hemisphere. Lepage transformed the chat-show format, however: Philip appeared inside the 'letter-box' horizontal rectangular slot created by masking the edges of the playing space with black cloth, and the director projected video of Philip's live performance on the upper edge of the cloth frame. By reproducing the real-time projections familiar from rock concerts, sporting events and modern political rallies, he invited spectators to consider the differences between the live performance within the movie-screen-like slot and the artificial, electronically created one above it. Still, the scene did not overtly comment on Québec; like his replacement of the Plebeians with car horns, Lepage devised an ironic treatment of the artificial spectacle of modern political processes in general, the kind that are easily recognizable by any of the Canadian or Northern European audiences who witnessed the *Cycle* tour. Indeed, he emphasized this irony by twice punctuating Philip's speech with another widely recognized sound, a boxing bell, suggesting that the vote-seeking was merely another spectacle of generalized political struggle with Coriolan as a hopeful Consul-pugilist.

Typically, the production's widely familiar, rather anonymous settings contributed to scenes that lacked a grand sense of occasion and that emphasized the play's personal dimensions. Coriolan's return to Rome after battle (2.1) was staged in a bar, created simply by lowering a countertop into the middle of the slot and dropping a red cloth for the background. The scene opened with Gagnon at the counter stage right, and Bissonnette and Bernier drinking stage left; all three faced out to the audience. Their initial debate seemed a one-sided dispute between longtime cocktail lounge rivals: Gagnon's Menenius clearly disliked these Tribunes personally, and he appeared to have already been drinking as he angrily spluttered his way through his long speech about 'convers[ing] more with the buttock of the night than the forehead of the morning' (49–51; 'connu oui pour ... préférer / le beau derrière de la nuit / au noble visage du matin' pp. 69–70). The grey-suited Bissonnette and Bernier acted more soberly, but Anne-Marie Cadieux, in her formal tiny black dress, substantial crystalline necklace and her brown hair swept up into a near-beehive, embellished Gagnon's almost louche barroom behaviour. While Marie Brassard's Virgilia (in a brown strapless evening gown and with a short, frumpy hairstyle) stood far stage right with her shoulders slumped and a dejected look on her face, Cadieux held a glass aloft in one hand and waved the other about with comic nonchalance as she barked, 'O, he is wounded, I thank the gods for't!' (118; 'oh il est blessé et j'en remercie dieu' p. 72). There was no great procession for Coriolan's entry: rather than shouts and flourishes, the small group (Limonchik's Valeria was also on stage) watched his 'return' on the bar's television, placed above the frame, out of spectators' view, and Philip and Cassistat got on stage during a brief blackout. Nor was there any pomp of exiting in state at the scene's conclusion. Instead, Lepage treated the personal aspects of the political ironically by having Cadieux assert her domestic and somewhat sexualized controlling relationship with Philip's Coriolan; her Volumnia kissed Philip's hand voluptuously before he angrily retracted it and told her, 'I had rather be their [the People's] servant in my way / Than sway with them in theirs' (199–200; 'j'aime mieux server à ma façon / que diriger à leur manière' p. 77). At that point Cadieux wagged her finger, then licked it to wipe Philip's face before pushing him off stage, as though she were sending a naughty little boy out to play. Proving that she was in charge of both her infantilized son and the bar itself, she then took her credit card from her purse and waved it imperiously at the bartender, drawing great laughter from the audience.

Cadieux intensified these histrionics in her attack on the Tribunes in 4.2, which took place in a restaurant, suggested by merely placing two dining tables with chairs and a large potted plant on stage. She turned Volumnia into a comic caricature of a domineering matron; painting in broad strokes, Cadieux made her Volumnia as easily legible to a wide audience as the simple restaurant setting itself was. Seated at one table with Brassard, Limonchik, Gagnon and Cassistat, Cadieux began her accusations against the Tribunes while she read her menu, hurling insults with a growl. After Brassard ineffectually slapped at Bissonnette, Cadieux rounded on him and Bernier, shrieking 'Ohhh!' as she scolded, '[O] I would my son / Were in Arabia, and thy tribe before him, / His good sword in his hand' (25–27; 'oh je voudrais que mon fils / soit devant toi l'arme à la main' p. 149). Although Gagnon's nervous Menenius tried to calm her, she continued to lecture them in a loud, scratchy voice, repeatedly thrusting her finger in the air, and getting laughs from the audience with each thrust. After Bernier and Bissonnette escaped her haranguing, the audience laughed appreciatively at Cadieux as she languidly and dismissively waved her finger at the weeping Brassard, and told her calmly, 'Leave this faint puling and lament' (55; 'plus de pleurs / plus de lamentations' p. 151). Finally, as the waiter came to take her order, she howled, 'In anger, Juno-like' (56; 'la rage! / comme junon!' p. 151), startling everyone on stage, and sending the audience into fits of laughter. The confrontation with the Tribunes, then, was not a serious denunciation of destructive political chicanery but an opportunity for Cadieux's Volumnia to attack them personally while making a humorous scene in an anonymous eatery, amongst a small group of the political elite.

Other anonymous settings in the production rendered publicly political scenes as intimate personal ones that carried a homoerotic overtone. Lepage turned war into sport by staging Martius' being named Coriolanus, as a post-game dressing-room scene simply by pushing a bench and some metal lockers on from stage left. The scene was staged only between Cassistat in dress uniform and Philip, naked except for a towel, which allowed the audience to gaze at his muscular torso while he flexed in an upstage mirror just stage right of the lockers. The soldiers who, in Shakespeare's script, cry 'Martius!' (1.10.40.1) were replaced by car horns. Nor was there any 'public' response from soldiers when Cassistat named Philip Coriolan; the latter responded shyly, and the demure voice with which he spoke 'Howbeit, I thank you' (1.10.70; 'mais je te remercie' p. 61) gave their exchange a subtly sexual feeling broken only by Philip's exasperated 'Have we no wine here?' (92; 'il n'y a pas de vin ici?' p. 61). This sexual undertone was explicit in Lepage's depiction of Aufidius' relationship with Paul-Patrick Charbonneau's lieu-tenant-conspirator, who replaced the Volsce Senators in Act 1. The scene's initial darkness was broken when Gérald Gagnon's Aufidius lit a cigarette and a floor lamp came on downstage left, illuminating a hotel room or bedroom. Again, the simple room could have been anywhere: besides the lamp, there was only a red-covered bed that took up the stage-left third of the screen-like slot. Gagnon, wearing a military dress uniform, sat on the edge of the bed next to Charbonneau, who wore only underpants and a sleeveless undershirt. Their discussion of the impending war with Rome was not about Aufidius' announcement of his intelligence reports with the Volsce leaders but a personal exchange between two lovers; nobody else appeared in the scene. After Charbonneau read the letter detailing Rome's military preparations, he reached out from the bed, tenderly pulled Gagnon to him and, gazing into one another's eyes, they kissed. The final scene (5.6) was set in this room, and Lepage revisited the sexual tone of 1.2 in the play's last moments by turning Cori-olan's assassination into a deadly *menage à trois* because the Volsce crowd's lines were represented by the mere noise of honking horns. The action began with Gagnon and Charbon-neau (in dress uniform) discussing the plot against Coriolan, and, although both Gagnon and Philip subsequently addressed the audience directly, looking out at the house as though the theatregoers were the Volsce Lords, their argument was a very personal one because they were alone on stage with Charbon-neau, who stood upstage of the bed clutching a briefcase. Having worked themselves into a fury as they accused one another, the two men grappled as Gagnon shouted, 'Insolent villain!' (130; 'l'insolence! l'insolence!' p. 218), and then heaved themselves on to the bed. Gaining the superior position, Philip tried to strangle Gagnon but they had equally tight grips on one another's throats. The spectacle of the two men thrusting their hips wildly into one another in this vain struggle was cut short when Charbonneau's lieutenant removed a pistol from his briefcase and approached the thrashing couple like a jealous lover, holding his weapon to the back of Philip's head for fifteen seconds before finishing the job.[10] Coriolan's death, was thus not so much political as it was a matter of the lieutenant consummating his relationship with Aufidius by annihilating Aufidius' sexualized relationship with Coriolan, and the bed consequently became the symbolic site of the link between sex and violent death.

Lepage had primed the audience for this intersection of sex and violent struggle in the riveting first-act battle between Philip and Gagnon. As the lights came up on the bare black space inside the screen-slot, an upstage mirror was angled into position, revealing the two men rolling nude into the frame as though they were floating in it, though they actually remained on the stage floor throughout the scene. They appeared to be crouching and, with their arms slightly raised like wrestlers, they angrily addressed each other harshly, shouting their lines over the sound of a drum pounding out a rapid heart-beat. When they finished speaking, a piercing alarm siren wailed and horns honked, as the two men punched, grappled, spun and rolled over each other in slow motion. Forty seconds into this fight, Charbonneau (wearing a dress uniform but in shirtsleeves) rolled on stage to help Gagnon and was mildly injured in the fray before the latter shouted at him, 'you have shamed me / In your condemnèd seconds' (1.9.14–15; 'je n'ai pas besoin d'aide / vous m'humiliez!' p. 57). The complete lack of scenery and costuming on the combatants presented theatregoers with the production's most radically anonymous setting that privileged the personal over the broadly social. More importantly, the nude wrestling match illustrates how, instead of directly addressing the historical relationships that affected Québécois cultural nationalism, *Coriolan*'s scenography reflected Lepage's talent for using actors' bodies to experiment with canonical character-based approaches to Shakespearean performance. As previous chapters have shown, such approaches, which circulate across national boundaries among mainstream Western practitioners and journalistic theatre critics, are grounded in traditions of psychological realism that elide the body of the performer and the character and privilege the dramatic text by linking the act of embodiment to the author's purportedly transhistorical intentions regarding character.[11] The nude fight, like much of *Coriolan*, is typical of Lepage's Shakespearean production insofar as it disrupted the effort to create the effect of subjectivity by putting that effect into competition with the materiality of the performers' bodies.[12] That is, while the men spoke the scripted words very much in character, and their fight did embody the hatred that their words denote, their speeches were brief and the scene's impact resulted from the spectacle of their actual performing bodies. The audience witnessed Philip's and Gagnon's muscles rippling and contracting on their stocky muscular frames as they shouted their lines. The sight of the two men became even more captivating in the silent hand-to-hand combat: bathed in a golden light, their heaving bodies glistened with perspiration as they pummelled one another in slow motion.

Lepage achieved richly meaningful effects throughout the production by ostentatiously manipulating the relationship between his actors' bodies and the technology of the theatre, particularly the cloth frame and the shallow playing space that the frame enclosed. The director made a virtue of the tight space by creating blocking patterns that ostentatiously contrasted the actors' restricted movement with the characters' emotional strain. Such counterpoint was especially pronounced in the production's most frenetically physical scene, 3.1, in which the Tribunes tell Coriolan that his Consulship has been revoked. Lepage ran the end of 2.3, when the Tribunes spoke on the telephone to the People into 3.1, and staged this action as though it took place in a pair of election war-rooms, created by cutting the frame in two (left and right) with a room-divider placed at the centre of the slot. The actors were crowded into the resulting cramped compartments: Bisonnette and Bernier sat behind a table speaking into a telephone stage right; Philip, Jacques-Henri Gagnon, Limonchik and Cassistat were squeezed around a matching table stage left. The split screen allowed Lepage to emphasize the frame by closing it down even more and he encouraged a horizontal perspective by inviting the audience to compare the action in one compartment to that in the other. The division further exaggerated the production's horizontal movement because the actors had only one exit in each compartment, and in order to enter the other screen an actor had to exit, disappear and reappear from the opposite wing. Lepage emphasized this necessity by staging numerous hasty exits and entrances, though he counterpointed the highly artificial blocking with the characters' deeply felt and violent emotions. Bernier and Bissonnette exited their war-room stage right and entered from stage left to confront Philip, both men assertively accusing him of despising the People. After Bernier's enraged Sicinius shouted, 'It is a mind / That shall remain a poison where it is, / Not poison any further' (88–90; 'des idées empoisonnées / qui devront rester privées' p. 113), Philip bitterly mocked him and exited with his three supporters as he angrily spoke, 'Whoever gave that counsel to give forth / The corn o'th'storehouse gratis, as 'twas used / Sometime in Greece' (115–117; 'je ne sais qui a repris / cette vieille idée grecque / de distribuer de la nourriture / aux classes inférieures' p. 114). However, Philip immediately returned and Lepage highlighted his manipulation of the frame by juxtaposing explosive physical activity against the limitations of the tiny playing space. As Philip shrieked, 'Hence, old goat!' (178; 'ne me touche pas / petit chien dégénéré' p. 116), he dragged Bissonnette off stage left and entered the stage-right room, followed by Bernier; Philip hurled Bissonnette to the ground and thrust Bernier off stage right; Gagnon entered from stage right, failed to calm Philip, and exited stage right just before Philip picked Bissonnette off the floor, smashed his head viciously on the table, kicked him brutally and exited stage right. Philip then returned to his stage-left room, and the scene ended with Cassistat and Gagnon urging him to act more diplomatically while Bernier tried desperately to make phone calls and revive Bissonnette in the stage-right compartment. Although the actors were committed to conveying their extreme passions throughout the scene, the action derived its interest from a combination of door-slamming farce and the ostentatious experimentation in visual perspective with which Lepage's scenography confronted the spectators.

This sense that the production was, in large part, a series of visual experiments was particularly evident in the signature effect of Lepage's manipulation of the frame, namely its cropping of the spectator's view of the actors' bodies. When the masking curtain material was lowered so that the aperture of the frame was lowered, or when performers stood on the tables that were frequently pushed into place in the middle of the stage and thereby moved their heads out of sight, Lepage denied his spectators access to the actors' faces, conventionally the most significant physical feature in conveying psychologically 'realistic' characters. While Lepage thus depersonalized the actors, *Coriolan* did not enact 'the "Death of the Character"' in any simple way (Hodgdon, '*Macbeth*' 161). Instead, the director put the fundamental goal of conventional mainstream Shake-spearean acting – producing the effect of interiority – 'into parentheses', frequently by contrasting actors whose faces were visible with those whose were not. The action immediately preceding Coriolan's and Aufidius' single combat represents a particularly creative and extended staging of the *process* of the performers' bodies becoming and unbecoming characters. Here the Roman troops massed before the walls at Antium were repre-sented by marionettes and the puppeteers who manipulated them. The masking cloth frame was lowered so that only the puppeteers' legs and hands were visible through the slot. Admit-tedly, the three-minute battle, which consisted mostly of small groups of puppet horsemen charging around each other, was hardly exhilarating compared to, say, the nude love-wrestle. More significant than the rather poor execution of the mari-onette battle is the fact that these faceless, characterless puppeteers, whose dark-trousered legs partly blended into the black background and seemed to be growing out of the top edge of the frame, is characteristic of Lepage's larger body of work where the performer becomes merely another element of the theatre's technology that the director can draw on in devising his image-driven *mise-en-scène*.[13] Yet when Philip's Coriolan, who had been battling off stage behind Antium's closed gates, tumbled into the frame from stage left with his bare upper body wet and blood-stained like a new-born infant's, spectators witnessed what might be called the 'Birth of the Character'. Once his face was in view his body assumed an individual personality, especially in comparison to the anonymous puppeteer's legs and the marionette representing Cominius, which he addressed in his crouching position. Unlike the legs and marionettes, Philip's body was not part of the theatre apparatus: his rib-cage heaved in unison with his angry speech that the audience could now see him mouthing, and the flexing muscles in his naked torso dupli-cated the intense emotion visible in his eyes, thereby eliding the performer's body with the character. Lepage immediately repeated and embellished the process. Philip first embraced the Cominius marionette; then, standing up to embrace Cassistat the puppeteer, his body became an extension of the frame as his face was invisible. A second later Philip twirled Cassistat around, pulled him crouching into the frame with him, and two characters came into being as both actors' now-visible faces gave their bodies individual subjectivity. More than in any other scene, Lepage here treated the playing space as a kind of chamber for transforming actors' bodies, a chamber that alternately generated psychologically realistic personalities and interred these characters within the theatrical apparatus.

Lepage used the frame ingeniously to dramatize the power struggle during the Roman women's embassy to Coriolan in 5.3. The scene began with Philip and Gagnon's Aufidius standing at the stage-right edge of the tables pushed into the frame. The women and Charbonneau, doubling as young Martius, entered walking on the table, so that Philip's shock and effort to steady himself were legible in his face. However, the women's faces were invisible until first Brassard and then Cadieux knelt supplicating into the frame on, respectively, Coriolan's 'Let it be virtuous to be obstinate' (26; 'l'obstination m'est une vertu' p. 196) and 'I melt' (28; 'je suis en train de fondre' p. 196). Such manipulation of visual perspective was crucial to the final, highly emotional exchange between mother and son. When Philip spoke Coriolan's 'Sink, my knee, i'th'earth' (50; 'j'oublie de m'agenouiller' p. 197), he clambered on to the table stage right into a kneeling position. The kneeling Cadieux stood, walked three paces towards him, then knelt back into the frame, touching his arm and saying gently, 'O, stand up blest' (52; 'lève-toi je te bénis' p. 197). With both Cadieux's and Philip's faces in the frame, the two shared an emotional bond as they spoke, until Cadieux's voice became husky with sorrow on 'Even he, your wife, this lady, and myself / Are suitors to you' (78–79; 'lui-même cette dame / ta femme moi ta mère / nous venons te supplier' p. 198). At that point Philip stood, severing the emotional contact; Cadieux made the rest of Volumnia's long appeals to the actor with his face out of the frame and hers in it so that he seemed cruelly indifferent while she became increasingly desperate. With bitter finality, she shrieked, 'I am hushed until our city be afire, / And then I'll speak a little' (182–183; 'je me tairai maintenant / jusqu'à ce que la ville brûle / alors je crierai ce que j'ai à dire' p. 203) and stood, beginning to walk off stage on the tables. After a ten-second pause, Philip dropped kneeling into the frame, crying, 'O mother, mother!' (183; 'ô maman maman' p. 203). The reversal of positions underscored Coriolan's defeat: Philip's eyes registered the despair in his voice as he addressed Cadieux, who had become the impersonal, superior figure. Lepage's use of the frame here thus actually intensified the emotional impact of the power shift from son to mother by reversing the contrast between one faceless, 'characterless' performer and the other whose face was visible and whose emotions the audience could track; the image of Cadieux's hand reaching down to stroke Philip's head as he resignedly spoke, 'All the swords / In Italy, and her confederate arms, / Could not have made this peace' (208–210; 'tout ce qu'il y a de soldats au monde n'aurait pu comme vous / me l'arracher cette paix' p. 205) did not project the irony that had characterized Cadieux's earlier domineering behaviour but was a thoroughly pitiful spectacle.

By experimenting with canonical, character-based Shake-spearean theatre using vaguely 'global' staging techniques that arguably blunt the production's local identity, *Coriolan* encour-aged what Denis Salter refers to as the *Cycle*'s 'hyper-aestheticisation of political difference' ('Between Wor(l)ds' 192). To a degree, British critical reaction to the production's Notting-ham Playhouse tour stop in November 1993 helped to decontextualize *Coriolan* by restricting its identity to its rela-tionship to Shakespeare's text. British reviewers typically assessed *Coriolan* according to a rhetoric of loss in which modish but hollow spectacle is substituted for the fullness of Shakespeare's 'original'.[14] Not surprisingly, this rhetoric of loss followed the logic that Shannon Steen and Margaret Werry iden-tify in criticisms of Lepage's *Elsinore*: when the actors were fully visible, they were deemed fully present as characters because their bodies were 'suture[d]' to those of their characters (Steen and Werry 146); when their faces were invisible, their bodies were read as being decoupled from character, as being part of the apparatus of theatre and therefore less than human. Yet, if such response decontextualized *Coriolan* by limiting its identity to a mere contest between traditional transatlantic modes of Shakespearean production and experimental international theatrical practices, other aspects of the response suggest the opposite, the localization of the production's aesthetics. It is in the differences between Québécois and British reviewers' reac-tion to *Coriolan* that we witness what Roland Robertson calls 'the "invention" of locality', a manifestation of those diverse forces that constitute the supposedly homogenous nature of global culture (35). The operation of these forces upon *Coriolan* produced, to use Robertson's phrasing, 'something like an "ideology of home" which has in fact come into being partly in response to the constant repetition and global diffusion of the claims that we now live in a condition of homelessness and root-lessness' (35). The 'ideologies of home' produced by *Coriolan*'s reception challenge the notion that Lepage's scenography is straightforwardly global, homogenous and anonymous.

Coriolan provoked locally meaningful response from the British critics who identified the actors' failure to elide their characters with their own bodies as an excess that signalled an assault on the national poet by colonial mimicry. The reviewers sexualized the performers and either described their bodily excesses using a foreign analogy or corrected them according to British cultural models. Paul Taylor coded the very frame as sexual, writing that it offered 'a peeping tom's perspective on the proceedings' (*The Independent* 26 November 1993). From this voyeuristic position, he regarded the battle between Coriolan and Aufidius as 'a nude love wrestle that makes the one in *Women in Love* look like a bad case of mutual indifference', employing a domestic standard of homoerotic performance to demean Lepage's supposed preference for 'a more narrowly psycho-sexual drama' (*The Independent* 26 November 1993). Michael Billington, meanwhile, reinforced what Barbara Hodgdon calls in another context this 'xenophobic blocking' strategy by invoking Tyrone Guthrie's production that opened the Nottingham Playhouse thirty years earlier (*The Shakespeare Trade* 182). Specifically, he cited the Playhouse's inaugural production directed as a domestic example of how archetypal sexuality served Shakespeare with canonical performances that did not threaten the playwright's textually inscribed meaning: 'Volumnia's Freudian lust and the homo-eroticism of warfare are ideas that have informed more conventional productions, including Guthrie's where [Ian] McKellen's Aufidius swooped on the dead body of his adversary' (*The Guardian* 26 November 1993). Such comments not only demonstrate the power of the body to disrupt Shakespeare's textual authority but they re-local-ized *Coriolan*'s disruption of those 'global' performance techniques that sustain this authority by reinforcing a sense of British cultural superiority.

Québécois response provides a fuller image of the diverse local concerns at stake in the performance of globalized Shakespeare in so far as it reflects the struggle that Lepage outlines in the quotations at the start of this chapter: the urge, on the one hand, to take part in global culture through an international repertoire that includes Shakespeare and, on the other, the powerful sense of Québec's double colonization by France and England/English Canada. In negotiating such conflicting influences, Québécois reaction localized *Coriolan*'s transnational identity by re-inscribing it with both the French and English colonial pasts that the director had hoped to surmount. For instance, the Québécois media diligently tracked Lepage's international successes at the Festival d'Automne in Paris in 1992.[15] Yet, while Québec journalists were careful to note favourable notices in French newspapers, they were less interested in Lepage's cosmopolitanism than they were in expressing their own relieved joy at gaining the colonial power's approbation (*Le Soleil* 26 October 1992, *Le Soleil* 15 January 1993). Specifically, by appealing to the authority of the Parisian media, the Québec journalists returned the director to the role of a subservient provincial whose success, as Michel Dolbec (quoting Lepage) came close to saying, depended upon the sanction of a scruti-nizing colonial authority: 'For a month and a half, the theatre of the Québécois director-actor-author was subjected to a "verita-ble X-ray exam", which he passed with success' ('Pendant un mois et demi, le théâtre du metteur en scène-acteur-auteur québécois a été soumis à un "véritable examen aux rayons X"', *Le Soleil* 5 December 1992).

Like the British critics, Francophone Québécois journalists judged *Coriolan* according to its supposed adherence to Shake-speare's scripted intentions, their deference to the playwright reinforcing the old colonial relationships to England and English Canada, and thus hindering Lepage's effort to deploy Shake-speare as a product of transnational culture. Unlike British reviewers, Québécois critics focused on the relationship between the playwright and national linguistic identity embodied in Garneau's translation, and most gauged the translation according to its perceived fidelity to Shakespeare's authoritative original, whether they understood Garneau to have respected the text or to have flattened the complexities of narrative and character (*Le Soleil* 31 May 1993; *Voir* 10 June 1993). However, Québécois reac-tion suggests that the set of relations amongst national concerns, global touring and Shakespeare's traditional stature produced a variety of local perspectives. Certain Québécois critics, for instance, proposed a symbiotic relationship between Shakespeare's and Garneau's scripts, either by arguing that Garneau honoured Shakespeare by liberating him from the deadening category of the classics (*La Presse* 31 May 1993) or that the translation made Shakespeare speak with North American rhythms (*Le Devoir* 28 January 1994). The harshest criticism, meanwhile, came from Robert Lévesque, who equated Garneau's purported failure to serve Shakespeare with a dated and insular nationalism, stating that the translations 'belong to the old arid and clumsy Québécois theatrical language of the nationalist era and are part of the vision of a poet who never ventures out of his own linguistic enclosure' ('appartient au passé ingrat et malhabile de la langue théâtrale québécoise des années nationalistes, et relève de la vision complaisante d'un poète qui ne sort pas de son clos linguistique', *Le Devoir* 7 June 1993). Lévesque's comments inspired a polemical response from Guy Marchand, who employed Shakespeare to buttress Québécois nationalist sentiment. Marchand questioned Lévesque's right to determine Shakespeare's intentions, while self-consciously needling him with a Québécois turn of phrase: 'what is comic is the critic's pretension to know what Shakespeare should be better than "the whole world, including his mother", as we say in good Québécois, this Québécois that Mr. Lévesque finds so out of place chez Le Grand Will' ('[C]e qui est comique, c'est la prétention du critique de savoir ce que doit être Shakespeare mieux que "tout le monde, y compris sa mère", comme on dit en bon québécois, ce québécois que M. Lévesque trouve si peu à sa place chez Le Grand Will' 63). Yet Marchand did not declare independence from a Shakespeare who is no longer relevant to Québécois nationalism, but used the authority that the playwright's ostensible intentions confer to defend Lepage's production. Specifically, Marchand praised the director for revealing Shakespeare's intentions with a modern parallel that implicitly endorsed Lepage's internationalism: 'He brought to light the ancient foundation of the boulevard that is hiding within this "dry drama", in transposing it to the milieus of this century's haute bourgeoisie that we ... encounter ... in all the capitals of the world' ('Il a fait ressortir de ce "drame sec", le vieux fond de boulevard qui s'y cachait, en le transposant dans les milieux d'une haute bourgeoisie de ce siècle qu'on ... rencontre ... dans toutes les capitales du monde', 65).

Scrutinizing the historical reception of *Coriolan*'s tour brings into focus important aspects of global Shakespearean theatre. *Coriolan's* production history is comprised of a series of geographically and chronologically discrete events and, perhaps, as Kidnie writes about 'the idea of "local"' concerning *Elsinore's* touring, 'in such a mobile geographical context', the production's significance 'breaks free of national boundaries associated with the author (Shakespeare) or auteur (Lepage) to attach itself instead to the particular *locales* at which' it was performed (133–134, italics original). Yet *Coriolan's* relative freedom to cross national boundaries – its apparent lack of specifically Québécois identity and its literal international touring – did not *necessarily* entail 'vanish[ing] down the memory-hole of revisionist history' or the production of 'absent identit[ies] from which absolutely *nothing* of value can ever be salvaged' (Salter, 'Between Wor(l)ds' 193, emphasis original). Québécois and British critics may have invoked Shakespeare's traditional literary authority, based on his supposed ability to portray transhistorical characters, but they used this trope to evoke quite different specific national identities. Experimental Shakespeare may have increased Lepage's prestige as a global theatre artist, but Québec critics incorporated this prestige into narratives about local identity. What such 'returns' to the local indicate is that the kind of late twentieth-century intercultural theatre that *Coriolan* represents was caught up in a set of relations in which 'home', the global and Shakespeare were not mutually exclusive entities, but sustained each other through the production of identities that may not have been firmly fixed but were nevertheless shaped by numerous and competing histories.

CHAPTER X

Bringing Shakespeare home or settling in comfortably? The new Globe's 2006 *Coriolanus*

The new Globe theatre's *Coriolanus*, which opened the company's season in May 2006, was the inaugural production under the theatre's new artistic director, Dominic Dromgoole. As Dromgoole was taking over from the Globe's original artistic director, Mark Rylance, who had left his imprint upon the theatre in its first decade up to 2005, comparisons between the two were inevitable. Michael Dobson was perhaps too harsh, though not wholly inaccurate, when remarking that, in the Globe's *Coriolanus*, '[t]he default settings established under Mark Rylance are clearly all still in place: the whole season has a moderately tenuous theme ...; the unfortunate actors in this opening production have to wear reconstructions of what somebody thinks Elizabethans would have worn when playing Romans; and the audience in the yard are continually having their space half-jokily invaded by bits of the action' ('Shakespeare Performances' 291). Although Dromgoole stated that he wished to 'ravish' the audience with the play's energy ('An Interview' 163), this *Coriolanus* appeared to be designed to fulfil a set of expectations related to a certain image of Globe performance: an approximately authentic early modern performance style that relied on period costuming and music, audience engagement, crowd-pleasing comedy and a belief in the architecture's suitability for Shakespeare's language; a directing style that 'got out of the way' of Shakespeare to let his words do the work; and (muted) claims about Shakespeare's relevance and insights into human nature. The Globe *Coriolanus* was not meant precisely to restore the play to its original performance conditions, but, by suggesting that goal with a 'low-concept' production, Dromgoole seemed to be reassuring audiences that they could expect a continuity of purpose under his directorship of the theatre.

The Globe project has always been a blend of disparate elements. Even before Dromgoole took over, the theatre had staged Shakespeare in early modern and modern dress, all-male and all-female Shakespeare, Shakespeare productions by visiting companies from Britain and from around the world, plays by Shakespeare's contemporaries and new works by British playwrights. Today, the Globe 'is a theme park, it is a living history, it is a heritage site, it is urban development, it is participatory experience. And it is theatre' (Worthen 84). This multi-faceted identity is the result of bringing together practitioners, playgoers and theatre historians in an effort to rebuild 'Shakespeare's' theatre and perform his plays in it. As the standard narrative goes, the new Globe was born of American actor Sam Wanamaker's dream of rebuilding the theatre on London's South Bank. Then, in collaboration with Wanamaker, academics tried to turn it into a 'laboratory' for testing scholarly hypotheses about early modern performance, and, though Wanamaker did not live to see it, the theatre quickly became a profitable venue, extremely popular with locals and tourists alike.[1] Over time, however, 'the position of the academic [at the Globe] has shifted, from the early enthusiastic and romantic participation of the scholar, to the involvement of the scholar as chronicler, to the placement of the scholar outside the experimental process as an "objective" critical observer' (Carson and Karim-Cooper 6).[2] However, as Farah Karim-Cooper points out, 'scholarship is [still] central to the Globe and to Globe Education's interest in discovery and its commitment to quality teaching' (131). What scholars on the 'outside' have criticized is the gap between claims to historical-theatrical authenticity and Rylance's belief that 'the function of Shakespeare's plays is to develop human consciousness through the performance and the experience of these strange tales' (qtd in Conkie 18). Arguably, it is Rylance's 'flexible' approach to Shakespearean authenticity that has proved to 'work' with audiences and that has made the Globe so commercially successful.

Dromgoole may seem to have been a surprising choice as artistic director for such a theatre. In 2005, he was not renowned for Shakespeare productions, since, in his capacity as artistic director at the Bush Theatre (1990–96) and the Oxford Stage

Company (1999–2005), he had been responsible for contemporary and twentieth-century plays. Nor did Dromgoole's 2006 memoir *Will and Me* necessarily make an explicit case for his directorship, despite him detailing his lifelong attachment to Shakespeare. The first section of the book outlines the importance of Shakespeare to English culture and politics, the influence of Shakespeare in his parents' and grandparents' lives and in his own life at school through university in the classroom and on stage. The second section, meanwhile, offers an account of the seven-day walk from Stratford-upon-Avon to the Globe Theatre in London that Dromgoole undertook with a friend, following in the footsteps, as it were, of Shakespeare. Throughout the book, Dromgoole laments what might be called falsified Shakespeare. For too long, he writes, directors have 'been trying and testing the patience of theatre's devotees with a relentless desire to be interesting' (46). Actors routinely spoil Shakespeare by 'inflecting, intoning and contorting the language towards their own twisted music' (49). Disillusionment with 'the Shakespeare industry', with its artificial 'political, academic and social costumes that people want to hang on the worlds imagined by a troubled and ambitious country boy 400 years ago' (167) even turned Dromgoole into a Shakespearean apostate for a while. It is arguably this concern to tout his longing for a 'genuine' Shakespeare that connects him with assertions of the Globe's authenticity.

Such claims to authenticity, which are usually connected to the building itself and the ways that the structure encourages audience participation in the theatre experience, remain central to the Globe's identity.[3] Journalists who have derided Globe audiences for their ignorance about theatrical decorum probably prove Christie Carson's point that the Globe offers a model of performance quite unlike that found at the Royal Shakespeare Company (RSC) and the National Theatre (NT); encouragement of sustained audience participation might be misinterpreted as 'a lack of reverence for the texts', but such participation could also 'be recognised as an approach to the text which assumes the development of mutual understanding' between actors and spectators (122).[4] The Globe's 'culture of response' (Conkie 45) is, of course, partly a function of the theatre's thrust stage, which puts the actors and playgoers in immediate proximity to each other. Belief in the power of this theatrical space to evoke an 'authentic' Shakespearean experience is connected to 'a rhetoric of the "death of the director" ... where s/he is required to efface their directorial control and cede it to the building itself, and to the notion of the universal Shakespeare, who will be revealed most clearly in an unadorned (or unmediated), authentic production' (Conkie 61). This model of performance is wholly consistent with the one that Dromgoole articulates in *Will and Me*: 'The sickness in English Shakespeare production, and in English theatre, is where a director chooses a style for a play and then relentlessly forces everything to fit. Find a world for the play and make it consistent, these halfwits spout' (172). Instead, he argues that directors should encourage a common-sense approach to acting: 'The better the play, the less you have to do. The more you do, the more you spoil it. Nowhere is this more pertinent than with Shakespeare ... Shakespeare will take you where you need to go' (49–50). In the same year that he published these sentiments, Dromgoole and his actors were publicly retailing an image of their production that sustained the Globe's identity as a venue in which a generalized authenticity derives from allowing Shakespeare's vaguely relevant text to speak for itself in 'Shakespeare's own' building and in collaboration with active theatregoers.[5]

The visual and aural aspects of the 2006 *Coriolanus* were integral to the conventionally authentic Globe experience. As the archival video reveals, there were no sets as such, though stools and benches were brought on for the women's sewing (1.3), Coriolanus' presentation to the Senate (2.2), the Tribunes greeting the Plebeians (4.6) and for Coriolanus and Aufidius to hear the Roman women's pleas (5.3).[6] In these regards, the theatre was left to 'speak for itself', so that spectators witnessed the production in the Globe's familiar unadorned state: the approximately round space of the amphitheatre encloses spectators but the open roof leaves them exposed to the elements; the carved wood of the roofed tiered seating that encircles the standing room of the yard is matched by the carving on the balcony that is set above the roofed stage. This stage, which thrusts into the yard to provide sightlines from three sides, has three doors set into the upstage wall. The underside of the roof, and both the pillars holding up the roof and those placed at the sides of the upstage doors and on the balcony, are richly ornamented with painted marbling and gilding. However, the theatre was not entirely unadorned: in 2.2, an Officer unfurled three crimson banners from the balcony, adding a ceremonial sumptuousness to the scene. Much more significantly, Dromgoole added, for the length of the production, two plain wooden ramps that curved out into the standing area from the downstage edge of the platform like a pair of parentheses. The actors, meanwhile, were dressed in a blend of early modern and Roman garb. The Patrician men and the Tribunes wore boots, doublets, hose and loose slops, often adding togas that gave the Tribunes in particular a donnish look. In battle, they added breastplates and swords, and Jonathan Cake's Coriolanus wore a cape that he lost in the course of fighting. The Plebeians were distinguished from the Patricians by the simpler and duller browns and tans of their early modern dress, and the Roman women, as in so many other *Coriolanus* productions of the previous several decades, wore plain full-length dresses. The music, too, was meant to evoke early modern performance, with live musicians playing the bagpipes, cornett, recorder, sackbut and shawm. The music was used in conventional ways: in battle, drums pounded and trumpets signalled the parley of 1.4; brass instruments indicated Coriolanus' processional entrances in 2.1 and 2.2. Dromgoole also employed music to establish mood, including recorders to set the domestic scene of the Roman women sewing (1.3), near-eastern cymbal-and-drum music at Aufidius' house to suggest the Volsces' otherness (4.5) and sombre drums and trumpet for the concluding funeral march. The music was also a means of engaging the audience. On the video, the crowd gave each of the pre-show tunes that the musicians played enthusiastic applause. They responded the same way to the celebratory music that accompanied the Plebeians' elation at Coriolanus' exile in 3.3 (which coincided with the start of the interval), and clapped joyfully and rhythmically to the music played for the lively jig at the conclusion of the tragedy.

The music was related to Dromgoole's alteration of the playing space, the type of alteration that would be repeated in future Globe productions.[7] This continued use of additional stage architecture has attracted criticism to the effect that Dromgoole has 'been developing grand schemes isolated from the material processes of their implementation' and that he has imposed his belief that the Globe is actually badly designed, rather than learning by trial and error how to work with the space as given

(Cornford 326). While it is hard to tell how much he consciously mistrusted the space for his first production in 2006, his staging of numerous exits and entrances on the ramps, which enabled him to make the crowd part of the play by bringing the action even further into the yard than the thrust stage allowed, had pronounced ideological implications. Dromgoole saw the ramps as a way of 'moving very easily from' the groundlings, whom he equated with 'the plebs, the common people, and the people in the seats', whom he equated with 'the "posher" people' in the play ('An Interview' 165). In effect, Dromgoole used the class distinctions that he understood to be inherent to the reconstructed early modern theatrical space to reinforce class animosity within the fictional world of the production, with the result that the 'common people' were implicated far more than the '"posher" people' in Martius' demise. From the start, Dromgoole established the dual nature of the crowd as both spectators and Romans (and later Volscians): before the play began, one Plebeian told the audience, 'Welcome to Rome', which drew cheers; another warned that the use of mobile phones would result in 'decapitation', drawing laughter; the tone became more serious when the Trevor Fox's First Citizen discussed the rebellion with other actors, whose placement in the yard maintained the standing crowd's identity as 'participants' in the uprising. In 2.3, Cake's presence in the yard intensified the enmity between classes. Wearing the long whitish gown of humility, Cake jumped into the crowd to seek votes for his Consulship from the actors planted there. Playgoers and actors alike were bunched together closely, and though Cake spoke most directly with the other actors, his loud angry delivery in his 'posh' accent seemed to be addressed to ticket-holders as well. Furthermore, Cake came into direct physical contact with the audience since he had to push his way through the paying crowd in order to get to the other cast members placed around the yard. After receiving the votes, Cake exited through the upstage-right doors on the platform, as far as possible from the area bounded by the ramps, and the Tribunes addressed the actors in the crowd for the rest of the scene, underlining the audience's role in Coriolanus' eventual exile.

The spectators' complicity in Coriolanus' ruin extended into the final scene. The actors in the crowd playing the Volsces called out for Coriolanus' death, and when the Conspirators on the platform stabbed him Cake plummeted from the stage into the pit, a thrilling moment that recalled Olivier's death-swoon from 1959. However, Olivier's swan dive occurred upstage; Dromgoole described Cake's spectacular dive into the yard as 'a consummation of his own death wish', since 'he ha[d] been inviting aggression from [the common people] all the way along' ('An Interview' 168). The Volsce 'common people' in fact shared with Aufidius the final assault on Coriolanus' body, combining collective and individual antipathy towards the lead. After Cake fell into their midst, the actors in the yard, screaming wildly, stomped and stabbed Coriolanus; Mo Sesay then leapt down, shouted a victorious 'Ooooooohhhh!' as he appeared to cut out his enemy's heart, and held the bloody organ aloft for all to see. During the final exchanges between Aufidius and the Volsce Lords, the actors once again drew the playgoers into the action by directly addressing themselves to those in the yard and the galleries. Finally, for the death march, much of the standing audience helped draw an enormous black cloth over the yard, which the actors took out of the back of the theatre in order to get Coriolanus 'off stage'.

Not all the staging overtly drew the audience into the play's fictional world, nor did Dromgoole claim to have no overarching concept for the production. Because he regarded the young Roman republic of *Coriolanus* to be 'very delicate', Dromgoole believed that 'the feeling [of the action] should ... [be] of something fragile and dangerously unstable' ('An Interview' 164). However, the fragility of an immature republic is not something that came across consistently in the performances of the Tribunes. Apart from several minutes of comic gloating in 4.6, neither Frank McCusker's Sicinius nor John Dougall's Brutus was exceptionally self-serving. Instead, they saw it as their duty to inform the People that Coriolanus was a real threat to the Plebeians: in 2.3, when Brutus asked the Citizens, 'Did you perceive / He did solicit you in free contempt / When he did need your loves?' (195–197), Dougall spoke with honesty rather than calculated manipulation; McCusker used the same honest tone for Sicinius' potentially cynical advice, 'You should have ta'en th'advantage of his choler / And passed him unelected' (194–195). What is more, in 3.1, Dougall told Robin Soans's Menenius 'Go not home' and McCusker continued 'Meet us on the market-place. We'll attend you there, / Where, if you bring not Martius, we'll proceed / In our first way' (334–336) not as a threat but in a conciliatory, compromising tone. They did lose some dignity when Margot Leicester's Volumnia treated them with contempt in 4.2, but, as in their confrontations with Cake's raging Coriolanus, they remained calm in response to Leicester's extremely angry matron so that the instability did not appear to reside in the Roman republic in general but was largely confined to the Martian clan. Similarly, apart from Coriolanus, who scolded the Citizens condescendingly throughout, the Roman noblemen were usually earnestly resolute in the execution of their public duties. Although both Joseph Marcell's Cominius and Soans's Menenius were scornful of the People and the Tribunes in Acts 4 and 5 when they feared Coriolanus' Volscian army, they were primarily appeasers. In particular, Soans treated the People in the opening scene with respect and in friendship, recounting the 'Tale of the Belly' with real seriousness; he did not even attempt humour or mockery when he called the First Citizen the 'great toe' of the rebellion (152).

Furthermore, the action only intermittently left the impression of a Rome that 'was a sort of frantic society ... that didn't have any sense of pause' (Dromgoole, 'An Interview' 165). Most scene endings and beginnings overlapped, giving the action real fluidity and speed. The large-framed and athletic Cake added excitement to scenes of conflict in Act 1 with his tremendous physical prowess. He charged relentlessly through the battles becoming more blood-soaked and dishevelled as the fighting progressed, and his individual combat with Sesay's Aufidius, which began as a sword fight but degenerated into vicious punching and kicking, was quite fierce. Similarly, the violence of 3.1, when the Tribunes tried to strip Coriolanus of his Consulship, was extensive, breaking out into full-blown pandemonium twice and briefer scuffles three more times, with shouting, club-carrying Plebeians on one side and a sword-wielding Cake on the other. However, in the play's opening scene, Cake merely had to chase one Citizen to scare off the less-than-rambunctious crowd of Plebeians, and he threw down Aufidius' Servingman effortlessly in 4.5. Furthermore, despite Cake's individual athleticism in Act 1, the group battle of 1.4 lasted a mere fifteen seconds and, with only ten soldiers in total, the cursory sword-clacking was neither spectacular nor thrillingly chaotic.

The production's extensive comedy, too, undercut Dromgoole's image of a Rome 'internally at war with itself' ('An Interview' 165). He explained that such humour was necessary in a long performance and that they were not 'doing anything which was not part of the writing' ('An Interview' 168). The latter assertion seems tenuous in light of, for instance, his 1.2: when Sesay could not find the letter outlining the political-military disposition in Rome, he played the episode for laughs, searching his clothes impatiently before a Senator passed him the letter; as Sesay departed, he handed the paper to one Senator who thrust it hard into another's chest, both getting the reaction they sought when the second Senator cried out 'Ooohh!' in a high-pitched voice. This humour is yet another convention of Globe Shakespeare, what Conkie calls '"boom boom" playing: the turning of ostensibly serious dramatic lines into comedy' (242). Conkie outlines how such comedy at the Globe has, at times, resulted in politically regressive performances (243–247), and, in the 2006 *Coriolanus*, much of the humour was indeed derived from or aimed at the Plebeians: the opening comedic warning to turn off mobile phones arguably undermined the seriousness of the 1.1 uprising; the audience's appreciative laughter at Cake waving his hand before his nose to indicate the Citizens' offensive smell undercut the threat they posed to Rome in that same scene; and, when Sesay's Aufidius had to strike and chase his soldier to get him to do his bidding at the end of Act 1, the comic servant diminished the gravity of the Volscian defeat. In fact, throughout, the Citizens, soldiers and servants were cowardly and bumbling. In Act 1, the Roman soldiers began to follow Cake into Corioles, shouting 'Ahhhhh!' as they charged upstage, but, when the doors closed in their faces, they intoned 'Ohhhh' in mock disappointment that humorously signalled their relief; when most did charge through the gates in the following scene, one cowardly soldier fled comically, greatly amusing the audience. As Cake's Coriolanus revealed himself to Sesay in Act 4, two drum-beats sounded (boom-boom) and a Volsce servant ducked low and retreated to the safety of the stage-right pillar. The audience, meanwhile, laughed repeatedly at the Roman Citizens' claims in Act 4 that they did not actually mean to banish Coriolanus, and in 5.4, the messenger bringing news of Volumnia's success drew more laughter when he narrowly recovered from a pratfall as he ran on stage. This broad humour might be understood as yet another means of kindly embracing the Globe audience by reassuring them that the tragedy is not unremittingly gloomy or serious; as Dromgoole remarked, he 'just wanted to release' the humour that appears 'even in the darkest of [Shakespeare's] tragedies' ('An Interview' 168). Still, because these incidents implicitly mocked the groundlings, with whom Dromgoole associated the 'lower classes', this kindly embrace made those standing in the yard complicit in the production's dubious approach to class by sneering at their own (real or fictional) 'inferior' status.

However, the comedy did extend to the central Patrician relationship in the play, that between Coriolanus and Volumnia. Whereas Cake was usually angrily and athletically demonstrative, Leicester was, from her first scene, in constant motion, always striding about the stage and gesturing grandly. Leicester's animation, combined with the frequently light tone of her speech, resulted in laughter, first when she laughingly imagined Hector's forehead spitting forth blood in 1.3, and later, when she thanked the gods for her son's injuries in a gruff, mock-angry voice and began enumerating those injuries over-enthusiastically in 2.1. The theatregoers also appreciated her more purposely histrionic moments, laughing at the very campy voice with which she spoke 'But oooooooo, thy wife!' (2.1.171) when pointing out Jane Murphy's Virgilia to Coriolanus. As in 1.3, Leicester's exaggerated vocalization here upstaged Murphy, rendering Virgilia something of a nonentity. In 3.2 Leicester developed these comic histrionics to reveal that her maternal anger was merely a hollow performance. Cake acted defiantly, speaking 'Well, I will do't [humble myself to the Plebeians]' (103) with jeeringly false conciliation, and later intoning 'I will not do't, / Lest I surcease to honour mine own truth' (122–123) with angry determination. However, Leicester hit back by speaking 'Do as thou list. / Thy valiantness was mine, thou suck'st from me, / But owe thy pride thyself' (130–132) gravely. After this browbeating, the sheepish voice with which Cake spoke, 'Mother, I am going to the market-place' (133) and 'Look I am going' (136) drew hearty laughter and applause from the crowd. The audience reacted the same way as Leicester sternly spoke her final line in the scene, 'Do your will' (139), and began to exit with dignity, but, behind Cake's back, skipped off stage while showing her crossed fingers to Soans's Menenius.

Dromgoole toned down the comedy somewhat for the individual struggle between Volumnia and Coriolanus in the women's embassy of 5.3. Cake's Coriolanus was visibly moved by Leicester's often passionate vocalization throughout Volumnia's two very long speeches (95–126 and 132–183), pointedly stopping himself from crossing to his mother when he visibly experienced a powerful desire to embrace her as she spoke, 'thou restrain'st from me the duty which / To a mother's part belongs' (168–169). Like other leads before him, Cake used an extended silence (approximately thirty seconds) during the hand-holding (183) to emphasize that his emotional anguish was the principal factor in his decision not to invade Rome. Nevertheless, Leicester performed parts of the encounter with her usual animation and the audience laughed at such lines as 'Thou hast never in thy life / Showed thy mother any courtesy' (161–162), 'This is the last' (173) and 'And then I'll speak a little' (183). The humour derived not so much from her tone of voice but from her physicality: on 'with no softer cushion than the flint' (53) she banged the stage with her hands; throughout her long speech beginning 'Should we be silent and not speak' (95–126), she waved her arms and shrugged her shoulders exaggeratedly; and on 'The man was noble / But with his last attempt he wiped it out' (146–147), she swept her arm in an arc, as though imagining words on a marquee. Such exaggerated gestures diminished her gravitas and tinged Volumnia's extremely long speeches with comic hypocrisy. Of course, unlike 3.2, the comedy of 5.3 switched to a seriousness that culminated in Cake's spectacular death fall in the last scene. However, what the director established in the last four scenes of the production was an alternation between seriousness and lightness. The tension of 5.4 was diminished by the messenger's near pratfall and then gave way to celebration of the women's success in 5.5, which was accompanied by strewn flowers and upbeat music. Similarly, the tragedy of 5.6 gave way to the celebratory curtain-call jig, when the cast filled the stage and in which the audience, as noted above, became part of the (post-)performance by cheering and clapping in time to the music and dancing actors.

Reaction to Dromgoole's attempt at a type of theatrical authenticity peculiar to the Globe reflects what Conkie discerns as the dual nature of performance at the theatre. On the one hand, 'authenticity invariably focuses political issues', like the class relationships in *Coriolanus*, 'even if the politics are, invariably, conservative or regressive' (Conkie 221). On the other hand, both 'the ugly or unsavoury elements of the plays and of the play-going experience ... have become too humanised and sanitised' at the theatre (Conkie 252). The lengthiest and most sophisti-cated response to the 2006 production appears in a self-consciously 'political' article by Peter Holland, in which he called this *Coriolanus* 'the most reactionary production of the play [he] had ever seen' (37). While Holland found '[t]he racial politics of' *Coriolanus*' publicity photograph, in which Cake kicks Sesay's black Aufidius in the face 'positively embarrassing' (37), his fury was primarily driven by the consequences of the Plebeians' easily manipulated comic stupidity: 'the patricians, RP-speaking, rational and ... clearly benign, could not but be the sympathetic centre of the politics of this divided society, for all the world like an old-fashioned Tory party, the core of a benevolent establishment' (38). As Holland noted (37), this polit-ical reaction was exceptional because virtually every critic who wrote about the production avoided commenting on political aspects external to the play's narrative. A couple of reviewers for American publications (*New York Times* 8 July 2006; Spates) made vague connections between *Coriolanus* and America and Britain's prosecution of the Iraq war, but most critics limited their reaction to measuring the production against 'Shake-speare'. Charles Spencer welcomed Dromgoole's appointment because the artistic director had 'expressed a robust distaste for excessively ... self-advertising director's theatre' (*Daily Telegraph* 12 May 2006). Furthermore, this 'straight-from-the-shoulder *Coriolanus*' supposedly showed that 'Dromgoole is going to get it right' (*Observer* 14 May 2006) as the new head because the production's 'energy and daring' brought the play to life without any 'annoying experimentalism or daft costumes' (*Sunday Times* 14 May 2006). Reviewers also appreciated that Dromgoole 'resist[ed] easy historical updating' but provided 'a sturdy run through the text' (*Daily Express* 11 May 2006), and that he gave the play 'no Marxist or other tilt' which, 'surely, is how Shake-speare would have wanted it' (*The Times* 12 May 2006). Most critics admired the stage extensions insofar as they understood the director to be using the space in conjunction with Shake-speare's intentions: the ramps provided 'an involving experience, literally, in that [they] co-opt[ed] the groundlings as the crowd of mutinous Roman citizens' (*The Independent on Sunday* 14 May

2006); and the extensions 'allow[ed] the standing spectators, representing the hydra-headed multitude, to be embraced by the action' (*The Guardian* 12 May 2006).

However, reviewers' main criterion for judging whether or not this *Coriolanus* was done as 'Shakespeare would have wanted it' was the performance of appropriately subtle and profound individuality. Many critics hedged their bets. Leicester, for instance, was 'marvellously communicative' but 'not remotely Juno-like' (*Financial Times* 12 May 2006); she lacked tremendous 'force . . . but she compensates with a sense of serene assurance, a blithe self-certainty' (*The Times* 12 May 2006); she was 'more like a peevish Mrs. Bennet [in *Pride and Prejudice*] worrying about her daughters than the flinty-hearted Roman matron rejoicing in her son's battle scars' (*Sunday Times* 14 May 2006). Reviewers focused mostly on Cake, especially his athleticism. He was 'a posh rugger-bugger' (*The Independent on Sunday* 14 May 2006), 'a rugby No 8, thick-skinned and always ready for a heave' (*Daily Mail* 12 May 2006), 'the cheerful, rugby-playing lad' (*Sunday Times* 14 May 2006) and 'Jonathan Beefcake' (*Daily Telegraph* 12 May 2006). At the same time, while reviewers did admire the emotional tension that Cake generated during his encounter with Leicester's Volumnia in 5.3, many were disappointed by what they perceived as the lead's failure to provide such psychological depth in the rest of his performance: Cake 'misses Coriolanus's crucial emotional dynamism' (*Evening Standard* 11 May 2006); he merely 'treats the tribunes with an infantile scorn, as though they were boys in a playground brawl rather than an increasingly powerful threat to his indoctrinated notions of heroism' (*Metro* 11 May 2006), and he 'does not attempt to show the godlike heights found by other characters in this hero' (*Financial Times* 12 May 2006).

Such criticisms notwithstanding, the 2006 *Coriolanus* represents a double accommodation. The first part of the accommodation was, of course, Dromgoole's adaptation to performance conditions that had become conventional at the Globe. The second part was the relatively widespread, if uneven, critical acceptance of those conventions as being conducive to enacting Shakespeare. It is true that, as Conkie observed of productions before Dromgoole took over, many journalists continued to use the lack of subtlety as a 'stick with which to beat' the director (252). It is also true that the majority of critics followed Dromgoole in approaching this *Coriolanus* on the Globe's terms, terms that have made the theatre immensely popular with playgoers. In particular, as noted above, the majority of reviewers appeared to be relieved by the transition from Rylance to Dromgoole; with the exception of Dobson, they lauded the continuity that the new artistic director's *Coriolanus* apparently signalled. This relief is likely because Dromgoole's rhetorical displacement of his directorial responsibility on to the theatre architecture (the extra ramps notwithstanding), the audience and Shakespeare's text manifested itself so tangibly in the stage action. The director's concept for the production was not especially novel, but his orthodoxy suited the reviewers quite well because they believed that it appeared to let Shakespeare (more or less) speak for himself. Reaction to the 2006 *Coriolanus* reveals the critical community following Dromgoole in settling comfortably into the Globe; overlooking past criticisms that the theatre's Shakespearean authenticity may be more closely linked to a tourist experience than to a desire for historical accuracy (Prescott), reviewers accepted that when the Globe is employed as a low-concept, non-directors' theatre venue it could be construed as a means of bringing Shakespeare home in the twenty-first century.

CHAPTER XI

Coriolanus as failed action hero

Ralph Fiennes's cinematic *Coriolanus*, released commercially in the winter of 2011–12, is another product of 'global Shakespeare', though one that draws on the aesthetics of the Hollywood movie rather than the avant-garde theatrical techniques of Robert Lepage's *Coriolan*. Fiennes, who made his directorial debut with and starred in this *Coriolanus*, produced the film at a time when some scholars had become ambivalent about popular culture Shakespeare. After the proliferation of Shakespeare films aimed at the mass market in the 1990s, the onset of the twenty-first century brought with it intimations that repeated and often trivializing citations of the playwright in popular venues have eroded his iconic status as his work becomes dispersed 'across all mass media ranging from advertising to popular music to fiction and comic books' (Burt, *'Shakespeare in Love'* 226).[1] But, despite the qualified prophecy that 'it may soon be time to speak of the Shakespeare apocalypse' (Burt, *'Shakespeare in Love'* 227), the 2011 *Coriolanus* proves that the playwright's name 'is still one to conjure with' in the cinema (Burnett and Wray 1).[2] Fiennes's screenwriter John Logan cut the script down to a two-hour film, but the Shakespeare the two men hoped to conjure was the old, universally relevant Bard whose narratives and characters they wanted us to hear speaking across time. This is not to say that the film simply evokes a traditionally British Shakespearean authority; shot at Serbian locations in ways that do not necessarily denote that country, comprised of a Briton-heavy but multinational cast in contemporary dress, and toured to various international film festivals, this *Coriolanus* suggests that form of cinematic Shakespeare which is 'free-floating, nationless, ... and homogenous' (Burnett 48). Yet it also embodies an aspect of what Richard Burt calls 'glo-cali-zation'; if the film blurs distinctions between the global and the local it also 'keeps "Cali" (as in California) or, more specifically, Hollywood, as the central point of discursive reference' ('Shakespeare, "Glo-cali-zation"' 16). Put another way, Fiennes's *Coriolanus* consolidates the cultural authority of Hollywood Shakespeare by drawing upon such typical features of the blockbuster as narrative clarity, frenetic editing techniques and an abundance of explosive violence. At the same time, the film complicates that most conventional of action movie motifs, the protagonist's 'journey', by making Coriolanus a failed action hero in denying him unambiguously heroic status.

In publicizing the film, Fiennes made clear, not surprisingly, his desire to produce a commercial work with broad appeal. He promoted *Coriolanus* using the cliché about *all* the plays' supposedly inherent accessibility: 'what's happening in Shakespeare's stories is always relevant' (Production Notes 8). Nevertheless, he claimed that he updated the film to the twenty-first-century world of economic strife, warfare and backroom politics specifically to allow audiences to overcome any fear of Shakespeare's foreignness by encountering in the film a world they witnessed 'every day ... in the paper or on television' (Carnevale). As the first decade of the twenty-first century began, the everyday news of the world was grim and getting worse. The triumphalism that had marked Western powers' entry into wars in Afghanistan (in 2001) and Iraq (in 2003) had turned into fatigue and distaste, especially for the perceived mendacity of those who advocated invading Iraq on the basis of its possession of weapons of mass destruction, weapons that never materialized. War-weariness was exacerbated by the global financial crisis of 2007–8, the worst economic downturn since the Great Depression; equity and housing markets collapsed, banks were bailed out and sovereign debt soared, leading eventually to numerous countries' governments slashing national budgets. Fiennes's contentions about the film's contemporaneity gained rhetorical force once *Coriolanus* was released. There may have been optimism about some revolutions in the 'Arab Spring' that began in late 2010 with the relatively peaceful removal of dictators in Tunisia, Egypt and Yemen, though conflicts in Libya and Syria proved far bloodier. The year 2011 saw the rise of the 'Occupy' movement, a somewhat amorphous participatory democracy movement that combined the use of electronic communication and camp-ins at locations around the globe in order to protest against (among other things) the alleged corruption of governments and major financial institutions.

Yet, when commenting on the film, the director avoided linking it with any specific conflict, even if filming in the Serbian capital raised the spectre of the Balkans war of the 1990s. Indeed, Fiennes claimed to value twenty-first-century Belgrade's architectural eclecticism because 'the events that happen in *Coriolanus* could happen anywhere, our Rome could be just about any city in the world' (Production Notes 11, 8). In creating this widely recognizable global nowhere-and-everywhere, the director took, he says, '[a] huge cue' from Baz Luhrmann's *Romeo + Juliet*, 'particularly, his [Luhrmann's] complete creation of a world that I couldn't tell you where it was but I knew it was somewhere today and I believed it' (Polowy). Although Fiennes had wanted to make the film ever since he performed Coriolanus on stage in a 2000 Almeida theatre production, he believed that Shakespeare's language represented a barrier, and that his words had to be rendered familiar for audiences not used to classical theatre. He therefore made a point of asserting his faith that the play could be pared back to its basics of narrative and character so that audiences would immediately recognize the film as 'a dynamic, political thriller with a kind of familial mother-son tragedy at the centre of it' (Carnevale). By manipulating elements of that quintessentially accessible Hollywood genre, the action film, Fiennes actually turned the universally relevant Bard into his globally relevant counterpart; he appeared to use *Coriolanus*, and Coriolanus' tarnished heroism, to comment pessimistically on a vaguely international blend of military adventurism, armed revolution and political protest, the same blend that the filmgoers who saw the film in cinemas around the world could have witnessed very recently 'in the paper or on television'.

Fiennes worked determinedly to shape his *Coriolanus* into an action film. The versatile actor has not distinguished himself as a belligerent action hero, but his Shakespearean career undoubtedly reflects his viability as a leading man: after a few years at the RSC taking principal roles in the late 1980s and early 1990s, he starred in productions that were clearly centred around him. This star status was the result of Fiennes's success in film, where he has proved his affinity for emotionally intense and conflicted protagonists, and he *has* distinguished himself as a compelling villain. His screen celebrity began with the role of Amon Göth, a Nazi concentration camp commandant in the Academy-award-winning *Schindler's List* (1993), and he probably would have been most widely recognized for his repeated turns as the evil wizard Voldemort in the hugely popular action-filled *Harry Potter* franchise, the last instalment of which was released in the summer of 2011 when *Coriolanus* was on the festival circuit. His Volumnia, Vanessa Redgrave, was perhaps the most distinguished working English actress in 2011, and her long and celebrated career on screen and on stage in modern and classical drama included a turn as Valeria opposite Laurence Olivier in 1959. If Redgrave was not primarily a Hollywood actress, the director did surround himself with men who had considerable blockbuster experience. Like Fiennes, his Menenius, Brian Cox, did Shakespeare in the 1980s and 1990s at the RSC and the National Theatre, but Cox has worked extensively as a character actor in spy-thrillers and fantasies such as *Troy* (2004), in which he portrayed a cartoonish Agamemnon. Fiennes's Aufidius, Gerard Butler, had virtually no profile as a Shakespearean, but would have been known to many moviegoers, in 2011, for starring four years earlier as the muscular King Leonidas in the hyper-kinetic *300*, a comic-book-based film. More important were Fiennes's choices of Barry Ackroyd as cinematographer and Logan as screenwriter. Ackroyd had recently shot two explosion-filled Iraq war dramas: *The Hurt Locker* (2008) about a bomb disposal unit (in which Fiennes has a minor role); and *The Green Zone* (2010), a big-budget military thriller. Logan, meanwhile, has a well-established career scripting commercial hits, including a screenwriting credit on the highly successful *Gladiator* (2000), which arguably spurred the post-millennial turn towards sword-and-sandal epics like *Troy* and *300*.

Logan's screenplay was instrumental in drawing out the similarities between Shakespeare's *Coriolanus* and contemporary action cinema. To give the film the 'strong narrative drive' that Fiennes desired, the screenwriter cut nearly two-thirds of the text and spread out the remaining incident and dialogue over more than double the number of scenes than there are in Shakespeare's script (Production Notes 8). The editing not only propels the action forward with the relentless pace of a 'thriller', but, as Fiennes hoped, it concentrates viewers' attention on the 'visceral dynamic of confrontation' between Coriolanus and three antagonistic forces: the Citizens, Aufidius and Volumnia (Production Notes 8). By radically reducing the dialogue and consequently the diversity of perspectives about Coriolanus, the screenwriter sharpens the focus on the hero's *direct* confrontation with his antagonists. In so doing, Logan simplifies the hero's 'journey' and accommodates it to the Hollywood movie's classic three-act structure: the hero's problems and conflicts are introduced; they are exacerbated, greatly testing the hero; the hero prevails (Bordwell 28). While Fiennes' Coriolanus is a failed action hero insofar as he *succumbs* to the conflicts his antagonists visit upon him, Logan's changes help clarify the preoccupations that the play shares with the action genre.[3] Action cinema may be associated with Hollywood but, as Lisa Purse notes, the genre 'resonates' globally, 'with and beyond its domestic audiences' by enacting 'a set of ideas celebrating an individualist heroism that can be traced back to classical mythology and equally to a Christian tradition to which "martyrdom and sacrifice are central"' (4–5).[4] Martin Fradley argues that the masochism of the typical martyred action hero is 'characterized by a form of paranoia' (235) about 'white male decentering and decline' that 'has become one of *the* master narratives in post-1960s American culture' (238, emphasis original). The hero becomes a stand-in for 'white masculinity as the "victim" of progressive social change' (Fradley 239), and, by mastering the physical risk to which he submits himself, he 'tap[s] into primal fantasies about dominating others, or being free from social and behavioral constraints' (Purse 3). The hero typically undergoes physical punishment and near feminization in the first part of his journey before remasculating during his third-act victory, a recuperation linked to 'the structural elements of melodrama' through '[a]ction cinema's generic tropes – character archetypes, moral polarisation, transparency of legibility, [and] spectacular and excessive *mise-en-scène*' (Fradley 241). Although Fiennes's Coriolanus does not successfully recuperate his masculinity in a simplistically melodramatic fashion, the generic tropes the film borrows from action cinema make it recognizably *akin* to a work like *Gladiator*, which, in Fradley's words, may project a 'sombre and elegiac *gravitas*' but the desperation with which it pursues a 'masculine utopia' actually 'renders its symptomatic hysteria as visibly as [the protagonist's] wounded body' (249).

The fight for Corioles is designed to display Martius submitting himself to risk in combat, thereby providing the spectators with the 'voyeuristic admiration of the hero's body and presence' that Paul Smith notes is a key aspect of the action film (156). The first phase of the battle, bracketed by the relatively peaceful conversations between Aufidius and a Senator in a Volscian bunker, and the women at Martius' elegant villa, establishes the environment of risk into which Martius thrusts himself. This environment has a topical aura in that it evokes scenes of urban warfare in, say, Iraq, that would have been familiar to moviegoers from newscasts of the last decade. Despite the apparent connection to contemporary politics, however, Fiennes's main concern is to allow the viewer clearly to follow the unfolding combat narrative while experiencing the disorientation of battle. The scene begins at the end of Shakespeare's 1.2 in Aufidius' bunker, with the sound of a screaming artillery shell that explodes when the shot cuts to the battlefield and we see debris flying out from a bombarded building. The hand-held camera (steadicam) whips around to capture a line of Roman soldiers running single-file along the street as a second shell explodes in flames behind them. The shaky camera tracks the soldiers' progress through the battered cityscape of crumbling, graffiti-covered walls, strewn rubble and burning cars. With the camera swiftly cutting between a wide range of differently angled long-shots and close-ups of the Romans and Volsces shooting at each other, the viewer's senses are assailed by the constant echo of automatic gunfire and by bullets sparking off balcony railings; shell casings pulse out of shuddering weapons, and soldiers on both sides fall dead in pools of blood. The first combat sequence ends with a bang and suspense: the Romans are knocked out by an explosion, leaving the viewer hanging when the scene cuts to the tranquil opulence of Martius' home.

The next phase of the battle, which occurs immediately after the women's conversation, concentrates more narrowly on Martius' individual submission to risk. Much of the incident in these sequences is characterized by what Geoff King calls the action film's '"impact aesthetic"', a style that relies on 'rapid editing and unstable camera work' (335). The impact aesthetic takes the viewers '"up close and personal", sometimes very much "down on the ground". The impression created is of a more subjective involvement in the action' (340). Our voyeuristic pleasure blends into an overwhelming empathy because the perpetually moving camera and quick edits appear to thrust the viewer into the hand-to-hand fighting. The camera follows Fiennes's Martius behind Corioles' 'walls' as he eliminates Volsce soldiers in a shot-up building; we feel as if we are with him, watching closely and listening to his laboured breathing when he destroys his enemies, losing his helmet and bloodying his shaved scalp in the process. The impact aesthetic is especially pronounced in the lone fight between Fiennes and Butler's Aufidius, and though we are meant, once more, to feel a kind of visceral empathy for Fiennes's exposure to physical danger, his mastery of risk here is not as decisive as it was in the earlier scenes. After heroically leading the Romans into another building through yet another street-fight, Fiennes confronts Butler in a smoke-filled foyer. The film works inexorably on the viewer's senses; the battle begins with sounds of tearing Velcro and unsheathed knives loudly amplified as the two men, surrounded by the other soldiers, strip off their flak vests and wield their blades. Most of the fight is filmed very close to the struggling bodies, and the camera's movements are exacerbated by quick edits, though the men also move rapidly across the frame, adding to the hectic motion. While Fiennes and Butler pummel, slash and yell, the viewer is given the sensation of being *in* the fight. We feel as though we, too, are being swirled around and tossed about by forces beyond our control; when the men slam into a wall, the rapid cuts and close shots make it seem as if *we* have been thrown into the wall; when the struggle devolves into a stalemate, the camera follows Fiennes and Butler down on to the ground, their bloody heads pressed together as they scream incoherently. Butler breaks the impasse by standing and hurling both himself and Fiennes through a window; the camera cuts to outside the building for the men's spectacular appearance, smashing through the window and tumbling to the ground out of the frame in a shower of tinkling glass. Straining the limits of credibility, the fight briefly resumes at ground level, with the camera up close to the two men, though their now-lethargic struggling is cut short by an exploding shell. It is here that Martius' mastery of risk, and thus his heroism, comes into question, since both combatants are helped away, though only Butler's Aufidius recovers and seems ready to keep fighting. Furthermore, Fiennes downplays the immediate individual rewards of Martius' risk by delaying his victorious naming as Coriolanus until he returns to Rome.

The techniques that Fiennes employs for the battle of Corioles might provide the visceral pleasure of experiencing combat *with* the hero, but to what end? The war zone might evoke Iraq, but the architecture is European, and the battle scenes could just as easily remind viewers of the Balkans war of the 1990s. This world is exactly the kind of urgently contemporary but placeless locale that Fiennes alluded to, and the relentless pace of the editing in depicting the Romans advancing towards their enemy make it difficult – and beside the point – for the viewer to locate this urban space: there are no shop or street signs visible, no landmarks to tell us precisely where we are. The distinction Fiennes does make between the two sides is a basic one that cuts across topical divisions: the Romans are invader-occupiers and the Volsces defender-insurgents. The Romans wear state-of-the-art combat gear, including Kevlar helmets, flak jackets and radio ear-sets, and use modern, telescope-sighted automatic rifles. The Volsces, by contrast, wear non-uniform fatigues and caps; they wield old-looking AK-47s, a Soviet-designed weapon favoured by numerous guerilla groups throughout the postwar era, and they draw the Romans into a booby-trapped bus, suggesting the kind of improvised explosive device 'insurgents' used against 'allied' forces in Afghanistan and Iraq in the first decade of the millennium. Martius thus proves himself by risking his life against an enemy that is the apparent underdog, one fighting off a militarily superior oppressor. Fiennes emphasizes this impression in the battle's coda, when the small band of surviving Volsces, led by Butler's exhausted Aufidius, discover a family slaughtered in their mini-van. Butler slumps to the ground, beaten by this image of wretchedness that the war has caused. Fighting back tears and breathing heavily, he speaks with angry determination, 'for where / I thought to crush him in an equal force, / True sword to sword, I'll potch at him some way / Or wrath or craft may get him' (1.11.13–16). By ending the Corioles scenes in this way, Fiennes implies that Aufidius' revenge is not simply a matter of personal animosity but is closely linked to the killing of his people. Thus the battles might not portray Martius as the '"victim" of progressive social change' but they do depict him as the leader of those forces bent on 'dominating others', those others being weaker – and in the case of murdered Volsce civilians unarmed – 'foes' defending their homes. This treatment might work against the moral polarization of protagonist and antagonist that is part of the action formula, but as the end of 'Act 1', it does establish the generic 'promise of major conflict' (Bordwell 28).

Of course, part of the major conflict is with the Plebeians, and the riots of 1.1 and 3.1 depict public protest as a form of battle. As elsewhere in the film, these scenes gain political urgency because, by the time the film screened in 2011 and 2012, they would have seemed lifted from contemporary news reports of, for instance, Greek protests against government austerity measures. However, once more, other than the Senate's classical architecture in 3.1 and the English 'Police' labels on riot shields, there is hardly any way to determine the scenes' specific locales. Coriolanus emerges as a kind of iconic dictatorial figure representing a general opposition to progressive social change, both because the Plebeians could be protestors from any Western nation and because the intensity of the scenes derives not so much from topicality as from sustained reliance upon the impact aesthetic. In Fiennes's 1.1 a large group of demonstrators, some carrying banners of Martius' silhouette crossed out in red, approach the fenced-off compound of the grain depot. As in Martius' knife-fight, the cinematography puts us in the thick of things, capturing close-ups of the black-clad riot police and the stick-wielding protestors. Shortly, a few young men smash the lock on the gate and the People stream forward, the shaky hand-held camera giving us a sense of the riot's dangerous swirl. Again, the viewer seems to be experiencing all of this first-hand as the camera cuts quickly between close shots of Citizens, an armoured military vehicle and police thumping protesters with batons. When both sides pause to regroup, Fiennes, in camouflage fatigues and a black beret, strides forward from the background, breaking through the ranks of riot police. He is never in any tangible danger here; he merely insults the People and exits back through the assembled police, who then disperse the rioters, banging out a menacing rhythm on their plastic shields. In 3.1 Fiennes's Coriolanus confronts the Citizens protesting outside the Roman Senate in the course of arguing with the two Tribunes; he grabs James Nesbitt's Sicinius, pushes him through the front doors and hurls him to the ground mere steps from the shouting demonstrators. A quickly cut assemblage of sweeping pans that temporarily blur the picture thrusts the viewer once more into the middle of the protest, though the hectic action is more sustained than it was in the grain riot and thus the sense of risk from the People is greater: the camera whips around everywhere as though it were trapped in the crowd, following Nesbitt to the ground and up again; close shots of the backs of heads, shoulders and raised arms rush through the frame; the perspective shuttles back and forth between close-ups of Nesbitt and Paul Jesson's Brutus addressing the People filmed over the shoulders of riot police and close-ups of the screaming crowd filmed from the perspective of the Senators, whose terrified faces we fleetingly see. Although Fiennes is hauled back behind the Senate doors by his supporters, he longs to expose himself to the risk of battling the crowd; with his brows furrowed low over piercing green eyes and his mouth stretched wide to release a lunatic bellow of wordless hatred, Fiennes's Coriolanus here is undoubtedly the hysterical opponent of progressive social change.

Fiennes's 'procession' to the Senate clearly signals that Martius is not 'brought to [the] breaking point' as Smith's action heroes are, by being *physically* broken (*Clint Eastwood* 156); the real risk for Martius does not reside in war, nor in domestic battles with the Plebeians, but in exposure to public rituals at home. Accompanied by a trumpet sounding august notes, the scene begins by projecting the kind of sombre gravitas Fradley alludes to with a close-up of Fiennes's highly polished black shoes and dark trouser legs on sunlit steps, and the camera remains in place, panning upwards to follow the returning hero as he climbs the stairs to the Capitol building with a purposeful, measured pace. The trumpet is matched by the stately images captured in the frame: the building's light stone classical pillars set off Fiennes's dark uniform, and the hero's centrality is underscored by two rows of saluting stiff-spined soldiers (dressed almost identically to him) standing on either side of the steps. The soldiers' symmetrical framing is repeated when Fiennes enters the building's airy, light-filled rotunda; the camera now tracks directly behind the actor as he walks through another gauntlet of his saluting comrades. We do not immediately fully see the crowd awaiting him at the end of a long red carpet. Instead, the camera cuts to a blurry close-up of Redgrave's face, which slowly comes into focus. Her pale blue eyes, gazing

[231]

intently at Fiennes, convey the deep emotional connection between mother and child, and she provides a moment of private, sober veneration by speaking in a wavering husky whisper, 'Before him / He carries noise, and behind him he leaves tears. / Death, that dark spirit, in's nervy arm doth lie, / Which being advanced, declines; and then men die' (2.1.154–157). The deferred establishing shot finally appears, allowing us to see that Fiennes's Martius has walked straight into a media event: numerous cameramen train their lenses on him to capture his every move, and the actor's apprehensive glances here imply that such publicity degrades the soldierly dignity of his heroic return. John Kani's Cominius, an older stay-at-home general, only now speaks the battlefield lines that give Martius his surname, 'call him, / With all th'applause and clamour of the host, / Caius Martius Coriolanus! / Bear th'addition nobly ever!' (1.10.63–66). The crowd intones in unison, 'Caius Martius Coriolanus' (1.10.67), and thus Martius becomes Coriolanus not in the immediate aftermath of battle but in a less masculinely heroic 'civilianized' political event that is meant for broadcast to all 'Rome'. The camera moves in for close-ups to capture the genuine emotion between son and mother and between husband and wife (Jessica Chastain's Virgilia) as they kiss, but the photographers' flashes burst repeatedly, reminding us of the scene's public nature. Shortly, the scene is reframed as a news item, which the film suggests is a downgrade from whatever solemnity there is in the 'live' event: the picture becomes grainier, and the serene trumpet that accompanied Martius' walk is replaced with pompous newscast music. As a title along the bottom of the screen reads, 'Will newly named general Coriolanus stand for Consulship?', real-life anchorman Jon Snow speaks in the portentous tones of the tele-prompted newsreader, 'I have seen the dumb men throng to see him, / And the blind to hear him speak . . . I never saw the like' (2.1.258–264).

This 'public' Rome is the realm of the conniving Tribunes, and two principal Citizens, Lubna Azabal's Tamora and Ashraf Barhom's Cassius, Plebeians that Fiennes and Logan single out or create to parallel the representatives of the People. Nesbitt and Jesson's Tribunes, aptly enough, watch the broadcast of Coriolanus' victorious return being transformed into a 'news item' while sipping wine in a bar. These two greying middle-aged men in grey suits are at home here, in a space that signals 'political backroom' without specifying exactly where they are; they relax among many other greying politicians lounging in their modern leather chairs, posed in front of a contemporary mural of the Roman Coliseum. Although they are unsettled by Coriolanus' rise, the men have no trouble rebuffing Cox's Menenius when he leaves his own cosy seat to pester them. Cox's understated sarcasm has little effect on them: when he speaks, with mock-unctuousness, 'I know you can do very little alone' (2.1.33), Jesson only cracks an amused but unconcerned smirk. If the Tribunes are part of the same backroom world that Patrician Menenius occupies, Fiennes ensures that we see the People they rule over as Martius' unequivocal antagonists, using Tamora and Cassius to accentuate and simplify the polarization between the hero and Rome's discontented populace. Although Logan's Coriolanus *Shooting Script* indicates that 'the resistance' (p. 2) members who gather early in 1.1 in a cramped apartment 'are not wild-eyed radicals' (p. 3), we get the overwhelming impression that they are undertaking a dangerously conspiratorial political rebellion. Ominous drums and clanging percussion sound as Azabal, a slight, grim-faced and dark-haired woman, walks quickly past apartment towers and graffiti-covered walls, looking over her shoulder to see if she is being followed on her way to the 'cell meeting' (Logan p. 2). Her suspenseful walk gives local 'Roman' habitation to contemporary global strife because it is intercut with newscast footage of food line-ups and rioters, though, as elsewhere in the film, these images do not point to any one specific location: there is nothing to indicate what contemporary city Tamora is actually in, and the footage is taken from around the world. Martius, too, is linked to this international unrest by including video of a uniformed Fiennes with the title 'General Martius suspends civil liberties' at the bottom of the screen. The director does sharpen the distinction between a liberty-suspending Martius and his progressive enemies by implying that this pale, green-eyed, received-pronunciation-speaking general is up against a resistance led by 'outsiders': when the straggly haired, goateed and foreign-accented Barhom (he is an Israeli) reminds the others, 'First, you know that Caius Martius is chief enemy to the people' (1.1.7–8), Azabal appears in the frame and confidently declares in her accented English (she is Belgian of Moroccan and Spanish parents), 'Let us kill him' (1.1.10). Fiennes sustains this conflict by bringing Martius and the two Citizens into explicit opposition at the grain riot. Fiennes stomps directly up to Barhom, the two stare down one another, and the latter coolly intones, 'We have ever your good word' in response to Fiennes's venomous 'What's the matter, you dissentious rogues, / That, rubbing the poor itch of your opinion, / Make yourselves scabs?' (1.1.161–163). Azabal's Tamora proves herself the more aggressive of the two opposition leaders by spitting out a large blob of saliva to rebut Fiennes's angry speech and glaring at him defiantly when he briefly turns on her.

However, neither Tamora nor Cassius is associated with any specific local or national identity, and, in fact, Fiennes does not push very far his representation of an Anglo-Saxon Martius fighting 'alien' elements within the state. Instead, the hero is set against the Plebeians as a general social class in the public ceremonies he undergoes. The relative composure that Coriolanus showed in the grain riot devolves into neurosis and eventually hysteria when he enters the Plebeians' territory on their terms. Wearing a dark suit and white shirt as his gown of humility, he addresses the Plebeians at an open-air market. The wobbly camerawork, with its quick blurring pans and close-ups of the People's nervous looks, conveys a sense of the building unease. This tension momentarily diminishes when Slobodan Boda Ninković's 'War Vet' (Logan p. 43) tells the crowd, 'He has done nobly, and cannot go without any honest man's voice' (2.3.128–129). As the People cry out, 'Amen!' and the police hold them back, Coriolanus appears to have regained his composure but, although he shakes Nesbitt's hand, he quickly snatches his own back before pushing through the now-cheering throng. The film re-pressurizes the atmosphere by introducing a menacing bass-string-and-drum soundtrack and by cutting frequently among shots of increasingly angry Citizens as the fearful Nesbitt and Jesson then work in concert with Azabal and Barhom to turn the crowd against Coriolanus. This pressure explodes, first in the riot of 3.1 discussed above, and second in the banishment scene (3.3), which Fiennes locates on the set of a day-time chat show. This latter scene is yet another media event, one meant to cast the People and the hero in the worst possible light as Coriolanus is brought to the breaking point. Jesson and Nesbitt act as pseudo-hosts, initially conspiring with Azabal and Barhom about how to assail Coriolanus. The People jeer and Azabal whistles, unsettling Fiennes's Coriolanus, whose eyes dart nervously as he sits stiffly in his chair on the stage, barely able to contain himself when feedback from his microphone raises a condescending laugh from the studio audience. Once the Tribunes successfully bait him with the charge of treason, Nesbitt eagerly seizes a microphone and tells the People, 'It shall be so!' (119). When Azabal seconds his call for banishment, the crowd begins chanting 'It shall be so' (120), and Nesbitt and Jesson enthusiastically join them, pointing their fingers arrogantly at Fiennes, drowning out Kani's dignified attempt to calm the situation. Under attack from this generically vulgar chat-show mob, Coriolanus unleashes his frenzied hatred for the People. Fiennes's face bunches, the veins throb visibly at the sides of his closely shaved head and his lips distend in loathing as he cries, 'Youuuuuu common cry of cuuuuuuuurs!' (121). The director films the brawling back-and-forth shouting-match morality of daytime television in a manner parallel to the knife-fight at Corioles: the unsteady hand-held camera stays close to Fiennes when he marches around the stage floor to yell at the crowd, giving us the sense that we are in the thick of his battle with the Citizens and ensuring that we do not miss any of his hysterical rant that represents a complete loss of gravitas. Still, if this hysterical outburst is the culmination of Coriolanus' abomination of the People or of 'progressive' forces, it is difficult to identify easily with either side; neither the crimson-faced reactionary 'action hero' nor the hooting Plebs garner much sympathy here.

Coriolanus-as-action-hero, who has survived, if not completely mastered, the battle-scene risks, and who has revealed his neurotic hatred for the People, now visibly undergoes a quasi-feminization in his exile. The film cuts from the Martian family's horrified and the Volsce soldiers' jubilant reactions to the televised chat-show confrontation to a close-up of Fiennes's dusty boots walking down a street. The shot evokes the returning hero's earlier march up the Senate stairs, and the tacit comparison between the august Senate and the litter-strewn ex-urban locale through which he now walks implies we are witnessing the full extent of the threat latent in Rome's public ceremonies. Like the other locations in the film, this one is contemporary but placeless: Coriolanus has fallen away from Rome and into an anonymous developing-world scene where we briefly glimpse children playing in the rubble and mangy dogs ambling about dilapidated bungalows; these creatures could just as easily be from Central America as from Central Europe and the nationless exile fits right in with this political jetsam. We follow Fiennes, dressed like a civilian backpacker in a wool cap, sweater and olive-grey anorak, watching him devolve into a ragged, hirsute stray: a wide-angle shot of the outcast, a puny figure set against a vast winter landscape of bare trees making his way along a muddy road, underscores his insignificance and his lonesome, wearying journey; the subsequent close-up reveals that his beard has grown, and the voice-over of his dialogue with Volumnia from 4.1, 'Nay, mother, I shall be loved when I am lacked' (16), indicates Coriolanus' sustaining obsession with the injustice of his banishment. By the time he arrives in sunny Antium, he has been completely transformed from the close-cropped soldier he once was into something resembling the scruffy Cassius he so opposed in Rome; his clothes are bleached out and his collar-length hair and thick brown beard frame his ever-intense eyes. While this transformation into the image of his Plebeian antagonist represents a decline from or pseudo-feminization of his once-heroic masculine self, his placelessness or lack of affiliation is implied in the resemblance between his ragged appearance and the rugged, anonymous countryside through which he has wandered. By contrast, Butler's Aufidius, whom Coriolanus spies on in the streets of Antium, is evidently at home here. Although the red-tiled houses and stone-paved squares of this vaguely Mediterranean town are no more easily recognizable as a specific place than are the streets of Corioles, Butler is grounded in this locale. The relaxed way in which he reciprocates the affection that ordinary people show him as they greet him from café tables clarifies his emotional response to the murdered family at Corioles. The contrast between the two men not only contributes to our sense of how abjectly lonely Coriolanus' exile is, but this Aufidius' devotion to his people underlines how the film qualifies the action genre's melodramatic polarization between an evil, calculating antagonist and a virtuous hero by calling into question Coriolanus' hatred of the Plebeians, his loyalty to Rome and perhaps even the nature of the heroism from which he has fallen.

Whatever the distinctions Fiennes draws between the hero and his Volsce antagonist, the film offers a visually potent representation of Coriolanus' fantasy of 'remasculating' in partnership with his old enemy, and gives us a glimpse of his attempt to create that 'masculine utopia' which, Fradley notes, is a key motif of the action film (249). Coriolanus' apparent remasculation is signalled mostly visually. The film cuts from the men's initial encounter in Aufidius' bunker, where the Volsce soldiers are eating, to a shot of Fiennes, shirtless but still hairy, looking pensive as he sits in the bunker's shower room. An older woman enters and, as she begins cutting his hair, the camera replicates Coriolanus' perspective, once more putting the viewer in his place by showing us close-ups of her arms reaching over his head and shots of his shorn hair on the bench next to him. Then Fiennes eliminates the woman from this scene, effecting an exclusively masculine (and sexually charged) sphere by alternating between shots of her and of Butler using the buzzing clippers. At first, the editing makes it seem as if Fiennes's Coriolanus is hallucinating, the camera trained now on the woman's shapeless dress, now on Butler's fatigues, his phallic knife prominent on his belt as he leans in to shear. But the camera cuts away from his perspective to show us a close-up of the two: we see Butler's muscular forearm tenderly cradling Fiennes's newly bald scalp as he gently runs the clippers along Fiennes's head, which is bowed in trusting submission; still in close-up, Fiennes momentarily gazes at his new ally with grave intimacy. Rather than comic servants relieving the seriousness of Coriolanus' transformation, the fantasy of a masculine community extends to the Volsce troops becoming Coriolanus clones in Fiennes's 4.7. The scene replays Coriolanus' shower-room cropping, though now the tone is ritualistic and loudly celebratory. It begins with the image of a barber's chair slowly spinning against the black night sky. Shot from below and illuminated by firelight so that it looms menacingly, the chair acquires a kind of totemic quality as we hear men shouting and the camera pans down to show an older skinheaded Volsce soldier laughing coarsely while he selects one of the young men for trimming. To the sound of blasting music, the barber kisses the sheepishly smiling young man, and elicits a cheer with the first pass of the clippers. Eventually, the compound fills with dancing Volsces, many shaved like Coriolanus; watching the sinister image of these muscular, tattooed soldiers swaying to the music and swilling liquor in the firelight, it *appears* that Coriolanus has exchanged the Rome of electronically regurgitated ceremonies for a world elsewhere of primal masculine rites more suited to the brutal spirit he displayed in battle.

The film's embassy by Menenius in 5.2 employs visually

dramatic contrasts and a grizzly epilogue to the scene to affirm that the hero has begun his third-act victory, that this masculine community, *initially*, offers Coriolanus his longed-for purity. Cox's Menenius, wearing his customary well-tailored suit and topcoat, is brought blindfolded to the Volsce compound. A close-shot builds suspense by panning slowly up the back of a shaved head, past a neckline dragon tattoo, and then cutting to Cox making his way through a crowd of skinheaded Volsces, the barrel fires reflected in their glaring eyes. Cox finds himself before Fiennes (the owner of the tattooed neck), who, seated in the barber's chair, looks like a cult leader surrounded by his sycophants, all of them utterly unlike Menenius in their sleeveless undershirts. Their verbal exchange is terse but moving; Cox quietly speaks, 'thou art preparing fire for us. Look thee, here's water to quench it' (70–71) with understated genuine emotion, a tear forming in his eye. Never moving from his chair, Fiennes replies, almost indifferently, 'Wife, mother, child, I know not. My affairs / Are servanted to others', and, 'Another word, Menenius, / I will not hear thee speak' (80–81, 89–90). Neither man needs to say more, since the images speak for them: Cox's face falls and he peers uncertainly at the bald Coriolanus lookalikes surrounding him; he glances back to their 'original' who stares with cold unflinching supremacy in close-up, before the camera cuts to a shot over Fiennes's shoulder to show Cox nodding his head with regretful understanding as he turns to be led away silently. The director follows through on this depiction of Coriolanus' apparently regained power by adding a squalid suicide scene. Sitting on a concrete embankment next to a canal, Cox slices his wrist with a pocket knife, the blood running past his fine French-cuffed shirt sleeves and spilling loudly on the dirty ground next to his scuffed expensive brogues. The next shot shows him, at dusk, sprawled in a slick of his own blood at the canal's filthy edge, this representative of Rome's conniving political class now looking like Coriolanus in exile when he was sleeping rough in trash-strewn wetlands.

Yet the film implies that the origins of Coriolanus' remasculation actually lie in the hero's feminizing vulnerability to which he was exposed in Rome, the vulnerability that undoes him. The head-shaving that Aufidius gives Coriolanus to help him regain his masculine self specifically mirrors Volumnia's treatment of her son in 2.1. Fiennes sets part of the scene in the family's bathroom, where the camera lingers in close-up on the hero's scar-covered back and two newly stitched wounds on his left arm. Redgrave gently bandages these wounds, and her attentive matron is solemnly pleased with her son when she softly speaks, 'I have lived / To see inherited my very wishes, / And the buildings of my fancy' (194–196). The scene is the first time we see Fiennes's Coriolanus out of uniform, so this is where his body is first openly eroticized, a sexualization characteristic of the action hero's emasculation (Smith, *Clint Eastwood* 156). Not only is he physically submissive here, as he is in the Volsce shower scene, but the director hints at something peculiarly illicit about this fetishization of his body. At precisely the moment Redgrave and Fiennes share a conspiratorial look on Coriolanus' 'good mother, / I had rather be their servant in my way / Than sway with them in theirs' (198–200), Chastain's Virgilia opens the door. She hesitates at the threshold, evaluating the situation with some ambiguous emotion in her eyes; no one speaks but, with Fiennes and Redgrave watching her, she retreats swiftly, closing the door behind her, having recognized that she is intruding upon some intimacy that excludes her.

To return to Fradley's formulation, the film renders visible the 'symptomatic hysteria' that drives the hero to seek a masculine utopia by making it clear that it is the illicit intimacy revealed in 2.1 that destroys Coriolanus in the women's supplication scene (5.3), which is set at the centre of the 'pure' masculine community, the Volsce compound. The women are escorted by the same thuggish soldiers who appeared in 5.2, but the action occurs in daylight, taking the malign edge off the previous scene, and Redgrave displays none of Cox's uncertainty. Although Redgrave does unleash the matriarch's fury in the scene, she breaks down Fiennes's Coriolanus with the same tenderness she displayed when bandaging his wounds; early in her supplication she approaches him as he sits defiantly in his barber chair, and places her hands softly on his splayed knees. The reaction shot of Butler averting his gaze, which evokes Chastain's uncertain stare in 2.1, indicates the disquieting closeness between parent and child. The director heightens our sense of their exclusionary bond through a series of close-ups of the two. The camera stays tight on Redgrave's beseeching face while she quietly and deliberately speaks, 'or else / Triumphantly tread on thy country's ruin, / And bear the palm for having bravely shed / Thy wife and children's blood' (116–119), her voice barely quavering with emotion. The camera cuts to a close-up of Fiennes to show the words finding their mark, as the emotion plays subtly across his face, the hint of a tear forming in his eye. His humiliating capitulation, too, is filmed in close-up, his kneeling Coriolanus desperately clutching Redgrave around the waist. If he is not explicitly feminized by his hysterical outburst, he is infantilized: Fiennes's searching eyes well with tears, and his mouth sags at the corners; pulling himself into the actress's coat, his face contorts with grief as he loudly sobs, 'O[, my] mother, mother!' (183). Until their dialogue ends, there are no reaction shots, except for those of Redgrave's Volumnia, evidently shocked by the depth of her son's infantilization.

The final two scenes complete Coriolanus' failure to remasculate and to become a successful action hero by portraying him as excluded from all communities. Fiennes reworks Shakespeare's 5.5 to reveal Coriolanus undone by one last Roman ceremony, signing the peace treaty with Cominius. Putting pen to paper, a tense Fiennes glances for a fraction of a second to his right. The reaction shot shows Redgrave, seated and wearing the grey dress uniform that Fiennes wore before his exile, watching her son carefully. Other one- and two-shots allow us to see Coriolanus' family and Rome's politicians staring intently at the signing. The ceremony over, the camera cuts back to establish the scene: the two signers are at a long table in the Senate foyer of 2.1, the Martian clan bunched apart from Fiennes on his right and the politicians grouped closely around Kani's left. When Redgrave stands, stamps her foot and crisply salutes on Kani's 'Behold our patroness, the life of Rome!' (1), we realize that Fiennes put himself in the scene to make explicit how isolated the warrior has become, for mother and son no longer share the same bond. Redgrave now scarcely moves her eyes in her child's direction, and Fiennes's Coriolanus, the dejection apparent on his face, can hardly compel himself to glance at his uniformed, saluting mother, who is now the very image of his former, masculine Roman self. The film contrasts Coriolanus' solemnly ceremonious exclusion from Rome with his murderous rejection by the Volsces, which takes place on the anonymous, abandoned rural highway where he has been returned after signing the treaty. Fiennes momentarily seems his old action-hero self, incapacitating several of the Volsces who attack him with their knives.

Unlike Volumnia in 5.5, Butler's Aufidius, who remains apart until Fiennes's Coriolanus is badly hurt, maintains to the end the bond they solidified in the shower room. The steadicam operator makes us feel like a participant in Aufidius' final emasculation of the hero, stepping in close and tracking clockwise around the men who stand toe-to-toe, their eyes locked on each other. There is no question of the scene's erotic charge: when Butler cradles Fiennes's head, as he did in the shower room, and thrusts his knife in, the sun flares in the camera lens like an orgasmic flash; his part done, Fiennes's eyes cross slightly in death while Butler's lips contract in satiation. We understand that the two are alone in their own sexualized masculine world together, because, except for the blowing wind, there is silence until Butler removes his knife with an amplified metallic swish and he gently lays down Fiennes on the pavement, kissing the dead man next to the yonic scar newly made on his cheek. The film's penultimate image, a wide shot of the wounded and exhausted Volsces and a depleted Butler kneeling behind Fiennes, who is sprawled on a road that stretches out into the hazy sunlit distance, seems almost to eulogize Coriolanus, to give the scene a tragic dignity that perhaps redeems and elevates the dead protagonist. But in the final shot, the director rejects any elegiac tone, holding firm to his anti-action-hero trajectory; Fiennes is dumped ignominiously and alone in a military vehicle's open cargo hold, the camera, located directly above, coldly framing this ugly piece of blood-smeared flesh against the grey of the hold's floor. Whatever the film's critique of the Tribunes' and the Plebeians' crass political manoeuvrings in the television studio, however bleak the film's depiction of Menenius' end as a backroom fixer, this last shot powerfully underscores Fiennes's reworking of what the conventional action hero stands for. All that Coriolanus embodies – the reactionary hysteria, the hypermasculine militarism – is, finally, rejected.

Reaction to *Coriolanus* was positive, though pedestrian. Critics praised the film for highlighting the play's eternal relevance: it 'vividly shows' that 'the play's topicality increases with every passing year' (*TLS* 20 January 2012); the film was well timed to cast light on the American Republican primaries (*New York Review of Books* 18 February 2012); '[l]ike all Shakespeare's plays, *Coriolanus* is astonishingly *au courant*' (McDonagh).

Reviewers admired Logan for clarifying but not harming the sacrosanct text, for 'sharply cut[ting] the text, removing the obscurer passages but retaining its lucidity ... and providing a sharp, graphic narrative' (*The Guardian* 22 January 2012), and, with Fiennes, they lauded him for his 'strikingly imaginative adaptation' (*The Telegraph* 16 October 2011), for 'hav[ing] the pulse of the play' and for 'tell[ing] a damn good story' (Edelstein). Actors were judged according to their basic characterization and ability to handle the verse: Fiennes's 'phrasing is so brilliant that you might be tempted to close your eyes if his physical performance weren't equally mesmerizing' (*New York Times* 1 December 2011); Redgrave 'makes clear' Volumnia's 'aristocratic hauteur, her zealous patriotism, her ferocious cult of martial honour' (*New York Review of Books* 18 February 2012); Cox 'steals the show ... [s]aying volumes with the arch of a brow and the tilt of his head, using a mirthless laugh for punctuation, Cox is the grease that keeps the wheels of this complicated narrative moving along' (*Los Angeles Times* 2 December 2011). The response *was* exceptional for frequent allusions to Ackroyd's work on *The Hurt Locker* but there was not much detailed discussion of the film's action motifs; with the exception of Katherine Duncan-Jones, who complained of the 'too-loud, too-violent, disaster-movie-like opening scenes', most reviewers were simply pleased with the meshing of action cinema and Shakespeare (*TLS* 20 January 2012).

This bland response reflects the longevity of relevance, character, narrative and language as critical categories of assessing Shakespeare, the same categories that animate the director's convictions about the film. Like all the directors in this book, Fiennes matched his conventional assumptions about Shakespeare to the artistic forms at his disposal, in this case, the highly popular medium of action cinema. His and Logan's departure from the hero's formulaically victorious third-act remasculation may have been slightly less respectful to action's traditions than it was to a particular understanding of Shakespeare, though it might seem ironic that this rejection of what the action hero symbolizes coincides with Fiennes's careful adherence to so much else that characterizes the genre. But, rather than dismantling the tenets of the Hollywood movie, *Coriolanus* cast a pall over Western military triumphalism *through* Western cinema's most triumphantly violent form. While this strategy is hardly unusual, this film proved the artistic, if not the overwhelming commercial, viability of a certain type of mass-market Shakespeare as a way to address global, though non-specific, political and economic crises.[5] Fiennes's *Coriolanus* did not quite bring about the Shakespeare apocalypse because, like all the productions in this book, it posits and was received as having a fundamentally 'hermeneutic' relationship to the play, not a trivially citational one. That is, despite removing two-thirds of the text, and despite its reliance on bombastic blockbuster cinematography, the film consolidated the playwright's traditional authority because the director took seriously the duty of proposing 'some interpretive and dialogical relation between the Shakespearean "original" and' his movie (Burt, *Shakespeare in Love* 226). Of course, this sense of duty is something that he shared with even overtly 'experimental' practitioners like Brecht and Berkoff. Far from killing the Bard, Fiennes's movie both indicates the resilience of Hollywood Shakespeare and strengthens the playwright's brand – based on star power, a cut script, 'respectfully' interventionist direction and spectacle – that has prevailed in the theatre, on screen and in journalistic response to *Coriolanus* productions for most of the postwar era.

NOTES

Preface and Chapter I

1 Unless otherwise stated, all citations to *Coriolanus* in this chapter are from Parker's edition of the play. Some productions have used a text with the spelling 'Marcius', but for consistency I have used the spelling 'Martius' throughout the book except when quoting scholars and reviewers who use the former spelling.

2 We cannot know how collectively the early modern actors actually spoke here, but they do speak with a unified purpose.

3 Ripley (79) attributes the comic additions to Cibber.

4 The comments in this paragraph are based on the 1811 prompt-book, held in the Folger Library. See also Ripley's discussion (117) of the existing texts related to Kemble's productions.

5 Ripley (135) takes the prompt-book's direction 'Everybody to the last Act' at the top of Act 5 to mean that all the supernumeraries from the ovation appeared in this scene.

6 The prompt-book for these productions is held in the Folger Library.

Chapter II

1 While the SMT had only been running for eighty years, Stanley Wells notes that in some years the company held more than one season (*Royal Shakespeare* 5).

2 See Howard's '"My Travail's History"'.

3 See also Hall's *Making an Exhibition*, 140–141. Ripley relates (391) that he was not able to locate the 1938 prompt-book.

4 The prompt-book is held in the archives at the Shakespeare Birthplace Trust in Stratford-upon-Avon. It is based on the 1958 Cambridge edition, edited by John Dover Wilson. All references to the text in this chapter are to that edition.

5 Wells asserts that all of 2.2 was deleted, though it was rehearsed (*Royal Shakespeare* 8–9). The prompt-book directions for 2.2 are all crossed out but the dialogue for much of 2.2 is not. The sound recording of the production, held in the British Library's sound archive, does not include 2.2 but other parts of the play not cut from the prompt-book are also missing from the recording. See Weinstein for a discussion of the recording.

6 The colour picture in Rich and Aronson's book (134) gives the best view of the set.

7 There is no video recording of the production; comments about line delivery are derived from the sound recording in the British Library.

8 The same omissions occur in the Tribunes' dialogue in 1.1 and 2.1; after

Martius and the others exit in both scenes, the tape cuts out, though much of their political calculation remains in the prompt-book.

9 See Olivier's own account of critics comparing him unfavourably to Gielgud in *On Acting* 70–74.

Chapter III

1 The note on 374 of Brecht's play-text gives a composition date of between 1951 and 1952.

2 The note on 265 of Brecht's 'Study' gives a date of 1953; the note on 265 of the play-text gives a date of 1954.

3 This information appears in the notes to the Ensemble version of the play; see Wekwerth and Tenschert, 'Shakespeare's *Coriolan*' 332.

4 See also, for instance, Grass's preface to the published version of the play; Schofield; and Ripley 307–312.

5 The script may have been authored or devised collectively but most publications, including the play-text in the *Collected Works* edition, attribute authorship to Brecht. For an account that vehemently questions Brecht's authorship of this and other works see Fuegi.

6 As the notes at the end of Wekwerth and Tenschert's script indicate, the published version of the play prints Dorothea Tieck's translation of Shakespeare's 1.4–1.10. See also the note on 396 of the Brecht script.

7 Setje-Eilers 368 notes that the uprising did, however, encourage artists to demand further freedoms.

8 See Jansohn for a history of the Shakespeare-Gesellschaft during the Cold War.

9 See Gunter, 'In Search' 183–186 for an account of the authorities shutting down Adolf Dresen's 'experimental' 1964 *Hamlet*.

10 There is no video recording of this production; the audio recording is held in the sound archive at the British Library. It is not clear if surtitles were used for the benefit of English-speaking audiences.

11 I attribute authorship to Wekwerth and Tenschert because, although the second note in the published script of the Ensemble's *Coriolanus* says that the script represents Brecht's corrections, Wekwerth and Tenschert directed the play, and were responsible for its final shape. See 'Shakespeare's *Coriolan*' 332.

12 Photographs of the production are in the National Theatre archive in London.

13 See also Brecht's 'The Modern Theatre Is the Epic Theatre'.

14 See the note on 42 of Brecht's 'The Modern Theatre Is the Epic Theatre'.

15 The script is vague with regards to how the Lictors prepared the scene for the triumphal procession, but photographs show the captured armour on display stands.

16 See Wekwerth 'Experiments' and Carlson.

17 The programme for the 1971 production is held in the National Theatre archive in London.

18 Photographs of the 1971 production are held in the National Theatre archive in London.

19 The recording is held in the sound archive at the British Library.
20 Photographs of the 1970 production are held in the Royal Shakespeare Company Archives in Stratford-upon-Avon.
21 The prompt-book for the 1970 production is held in the Royal Shakespeare Company archive in Stratford-upon-Avon.

Chapter IV

1 According to the Office for National Statistics, work-days lost to strikes annually in Britain increased from 2.78 million in 1967 to 23.9 million in 1972. For more on labour unrest in the early 1970s, see Whitehead 70–98. For an account of the miner's strike, see Taylor, *The NUM* 49–109.
2 Beauman reports that attendance for Aldwych plays had been up to 82 per cent capacity for the 1970–71 season (314).
3 See Addenbrooke 151–152 and 156–159, and Beauman 295–297.
4 For critics making a connection between the two seasons see Crick; Elsom 'Roman'; and Hurren, 'Roman Balance'.
5 For Hall's comments on his 'radical' politics and the need to make Shakespeare's works relevant, see Addenbrooke 66. See the policy statement in *Royal Shakespeare Theatre Company 1960–1963* (8) for an articulation of the ideology of modern relevance. Hall reiterates these ideas in his interview with Berry, but refers to himself there as an exponent of 'classicism' (208–209). For Nunn's comments on his desire to create 'politically aware' and popular theatre in an ensemble context, see Addenbrooke 182–183. Nunn distances himself from a 'political' approach to theatre, however, in 'Director in Interview' (16). See also Sinfield's 'Royal Shakespeare' and McCullough.
6 The prompt-books for the 1972 and 1973 productions are based on Hibbard's Penguin edition of *Coriolanus*. Unless otherwise stated, all scene and line references to the play in this chapter are to that edition.
7 See the first note.
8 Nunn acknowledged that the power cuts from the strike set back construction of the new stage at Stratford (Nunn and Jones 57).
9 See Rutter's *Enter the Body* 75–81 for more on these issues in relation to the 1972 *Antony and Cleopatra*.
10 During a 1972 interview, Nunn paraphrased this passage from Nietzsche (Nunn and Morley 26).
11 I would like to thank Alexander Leggatt, who saw the production, for relating this detail to me during a conversation in January 2003.
12 Oakes relates that Williamson stopped a London performance of *Inadmissible Evidence* 'after a gruelling run of matinees and damn[ed] the show's management as "a second-rate Mikado with a whip"'. Apparently, Williamson also physically assaulted the impresario David Merrick.
13 The sound recording of the 1973 production is held in the British Library's sound archive. There is no film recording of the 1973 production. The archive does not contain a recording of the 1972 production.
14 The prompt-book directions do not indicate when he acquired this necklace, or what it represented.

15 In 1973 John Nettleton replaced Westwell as Sicinius and Philip Locke replaced James as Brutus, which may have affected changes in critical opinion.

Chapter V

1 In this section of the chapter, scene and line numbers follow G.R. Hibbard's Penguin edition of the play, upon which the RSC prompt-book is based. The prompt-book is in the Shakespeare Birthplace Trust archive in Stratford-upon-Avon.
2 He won it for performances in *Coriolanus*, the *Henry VI* plays and *Wild Oats*. See Daniell for an account of the European tour.
3 For more on the Arts Council under Conservative governments during the 1980s, see Sinclair 247–333.
4 The text was only cut by approximately 265 lines. For more on his 'relaxed' directorial approach, see Beauman 324; Breen; Hampton-Reeves and Rutter 80–107; and Mulryne 331–332.
5 There is no film of the production. The sound recording is housed in the British Library sound archive.
6 Daniell (35) describes this final moment in 4.1 from the tour, when Jill Baker played Virgilia. It is not clear from the 1977 prompt-book whether or not Chandler did the same in performances in England.
7 Scene and line numbers follow the BBC script in the BBC portion of the chapter.

Chapter VI

1 For more on the National Theatre see Callow; Cook, *The National Theatre*; Elsom and Tomalin; Lewis, *The National*; and the National Theatre, *The Complete Guide*.
2 After the London staging closed in August 1985, the company toured *Coriolanus* to the Herod Atticus Theatre in Athens for a two-night run in mid-September.
3 Accounts of the difficulties experienced in opening the South Bank complex appear in Elsom and Tomalin 273–280, 299–301, 304–307; Fay 235–237; and Lewis, *The National* 89–90, 108–110. For more on strikes at the National, see Elsom and Tomalin 282; Fay 238–239, 241, 274–275; Hall, *Diaries* 248–253, 296–299, 302–305, 421–435; Hall, *Making an Exhibition* 293, 300–302; Lewis, *The National* 115–117, 124–125, 127–130. Hall discusses voting Tory in his *Diaries* 434. For accounts of the *Romans in Britain* scandal, see Fay 278–282; Hall, *Making an Exhibition* 314–315; and Lewis, *The National*.
4 See Kavanagh 123–150 for a discussion of the abandonment of consensus by both left- and right-wing constituencies in the 1970s. See also Harrison, 'The Rise' for a discussion of postwar consensus. For accounts of such changes in Britain during the 1970s and 1980s, see Harrison's *Finding A Role?*; Kavanagh; and Vinen.
5 For more on the alternative theatre movement of the 1970s, see Itzin,

Stages in the Revolution. Kershaw offers an account of alternative and community theatre in Britain from the 1960s to the 1980s on 93–205. See Peacock 2–5 for the effect that the abandonment of consensus politics by the radical left had on oppositional theatre in Britain in the 1970s. For accounts of the Arts Council's funding of 'alternative' theatre, see Sinclair 148–176; and Witts 318–329.

6 Peacock offers an account of British theatre during the Thatcher era. Sinclair notes on 273 that half the Arts Council's Drama Panel resigned in frustration after being consistently ignored by senior Council officers. See also Fay 303–309; Lewis, *The National* 172–182; and Hall, *Making an Exhibition* 332–335.

7 For accounts of the strike, see Adeney and Lloyd; Taylor, *The NUM* 173–234; and Wilsher et al.

8 See Adeney and Lloyd 202–217; Taylor, *The NUM* 214–228; and Vinen 165.

9 See Bedford 139–142, 151–153; Hall, 'J'accuse' 7; Worth.

10 The prompt-book is based on Hibbard's edition of the play. All line and scene references in this chapter are keyed to Hibbard's edition.

11 The sound recording of the production is held in the British Library's sound archive. There is no film of the production.

12 Bedford remarks that McKellen suggested during rehearsal that Coriolanus should present his son to Aufidius but that the idea was rejected at the time because the scene was supposed to be 'about the ladies' (300).

Chapter VII

1 For general histories of Hungary that include accounts of the Kádár era, see Kontler; Lendvai; and Molnár, *Concise*. For accounts of twentieth-century Hungarian history that include lengthy analyses of the country under Kádár, see Congdon and Király; Gyáni et al.; Molnár, *From Béla Kun*; and Tőkés. See also Gough.

2 For an account of the Hungarian theatre under this form of communism see Márkus, 'War'; and Schandl, especially 1–32.

3 For accounts of reformers within the communist party and the activities of intellectual dissidents, see Gough 212–58; Molnár, *From Béla Kun* 199–211; Tőkés 167–209.

4 For accounts of Shakespeare in Hungary, see Dávidházi, 'Camel, Weasel, Whale'; Dávidházi, *Romantic*; Dávidházi, 'Weimar'; Klein and Dávidházi, eds; Márkus, 'War'; Reuss; Schandl.

5 His script is based on a translation by Eörsi István. References to scene numbers and to quotations in English from the play in this chapter follow Parker's edition. Because the typed prompt-book, which is Székely's director's script, does not include line numbers, I use page numbers after the parenthetically cited Hungarian dialogue as the most precise way to indicate that dialogue's location in Székely's script. The prompt-book is held in the archive of the Országos Színháztörténeti Múzeum és Intézet in Budapest.

6 The video is of a television broadcast of the production. The broadcast

used Székely's text of the script, which indicates cuts, textual alterations and blocking. Comparisons of production photographs, the director's script and the video reveal that the broadcast performance was very similar to the stage production. The video is in the archives of the Országos Színháztörténeti Múzeum és Intézet in Budapest.

7 Schandl covers these productions in her chapters 2, 3, 7 and 8. Especially significant was Cserhalmi's turn as Hamlet in an experimental 1981 production, which the actor described as encapsulating the struggle their postwar generation of intellectuals faced between futile action and equally futile inaction in a functional but profoundly decaying society (Schandl 57–58). This opinion was echoed by *Hamlet's* director and Cserhalmi's close friend Gábor Bódy, who committed suicide shortly after Székely's *Coriolanus* opened in 1985. Bódy must have felt the dilemma of his society's artists sharply considering that he may have been informing on colleagues since the 1970s (Schandl 63–64).

8 I am very grateful to Ágnes Juhász-Ormsby for providing the translations of the reviewers' comments.

Chapter VIII

1 For accounts of this scandal, see Walsh; and 'Iran-Contra Affair' in Levy. For an account of the impact of the scandal on Bush's 1988 presidential campaign, see Parmet 305–320.

2 For accounts of the NYSF's history and Papp's role in it, see Epstein; Lennox; Little; and Turan and Papp. Epstein offers a general account of the Marathon on 429–439.

3 For discussions of this tradition, see Cartelli; and Sturgess.

4 The radio programme script for *Coriolanus*, held in the New York Public Library's Billy Rose Theatre Collection, adopted the same carnival-barker-cum-authentically-Jacobean tone.

5 For other overviews of Berkoff's career, see Cross; and Currant.

6 Berkoff explains these ideas more fully in 'Three Theatre Manifestos'. See Cross; Currant; and Rosen for more on Berkoff's directorial style.

7 Scholars have noted Berkoff's tendency to maintain exceptional control over his productions, and have questioned his commitment to his avowed democratic principles. As Rosen argues (102–103), Berkoff places himself at the centre of his own stagings, often taking over the lead role himself, as he did for a 1995 *Coriolanus* in Leeds (though not for his other stagings of the play in Germany in 1991 and Australia in 1996). For an account of the German production, see Berkoff's *Coriolanus in Deutschland*.

8 As Cross suggests, Berkoff has actually 'needed the theatre Establishment as something to defy . . . in order to define and create both his own dramaturgical and performance style and his "outsider" persona' (83). Besides his role as Hitler, he also plotted against America as Soviet General Orlov in the 1983 James Bond vehicle *Octopussy*, and played Soviet Colonel Podovsky, who tortured Sylvester Stallone's hero John Rambo in *Rambo: First Blood Part II* (1985).

9 According to Masha Leon, Paul Hecht's Menenius also had a homburg, a cane and a fur-trimmed black overcoat (*The Forward* 6 January 1989).

10 He made twenty-nine clarifying alterations, which often follow the glosses in Brower's Signet edition. Because Brower's edition served as the basis for the prompt-book, all references to the play in this chapter are from that edition.

11 The programme and prompt-book are held in the New York Public Library's Billy Rose Theatre Collection.

12 The same effect occurs in 3.1 to 'All's' lines, in 4.5 to the First Serving-man's speech, and the First Watch's lines in 5.2.

13 More specifically, his headwear seemed derived from rap music's African-inspired fashion of the late 1980s, while the rest of his outfit looked like a combination of rap artist Grandmaster Flash in his political music video 'The Message' (1982) and the S1Ws, a security detail dressed in military fatigues which came to perform with the political rap group Public Enemy in the 1980s.

Chapter IX

1 For accounts of these events, see McRoberts 190–244.

2 For an account of the *Cycle*, see Salter, 'Between Wor(l)ds'.

3 Unless otherwise stated, all translations in this chapter are mine.

4 For discussions of Shakespeare and globalization, see Massai; Kujawin-ska-Courtney and Mercer; and Worthen. For discussions of Lepage's Shakespearean work, see Fricker; Hodgdon, '*Macbeth*'; Hodgdon, *The Shakespeare Trade*; Kidnie; Knowles; Lieblein; Salter, 'Between Wor(l)ds'; and Steen and Werry.

5 The FTA programme, pp. 6–8, indicates that the plays are written in three different types of Québécois.

6 The *Cycle* toured to France, Switzerland, Germany and within Québec. It was co-produced with the Am Turm Theatre in Frankfurt, the Théâtre Maubeuge (France), the Festival d'Automne in Paris, the Zürcher Theater Spektakel, Montréal's FTA and Théâtre Repère, the Québec company with which Lepage often worked. *Coriolan* was co-produced in Nottingham with the Nottingham Playhouse. For an account of the dual Québécois and international identities of Lepage's current company, ExMachina, see Harvie and Hurley.

7 For more on the language in Garneau's *Macbeth*, see Brisset 109–161.

8 Garneau either deletes or alters references to the Graeco-Roman world from forty-two places in Shakespeare's script. Typical of Garneau's trans-lation is his prosaic rendering of Cominius' 'You shall not be / The grave of your deserving' (1.10.19–20), Coriolanus' 'and at all times / To under-crest your good addition / To th' fairness of my power' (1.10.71–73) and his 'For they do prank them in authority / Against all noble sufferance' (3.1.24–25), respectively as 'je ne te laisserai pas enterer tes mérites' (p. 59), 'je porterai le nom que tu me donnes / avec fierté' (p. 61) and 'parce qu'ils font croire / aux pauvres gens / qu'ils ont quelque chose à dire / sur la conduite du monde' (p. 109). Throughout the chapter, all

English quotations from *Coriolanus* are from Parker's edition, and I follow his scene and line numbering for English quotations. All quotations from *Coriolan* are from Garneau's published translation. I cite Shakespeare's text as an approximate equivalent of Garneau's language. Because Garneau does not employ line numbers, I use his page numbers after the parenthetically cited French dialogue as the most precise way to indicate each quotation's location in the French text.

9 Because no prompt-book exists for the production, information about cuts and scenography is derived from the video of a 1993 performance in Montréal at the FTA, now held in the archive of ExMachina in Québec City.

10 The archived video cuts out before the shooting, but Paul Taylor indicates that, in the Nottingham mounting, Coriolan was shot (*The Independent* 26 November 1993). However, Michael Coveney indicates that, in the Montréal run, he was stabbed (*The Observer* 6 June 1993).

11 For more on this issue in relation to Lepage's theatre, see Steen and Werry 146.

12 For more on how Lepage disrupts the effect of subjectivity by putting the effect into conflict with the materiality of his performers' bodies, see Hodgdon, 'Macbeth'.

13 Philip and Cassistat seem to have operated the marionettes that represented their characters in these scenes. For an extended account of Lepage's approach to *mise-en-scène*, see Dundjerović.

14 *The Guardian* 26 November 1993; *TLS* 10 December 1993; *Weekend Telegraph* 27 November 1993; *The Independent* 26 November 1993.

15 In addition to the *Cycle* plays, Lepage toured his *Le Polygraphe* and *Les Aiguilles et L'Opium* to France.

Chapter X

1 See Barry Day for an exhaustive history of the new Globe's creation. Gurr and Orrell; and Mulryne and Shewring, eds, provide discussions of early modern performance conditions at the Globe as well as accounts of the building and uses of the new Globe.

2 See also Conkie 186–201; and Karim-Cooper.

3 For critiques of various aspects of such authenticity, see Conkie passim; Cornford; Escolme 62–73; Shaugnessy 1–4; Silverstone; and Worthen 79–116.

4 For more on the critics' treatment of spectators at the Globe see Prescott.

5 See the rehearsal blogs by Leicester; Marcell; and Sesay. See also interviews with Cake and Dromgoole.

6 Observations about the stage action are derived from the archival performance video housed at the Globe theatre offices in London. All scene and line numbers and quotations are from Parker's edition.

7 See Cornford for alterations to the Globe during Dromgoole's tenure.

Chapter XI

1 See, for instance, Burt's 'To E- or Not to E-?'; Jess-Cooke; and Taylor, 'Afterword'.

2 Burnett and Wray (1) cite both Burt's and Taylor's scepticism about the future of Shakespeare's cultural authority.

3 With the exception of Volumnia's thirty-six-line diatribe to her son in 5.3, there are only a handful of speeches longer than ten lines in the screenplay, and most are under five. Characters whose perspectives on Coriolanus are greatly curtailed or eliminated include Cominius, the Tribunes, the Citizens, the two Officers in 2.2 and the Volsce Servingmen, who are gone from 4.5. Unless otherwise specified, quotations from *Coriolanus* and references to scene and line numbers in the play follow Parker's edition. Logan's additional character or stage directions are from his Coriolanus *Shooting Script*. Because Logan's script does not indicate line numbers, I cite it using its page numbers.

4 She is quoting Tasker 39.

5 Both *The Hurt Locker* and *The Green Zone* arguably do something very similar.

APPENDIX

Major actors and staff for twentieth- and twenty-first-century productions discussed in this volume

The Shakespeare Memorial Theatre, Stratford-upon-Avon, 1959

Director   Peter Hall

Coriolanus	Sir Laurence Olivier	*Brutus*	Peter Woodthorpe
Volumnia	Dame Edith Evans	*Sicinius*	Robert Hardy
Aufidius	Anthony Nicholls	*Cominius*	Paul Hardwick
Virgilia	Mary Ure	*Titus Lartius*	Donald Eccles
Menenius	Harry Andrews	*Valeria*	Vanessa Redgrave

The Berliner Ensemble at the National Theatre Company, London, 1965

Directors   Manfred Wekwerth and Joachim Tenschert

Translated and adapted by
Bertolt Brecht, Manfred Wekwerth and Joachim Tenschert

Coriolanus	Ekkehard Schall	*Sicinius*	Martin Flörchinger
Volumnia	Helene Weigel	*Cominius*	Bruno Carstens
Aufidius	Hilmar Thate	*Titus Lartius*	Siegfried Weiss
Virgilia	Renate Richter	*Valeria*	Barbara Berg
Menenius	Wolf Kaiser	*Spurius*	Willi Schwabe
Brutus	Günter Naumann	*Calvus*	Stefan Lisewski

The Royal Shakespeare Company, Aldwych Theatre London, 1970
The Plebeians Rehearse the Uprising

Director   David Jones
Author   Günter Grass
Translator   Ralph Manheim

The Boss	Emrys James	*Kozanka*	David Bailie
Volumnia	Peggy Ashcroft	*Wiebe*	Michael Gambon
Erwin	Nicholas Selby	*Damaschke*	Roger Rees
Podulla	Geoffrey Hutchings	*Hairdresser*	Lisa Harrow
Litthenner	Peter Geddis		

National Theatre Company, London, 1971

Produced by the National Theatre Company at the Old Vic, London,
beginning 6 May 1971

Directors   Manfred Wekwerth and Joachim Tenschert

Coriolanus	Anthony Hopkins	*Brutus*	Bernard Gallagher
Volumnia	Constance Cummings	*Sicinius*	Charles Kay
Aufidius	Dennis Quilley	*Cominius*	Michael Turner
Virgilia	Anna Carteret	*Titus Lartius*	Kenneth Mackintosh
Menenius	John Moffatt	*Valeria*	Maggie Riley

Royal Shakespeare Company, Stratford-upon-Avon, 1972

Director   Trevor Nunn with Buzz Goodbody

Coriolanus	Ian Hogg	*Brutus*	Gerald James
Volumnia	Margaret Tyzack	*Sicinius*	Raymond Westwell
Aufidius	Patrick Stewart	*Cominius*	Clement McCallin
Virgilia	Rosemary McHale	*Titus Lartius*	John Bott
Menenius	Mark Dignam	*Valeria*	Edwina Ford

Royal Shakespeare Company, London, 1973

Director   Trevor Nunn with Buzz Goodbody and Euan Smith

Coriolanus	Nicol Williamson	*Brutus*	Philip Locke
Volumnia	Margaret Tyzack	*Sicinius*	John Nettleton
Aufidius	Oscar James	*Cominius*	Nicholas Selby
Virgilia	Wendy Allnutt	*Titus Lartius*	Walter Brown
Menenius	Mark Dignam	*Valeria*	Edwina Ford

Royal Shakespeare Company, Stratford-upon-Avon, 1977; London, 1978; on tour, 1979

Director   Terry Hands

Coriolanus	Alan Howard	*Sicinius*	John Burgess,
Volumnia	Maxine Audley		Tim Wylton
Aufidius	Julian Glover,	*Cominius*	Jeffery Dench,
	Charles Dance		Bernard Brown
Virgilia	Fleur Chandler,	*Titus Lartius*	Bernard Brown,
	Jill Baker		Roy Purcell
Menenius	Graham Crowden	*Valeria*	Yvonne Coulette,
Brutus	Oliver Ford-Davies		Ruth Rosen

The British Broadcasting Corporation, 1984

Director   Elijah Moshinsky

Coriolanus	Alan Howard	*Brutus*	Anthony Pedley
Volumnia	Irene Worth	*Sicinius*	John Burgess
Aufidius	Mike Gwilym	*Cominius*	Patrick Godfrey
Virgilia	Joanna McCallum	*Titus Lartius*	Peter Sands
Menenius	Joss Ackland	*Valeria*	Heather Canning

National Theatre Company, London, 1984

Director   Peter Hall

Coriolanus	Ian McKellen	*Brutus*	James Hayes
Volumnia	Irene Worth	*Sicinius*	David Ryall
Aufidius	Greg Hicks	*Cominius*	John Savident
Virgilia	Wendy Morgan	*Titus Lartius*	Basil Hensen
Menenius	Frederick Treves	*Valeria*	Judith Paris

Katona József Theatre, Budapest, 1985

Director   Gábor Székely
Translated by   István Eörsi

Coriolanus	György Cserhalmi	*Brutus*	Géza Balkay
Volumnia	Erzsi Máthé	*Sicinius*	Zoltán Papp
Aufidius	Károly Eperjes	*Cominius*	László Vajda
Virgilia	Erika Bodnár	*Titus Lartius*	György Dörner
Menenius	Ádám Rajhona	*Valeria*	Mária Ronyecz

New York Shakespeare Festival, New York, 1988

Director   Steven Berkoff

Coriolanus	Christopher Walken	*Brutus*	Andre Braugher
Volumnia	Irene Worth	*Sicinius*	Larry Bryggman
Aufidius	Keith David	*Cominius*	Moses Gunn
Virgilia	Ashley Crow	*Titus Lartius*	Thomas Kopache
Menenius	Paul Hecht	*Valeria*	Sharon Washington

Théâtre Repère at the Festival d'automne, Paris, 1992; Nottingham, 1993; Festival de Théâtre des Ameriques, Montréal, June 1993; Québec City, 1994

Director   Robert Lepage
Translated by   Michel Garneau

Coriolanus	Jules Philip	*Brutus*	Normand Bissonnette
Volumnia	Anne-Marie Cadieux	*Sicinius*	Éric Bernier
Aufidius	Gérald Gagnon	*Cominius*	Carol Cassistat
Virgilia	Marie Brassard	*Valeria*	Macha Limonchik
Menenius	Jacques-Henri Gagnon		

Shakespeare's Globe Theatre, London, 2006

Director   Dominic Dromgoole

Coriolanus	Jonathan Cake	*Brutus*	John Dougall
Volumnia	Margot Leicester	*Sicinius*	Frank McCusker
Aufidius	Mo Sesay	*Virgilia*	Jane Murphy
Cominius	Joseph Marcell	*Titus Lartius*	Ciaran McIntyre
Menenius	Robin Soans	*Valeria*	Akiya Henry

Hermetof Pictures, Magna Films, and Icon Entertainment International, 2011

Director   Ralph Fiennes
Screenplay by   John Logan

Coriolanus	Ralph Fiennes	*Brutus*	Paul Jesson
Volumnia	Vanessa Redgrave	*Sicinius*	James Nesbitt
Aufidius	Gerard Butler	*Cominius*	John Kani
Virgilia	Jessica Chastain	*Titus Lartius*	Dragan Mićeanović
Menenius	Brian Cox		

BIBLIOGRAPHY

Addenbrooke, David. *The Royal Shakespeare Company: The Peter Hall Years*. London: Kimber, 1974.

Adelman, Janet. *Suffocating Mothers: Fantasies of Maternal Origin in Shakespeare's Plays,* Hamlet *to* The Tempest. New York and London: Routledge, 1992.

Adeney, Martin and John Lloyd. *The Miner's Strike 1984–5: Loss Without Limit*. London: Routledge & Kegan Paul, 1986.

An Authentic Narrative of Mr. Kemble's Retirement from The Stage. 1817.

Arnold, Oliver. *The Third Citizen: Shakespeare's Theater and the Early Modern House of Commons*. Baltimore: Johns Hopkins University Press, 2007.

Beauman, Sally. *The Royal Shakespeare Company: A History of Ten Decades*. Oxford: Oxford University Press, 1982.

Bedford, Kristina. *Coriolanus at the National*. London and Toronto: Associated University Presses, 1992.

Berkoff, Steven. Coriolanus *in Deutschland*. Oxford: Amber Lane Press, 1992.

—— *Free Association: An Autobiography*. London: Faber, 1996.

—— *Overview*. London: Faber and Faber, 1994.

—— 'Three Theatre Manifestos'. *Gambit International Theatre Review* 32 (1978): 7–21.

Berliner Ensemble. *Coriolanus*. Programme. London, 1965.

—— *Coriolanus*. Production photographs. London, 1965.

Blakemore, Michael. *Arguments with England: A Memoir*. London: Faber and Faber, 2004.

Bordwell, David. *The Way Hollywood Tells It: Story and Style in Modern Movies*. Berkeley and Los Angeles: University of California Press, 2006.

Bradley, A.C. '"Coriolanus" (British Academy Lecture 1912)'. Coriolanus: *Critical Essays*. Ed. David Wheeler. New York and London: Garland, 1995. 25–45.

Brecht, Bertolt. *Coriolanus*. Trans. Ralph Manheim. *Collected Plays*. Volume 9. Eds Ralph Manheim and John Willett. New York: Pantheon, 1972. 57–146, 374–400.

—— 'The Modern Theatre Is the Epic Theatre'. *Brecht on Theatre*. Ed. and trans. John Willett. New York: Hill and Wang, 1989. 33–42.

—— 'Study of the First Scene of Shakespeare's "Coriolanus"'. *Brecht on Theatre*. Ed. and trans. John Willett. New York: Hill and Wang, 1989. 252–265.

Breen, Phillip. 'Terry Hands'. *The Routledge Companion to Directors' Shakespeare*. Ed. John Russell Brown. London and New York: Routledge, 2008. 160–173.

Brisset, Annie. *A Sociocritique of Translation: Theatre and Alterity in Quebec, 1968–1988*. Trans. Rosalind Gill and Roger Gannon. Toronto: University of Toronto Press, 1996.

Bulman, James C. 'The BBC Shakespeare and "House Style"'. *Shakespeare on Television: An Anthology of Essays and Reviews*. Eds J.C. Bulman and H.R. Coursen. Hanover, NH, and London: University Press of New England, 1988. 50–60.

Burnett, Mark Thornton. *Filming Shakespeare in the Global Marketplace*. Houndmills, Basingstoke; New York: Palgrave Macmillan, 2007.

Burnett, Mark Thornton and Ramona Wray. 'Introduction'. *Screening Shakespeare in the Twenty-first Century*. Eds Mark Thornton Burnett and Ramona Wray. Edinburgh: Edinburgh University Press, 2006. 1–12.

Burt, Richard. 'To E- or Not to E-? Disposing of Schlockspeare in the Age of Digital Media'. *Shakespeare after Mass Media*. Ed. Richard Burt. Houndmills and New York: Palgrave, 2002.

—— 'Shakespeare, "Glo-cali-zation," Race, and the Small Screens of Post-popular Culture'. *Shakespeare, the Movie, II: Popularizing the Plays on TV, Video, and DVD*. Eds Richard Burt and Lynda E. Boose. London and New York: Routledge, 2003. 14–36.

—— 'Shakespeare in Love and the End of the Shakespearean: Academic and Mass Culture Constructions of Literary Authorship'. *Shakespeare, Film, Fin de Siècle*. Eds Mark Thornton Burnett and Ramona Wray. New York: St Martin's, 2000. 203–231.

Cake, Jonathan. 'An Interview with Jonathan Cake, Starring as Coriolanus at Shakespeare's Globe Theatre in 2006'. *Lectures de Coriolan de William Shakespeare*. Eds Delphine Lemonnier-Texier and Guillaume Winter. Rennes: Presses Universitaires de Rennes, 2006. 171–180.

Callow, Simon. *The National: The Theatre and Its Work, 1963–1997*. London: Nick Hern, 1997.

Carlson, Harry G. 'Dialogue: Berliner Ensemble'. *The Drama Review* 12.1 (1967): 112–117.

Carnevale, Rob. 'Coriolanus – Ralph Fiennes Interview'. *IndieLondon*. N.d. www.indielondon.co.uk/Film-Review/coriolanus-ralph-fiennes-interview. Accessed 8 February 2012.

Carson, Christie. 'Democratising the Audience?' *Shakespeare's Globe: A Theatrical Experiment*. Eds Christie Carson and Farah Karim-Cooper. Cambridge: Cambridge University Press, 2008. 115–126.

Carson, Christie and Farah Karim-Cooper. 'Introduction'. *Shakespeare's Globe: A Theatrical Experiment*. Eds Christie Carson and Farah Karim-Cooper. Cambridge: Cambridge University Press, 2008. 1–12.

—— eds. *Shakespeare's Globe: A Theatrical Experiment*. Cambridge: Cambridge University Press, 2008.

Cartelli, Thomas. *Repositioning Shakespeare: National Formations, Postcolonial Appropriations*. London and New York: Routledge, 1999.

Cavell, Stanley. *Disowning Knowledge in Six Plays of Shakespeare*. Cambridge and New York: Cambridge University Press, 1987.

Charney, Maurice. 'Alan Howard in Moshinsky's *Coriolanus*'. *Shakespeare on Film Newsletter* 9.1 (December 1984): 1, 5.

Cohn, Ruby. *Modern Shakespeare Offshoots*. Princeton: Princeton University Press, 1976.

Coleman, Terry. *Olivier*. New York: Henry Holt, 2005.

Congdon, Lee W. and Béla K. Király, eds. *The Ideas of the Hungarian Revolution: Suppressed and Victorious 1956–1999*. Trans. Judit Zinner. Boulder, CO: Social Science Monographs, 2002.

Conkie, Rob. *The Globe Theatre Project: Shakespeare and Authenticity*. Lewiston, NY: Edwin Mellen Press.

Cook, Judith. *The National Theatre*. London: Harrap, 1976.

—— *Shakespeare's Players: A Look at Some of the Major Roles in Shakespeare and Those Who Have Played Them*. London: Harrap, 1983.

Cornford, Tom. 'Reconstructing Theatre: The Globe under Dominic Dromgoole'. *New Theatre Quarterly* 26.4 (November 2010): 319–328.

Cox, Frank. '*Coriolanus*'. *Plays and Players* 19.9 (June 1972): 36–39.

Crick, Bernard. 'The Politics of Rome'. *Times Higher Educational Supplement* 21 December 1973.

Cross, Robert. *Steven Berkoff and the Theatre of Self-Performance*. Manchester: Manchester University Press, 2004.

Currant, Paul Brian. *The Theatre of Steven Berkoff*. Dissertation University of Georgia, 1991. Ann Arbor: UMI, 1991. ATT 9133468.

Cushman, Robert. '*Coriolanus*'. *Plays and Players* 18.9 (June 1971): 34–35, 59.

Daniell, David. '*Coriolanus' in Europe*. London: Athlone Press, 1980.

Dávidházi, Péter. 'Camel, Weasel, Whale: The Cloud-scene in *Hamlet* as a Hungarian Parable'. *Shifting the Scene: Shakespeare in European Culture*. Eds Ladina Lambert and Balz Engler. Newark, DE: University of Delaware Press, 2004. 95–110.

—— *The Romantic Cult of Shakespeare: Literary Reception in*

Anthropological Perspective. Houndmills, Basingstoke; New York: Palgrave Macmillan, 1998.

—— 'Weimar, Shakespeare, and the Birth of Hungarian Literary History'. *Shakespeare Jahrbuch* 141 (2005): 98–118.

Day, Barry. *This Wooden 'O': Shakespeare's Globe Reborn: Achieving An American's Dream*. New York: Limelight, 1998.

Dennis, John. *The Invader of His Country: Or, The Fatal Resentment. A Tragedy*. 1720.

Dobson, Michael. 'John Philip Kemble'. *Garrick, Kemble, Siddons, Kean. Great Shakespeareans Volume II*. Ed. Peter Holland. London and New York: Continuum, 2010. 55–104.

—— 'Shakespeare Performances in England, 2006'. *Shakespeare Survey* 60 (2007): 284–319.

Dromgoole, Dominic. 'An Interview with Dominic Dromgoole, Artistic Director at Shakespeare's Globe Theatre, Director of *Coriolanus* in 2006'. *Lectures de Coriolan de William Shakespeare*. Eds Delphine Lemonnier-Texier and Guillaume Winter. Rennes: Presses Universitaires de Rennes, 2006. 163–169.

—— *Will and Me: How Shakespeare Took Over My Life*. London and New York: Allen Lane, 2006.

Dundjerović, Aleksandar Saša. *The Theatricality of Robert Lepage*. Montréal and Kingston: McGill-Queen's University Press, 2007.

Eastman, Nate. 'The Rumbling Belly Politic: Metaphorical Location and Metaphorical Government in *Coriolanus*'. *Early Modern Literary Studies* 13.1 (May 2007): 2.1–39.

Eddershaw, Margaret. *Performing Brecht: Forty Years of British Performance*. London and New York: Routledge, 1996.

Edelstein, David. 'A Dangerous Man'. *New York Magazine* 27 November 2011. http://nymag.com/movies/reviews/coriolanus-hugo-edelstein-2011-12/. Accessed 6 January 2012.

Elsom, John. 'Roman Nights'. *Listener* 8 November 1973.

Elsom, John and Nicholas Tomalin. *The History of the National Theatre*. London: Jonathan Cape, 1978.

Epstein, Helen. *Joe Papp: An American Life*. New York: Little, Brown, and Company, 1994.

Escolme, Bridget. *Talking to The Audience: Shakespeare, Performance, Self*. New York: Routledge, 2005.

Fay, Stephen. *Power Play: The Life and Times of Peter Hall*. London: Hodder and Stoughton, 1995.

Fenwick, Henry. 'The Production'. *Coriolanus*. London: British Broadcasting Corporation, 1984. 18–30.

Festival de Théâtre des Amériques. *Coriolan* Programme. Montréal, 1993.

Forrest, Edwin. *Coriolanus* Prompt-book, 1863.

Fradley, Martin. 'Maximus Melodramaticus: Masculinity, Masochism and White Male Paranoia in Contemporary Hollywood Cinema'. *Action and Adventure Cinema*. Ed. Yvonne Tasker. London and New York: Routledge, 2004. 235–251.

Fricker, Karen. 'Robert Lepage'. *The Routledge Companion to Director's Theatre*. Ed. John Russell Brown. London and New York: Routledge, 2008. 233–250.

Fuegi, John. *Brecht and Company: Sex, Politics, and the Making of Modern Drama*. 2nd ed. New York: Grove, 2002.

Garganigo, Alex. '*Coriolanus*, the Union Controversy, and Access to the Royal Person'. *Studies in English Literature 1500–1900* 42 (2002): 335–359.

Garneau, Michel, trans. *Coriolan*. By William Shakespeare. Montréal: VLB, 1989.

—— *Macbeth*. By William Shakespeare. Montréal: VLB, 1978.

Garton Ash, Timothy. 'Revolution in Hungary and Poland'. *New York Review of Books* 17 August 1989. www.nybooks.com/articles/archives/1989/aug/17/revolution-in-hungary-and-poland. Accessed 7 May 2010.

George, David. '*Coriolanus* at the Blackfriars?' *Notes and Queries* 38 (1991): 489–492.

—— '*Coriolanus'* Triumphal Entry into Rome'. *Notes and Queries* 43 (1996): 163–165.

Gerard, Jeremy. 'From Papp, All of Shakespeare'. *New York Times* 4 November 1987.

Germanou, Maro. 'Brecht and the English Theatre'. *Brecht in Perspective*. Eds Graham Bartram and Anthony Waine. London and New York: Longman, 1982. 208–224.

Goldberg, Jonathan. *James I and the Politics of Literature: Jonson, Shakespeare, Donne, and Their Contemporaries*. Baltimore: Johns Hopkins University Press, 1983.

Gough, Roger. *A Good Comrade: János Kádár, Communism and Hungary*. London and New York: I.B. Tauris, 2006.

Grass, Günter. *The Plebeians Rehearse the Uprising: A German Tragedy*. Trans. Ralph Manheim. London: Secker and Warburg, 1967.

Gunter, Lawrence. 'Brecht and Beyond: Shakespeare on the East German Stage'. *Foreign Shakespeare: Contemporary Performance*. Ed. Dennis Kennedy. Cambridge: Cambridge University Press, 1993. 109–139.

—— 'In Search of a Socialist Shakespeare: *Hamlet* on East German Stages'. *Shakespeare in the Worlds of Communism and Socialism*. Eds Irena Makaryk and Joseph G. Price. Toronto: University of Toronto Press, 2006.

Gurr, Andrew and John Orrell. *Rebuilding Shakespeare's Globe*. London: Weidenfeld and Nicolson, 1989.

Gyáni, Gábor et al., eds. *Social History of Hungary from the Reform Era to the End of the Twentieth Century*. Trans. Mario Fenyo. Boulder, CO: Social Science Monographs, 2004.

Habicht, Werner. 'Shakespeare and the Berlin Wall'. *Shakespeare in the Worlds of Communism and Socialism*. Eds Irena Makaryk and Joseph G. Price. Toronto: University of Toronto Press, 2006. 157–176.

Hall, Peter. Interview with Ralph Berry. *On Directing Shakespeare: Interviews with Contemporary Directors*. Ed. Ralph Berry. Rev ed. London: Hamish Hamilton, 1989. 208–216.

—— 'J'accuse'. *Plays and Players* 379 (April 1985): 6–7.

—— 'The Job He Liked Best'. *Olivier: In Celebration*. Ed. Garry O'Connor. London: Hodder and Stoughton, 1987. 118–122.

—— *Making an Exhibition of Myself*. 2nd ed. London: Oberon, 2000.

—— *Peter Hall's Diaries: The Story of a Dramatic Battle*. Ed. John Goodwin. London: Hamish Hamilton, 1983.

—— 'Shakespeare and the Modern Director'. *Royal Shakespeare Theatre Company 1960–1963*. Ed. John Goodwin. London: Max Reinhardt, 1964. 41–48.

—— 'We Will Mount a Fight for Our Arts'. *Sunday Times* 3 March 1985.

Hamburger, Maik. '"Are You a Party in this Business?": Consolidation and Subversion in East German Shakespeare Productions'. *Shakespeare Survey* 48 (1995): 171–184.

Hampton-Reeves, Stuart and Carol Chillington Rutter. *The Henry VI Plays*. Manchester: Manchester University Press, 2006.

Harrison, Brian. *Finding a Role? The United Kingdom 1970–1990*. Oxford: Oxford University Press, 2010.

—— 'The Rise, Fall, and Rise of Political Consensus in Britain since 1940'. *History* 84 (1999): 301–324.

Harvie, Jennifer and Erin Hurley. 'States of Play: Locating Québec in the Performances of Robert Lepage, ExMachina, and the Cirque du Soleil'. *Theatre Journal* 51 (1999): 299–315.

Hayman, Ronald. *Brecht: A Biography*. London: Weidenfeld & Nicolson, 1983.

Hewson, David. 'National Theatre to Close One Stage and Cut Jobs'. *The Times* 8 February 1985.

Higgins, John. 'Hands Full for Terry Hands'. *The Times* 19 October 1977.

Hindle, Steve. 'Imagining Insurrection in the Seventeenth-century: Representations of the Midland Rising of 1607'. *History Workshop Journal* 66 (2008): 21–61.

Hodgdon, Barbara. '*Macbeth* at the Turn of the Millennium'. *Shakespearean Illuminations: Essays in Honor of Marvin Rosenberg.* Eds Jay L. Halio and Hugh Richmond. Cranbury, NJ; London; and Mississauga, ON: Associated University Presses, 1998. 147–163.

—— *The Shakespeare Trade: Performances and Appropriations.* Philadelphia: University of Pennsylvania Press, 1998.

Hogg, Ian. 'Coriolanus'. *Shakespeare in Perspective.* Vol. 2. Ed. Roger Sales. London: Ariel Books, 1995. 240–250.

Holden, Anthony. *Olivier.* London: Max Press, 2007.

Holderness, Graham. 'Boxing the Bard: Shakespeare and Television'. *The Shakespeare Myth.* Ed. Graham Holderness. Manchester: Manchester University Press, 1988. 173–189.

Holland, Peter. 'It's All About Me. Deal With It'. *Shakespeare Bulletin* 25.3 (2007): 27–39.

Hollington, Michael. *Günter Grass: The Writer in a Pluralist Society.* London and Boston: Marion Boyars, 1980.

Howard, Tony. '"My Travail's History": Perspectives on the Roads to *Othello*, Stratford-upon-Avon 1959'. *Shakespeare Bulletin* 28.1 (2010): 93–110.

Hurren, Kenneth. 'Roman Balance'. *The Spectator* 22 April 1972.

Itzin, Catherine. *Stages in the Revolution: Political Theatre in Britain since 1968.* London: Eyre Methuen, 1980.

Jagendorf, Zvi. '*Coriolanus*: Body Politic and Private'. Coriolanus: *Critical Essays.* Ed. David Wheeler. New York and London: Garland, 1995. 229–250.

Jansohn, Christa. 'The German Shakespeare-Gesellschaft During the Cold War'. *German Studies at the Turn of the Twenty-First Century.* Ed. Christa Jansohn. Newark: University of Delaware Press, 2006. 272–291.

Jess-Cooke, Carolyn. 'Screening the McShakespeare in Post-Millennial Shakespeare Cinema'. *Screening Shakespeare in the Twenty-first Century.* Eds Mark Thornton Burnett and Ramona Wray. Edinburgh: Edinburgh University Press, 2006. 163–184.

Jones, David. 'Director in Interview'. *Plays and Players* 17.11 (August 1970): 20–21.

Jones, Gordon. 'Nahum Tate Is Alive and Well: Elijah Moshinsky's BBC Shakespeare Productions'. *Shakespeare on Television: An Anthology of Essays and Reviews.* Eds J.C. Bulman and H.R. Coursen. Hanover, NH, and London: University Press of New England, 1988. 192–200.

Kahn, Coppélia. *Roman Shakespeare: Warriors, Wound, and Women.* London and New York: Routledge, 1997.

Karim-Cooper, Farah. 'Introduction to Part II'. *Shakespeare's Globe: A Theatrical Experiment.* Eds Christie Carson and Farah

Karim-Cooper. Cambridge: Cambridge University Press, 2008. 129–133.

Katona József Theatre. *Coriolanus*. Production video. Budapest, 1985.

—— *Coriolanus*. Programme. Budapest, 1985.

—— *Coriolanus*. Director's script. Budapest, 1985.

Kavanagh, Dennis. *Thatcherism and British Politics: The End of Consensus?* 2nd ed. Oxford: Oxford University Press, 1990.

Kemble, John Philip. *Shakespeare's Coriolanus; Or, The Roman Matron*. 1806.

Kershaw, Baz. *Politics of Performance: Radical Theatre as Cultural Intervention*. London and New York: Routledge, 1992.

Kidnie, Margaret Jane. 'Dancing With Art: Robert Lepage's *Elsinore*'. *World-Wide Shakespeares: Local Appropriations in Film and Performance*. Ed. Sonia Massai. London and New York: Routledge, 2005. 133–140.

Kiernan, Pauline. *Staging Shakespeare at the New Globe*. Houndmills, Basingstoke: Macmillan, 1999.

King, Geoff. 'Spectacle and Narrative in the Contemporary Blockbuster'. *Contemporary American Cinema*. Eds Linda Ruth Williams and Michael Hammond. London and Boston: Open University Press, 2006. 334–349.

Kiscsatári, Marianna. 'Annus Mirabilis: A Year in Photos. Part 1: As 1988 Turned into 1989'. *The Hungarian Quarterly* 193 (2009): http://hungarianquarterly.com/no193/7.shtml. Accessed 19 May 2010.

Kitchin, Laurence. *Mid-Century Drama*. London: Faber and Faber, 1962.

Klein, Holger and Péter Dávidházi, eds. *Shakespeare and Hungary*. *Shakespeare Yearbook* 7 (1996).

Knowles, Ric. *Shakespeare and Canada: Essays on Production, Translation, and Adaptation*. Brussels: Peter Lang, 2004.

Koltai, Tamás. 'Realpolitik or the Chances of Personality'. *The New Hungarian Quarterly* 101 (1986): 194–199.

Kontler, László. *A History of Hungary: Millennium in Central Europe*. Houndmills, Basingstoke; New York: Palgrave Macmillan, 2002.

Kramer, Mimi. 'Director's Tragedy'. *New Yorker* 12 December 1988: 139–140.

Kroll, Jack. 'Dynamite in Ancient Rome'. *Newsweek* 12 December 1988: 43.

Kujawinska-Courtney, Krystyna and John M. Mercer, eds. *The Globalization of Shakespeare in the Nineteenth Century*. Lewiston, NY: Edwin Mellen, 2003.

Lambert, J.W. 'Plays in Performance'. *Drama* 102 (1971): 15–30.

Leeson, Bob. 'How They Carry on Brecht's Work'. *Daily Worker*. N.d.

Lehnhof, Kent. '"Rather Say I Play the Man I Am": Shakespeare's *Coriolanus* and Elizabethan Antitheatricality'. *Selected Papers from The West Virginia Shakespeare and Renaissance Association* 23 (2000): 31–41.

Leicester, Margot. 'Rehearsal Notes: 2'. www.globe-education.org/print/1146. Accessed 13 May 2011.

—— 'Rehearsal Notes: 5'. www.globe-education.org/print/1149. Accessed 13 May 2011.

Lendvai, Paul. *The Hungarians: A Thousand Years of Victory in Defeat*. Trans. Ann Major. London: Hurst & Co., 2003.

Lennox, Patricia. 'Joseph Papp'. *The Routledge Companion to Director's Shakespeare*. Ed. John Russell Brown. London and New York: Routledge, 2008. 307–322.

Lepage, Robert. *Robert Lepage: Connnecting Flights: Robert Lepage in Conversation with Rémy Charest*. Trans. Wanda Romer Taylor. Toronto: Knopf, 1998.

Levy, Peter B. 'Iran Contra Affair'. *Encyclopedia of the Reagan–Bush Years*. New York: Greenwood Press, 1996.

Lewis, Peter. *The National: A Dream Made Concrete*. London: Methuen, 1990.

Lieblein, Leanore. 'Theatre Archives at the Intersection of Production and Reception: The Example of Québécois Shakespeare'. *Textual and Theatrical Shakespeare: Questions of Evidence*. Ed. Edward Pechter. Iowa City: University of Iowa Press. 164–180.

Little, Stuart W. *Enter Joseph Papp: In Search of a New American Theater*. New York: Coward, McCann and Geoghegan, 1974.

Loehlin, James. 'Brecht and the Rediscovery of *Henry VI*'. *Shakespeare's History Plays: Performance, Translation, and Adaptation in Britain and Abroad*. Ed. Ton Hoenselaars. Cambridge: Cambridge University Press, 2004. 133–150.

Logan, John. Coriolanus: *The Shooting Script*. New York: Newmarket Press, 2011.

Marcell, Joseph. 'Rehearsal Notes: 5'. www.globe-education.org/print/1157. Accessed 13 May 2011.

Marchand, Guy. 'Lévesque et la Trilogie de Lepage: Comme Alonso dans l'île de Prospéro'. *Jeu* 67 (1993): 63–67.

Marcus, Leah S. *Puzzling Shakespeare: Local Reading and Its Discontents*. Berkeley: University of California Press, 1988.

Margaretthatcher.org. www.margaretthatcher.org/document/106689. Accessed 19 December 2010.

Márkus, Zoltán. '"Loyalty to Shakespeare": The Cultural Context of the 1952 *Hamlet*-Production of the Hungarian National Theatre'.

Shakespeare and Hungary. Shakespeare Yearbook 7 (1996): 169–189.

—— 'War, Lechery, and Goulash Communism: *Troilus and Cressida* in Socialist Hungary'. *Shakespeare in the Worlds of Communism and Socialism*. Eds Irena R. Makaryk and Joseph G. Price. Toronto, Buffalo and London: University of Toronto Press, 2006. 246–269.

Marshall, Cynthia. 'Wound-man: *Coriolanus*, Gender, and the Theatrical Construction of Interiority'. *Feminist Readings of Early Modern Culture: Emerging Subjects*. Eds Valerie Traub, M. Lindsay Kaplan and Dympna Callaghan. Cambridge and New York: Cambridge University Press, 1996. 93–118.

Massai, Sonia, ed. *World-wide Shakespeares: Local Appropriations in Film and Performance*. London and New York: Routledge, 2005.

McConachie, Bruce. 'Forrest, Edwin'. *American National Biography*. Oxford: Oxford University Press, 1999.

—— *Melodramatic Formations: American Theatre and Society, 1820–1870*. Iowa City: University of Iowa Press, 1992.

McCullough, Christopher J. 'The Cambridge Connection: Towards a Materialist Theatre Practice'. *The Shakespeare Myth*. Ed. Graham Holderness. Manchester: Manchester University Press, 1988. 112–121.

McDonagh, Maitland. 'Film Review: Coriolanus'. *Film Journal International*. 23 January 2012. www.filmjournal.com/film journal/content_display/reviews/specialty-eleases/e3i9bf3dca739 728f07ede61baf9d3c64d2. Accessed 8 February 2012.

McGugan, Ruth. *Nahum Tate and the* Coriolanus *Tradition in English Drama. With a Critical Edition of Tate's* The Ingratitude of A Common-Wealth. New York and London: Garland, 1987.

McRoberts, Kenneth. *Misconceiving Canada: The Struggle for National Unity*. Oxford: Oxford University Press, 1997.

Miller, Anthony. 'Domains of Victory: Staging and Contesting the Roman Triumph in Renaissance England'. *Playing the Globe: Genre and Geography in English Renaissance Drama*. Eds John Gillies and Virginia Mason Vaughan. London and Cranbury, NJ: Associated University Presses, 1998. 260–287.

Miller, Shannon. 'Topicality and Subversion in William Shakespeare's *Coriolanus*'. *Studies in English Literature, 1500–1900* 32.2 (1992): 287–310.

Molnár, Miklós. *A Concise History of Hungary*. Trans. Anna Magyar. Cambridge: Cambridge University Press, 2001.

—— *From Béla Kun to János Kádár: Seventy Years of Hungarian Communism*. Trans. Arnold J. Pomerans. New York, Oxford, Munich: Berg, 1990.

Mulryne, J.R. '*Coriolanus* at Stratford-upon-Avon: Three Actors' Remarks'. *Shakespeare Quarterly* 29 (1978): 323–332.

Mulryne, J.R. and Margaret Shewring, eds. *Shakespeare's Globe Rebuilt*. Cambridge: Cambridge University Press, 1997.

Munn, Michael. *Lord Larry: The Secret Life of Laurence Olivier, A Personal and Intimate Portrait*. London: Robson Books, 2007.

National Theatre. *The Complete Guide to Britain's National Theatre*. London: Heinemann, 1977.

—— *Coriolanus*. Production photographs. London, 1971.

—— *Coriolanus*. Production photographs. London, 1984.

—— *Coriolanus*. Programme. London, 1971.

—— *Coriolanus*. Programme. London, 1984.

—— *Coriolanus*. Prompt-book. London, 1971.

—— *Coriolanus*. Prompt-book. London, 1984.

—— *Coriolanus*. Sound recording. London, 1971.

—— *Coriolanus*. Sound recording. London, 1984.

New York Shakespeare Festival. Adverstisement for Shakespeare Marathon. *New York Times* 8 November 1987.

—— *Coriolanus*. Programme. New York, 1988.

—— *Coriolanus*. Prompt-book. New York, 1988.

—— *Coriolanus*. Radio advertisement script. New York, 1988.

Nunn, Trevor. 'Director in Interview'. *Plays and Players* 17.12 (September 1970): 16–17, 21.

—— Interview with Ralph Berry. *On Directing Shakespeare: Interviews with Contemporary Directors*. Ed. Ralph Berry. Rev ed. London: Hamish Hamilton, 1989. 60–81.

Nunn, Trevor and David Jones. 'Writing on Sand'. *Theatre 73*. Ed. Sheridan Morley. London: Hutchinson, 1973. 54–67.

Nunn, Trevor and Christopher Morley. 'Direction and Design'. *Plays and Players* 19.12 (September 1972): 23–27.

Oakes, Philip. 'Return to the Arena'. *Sunday Times* 21 October 1973.

Office for National Statistics. 'Working Days Lost, 1901 to 1998: Social Trends 30'. www.statistics.gov.uk/statbase/xsdownload. asp?vlnk=134. Accessed 25 August 2010.

Olivier, Laurence. *Confessions of an Actor*. New York: Simon and Schuster, 1982.

—— *On Acting*. New York: Simon and Schuster, 1986.

Ormsby, Robert. '*Coriolanus*, Antitheatricalism, and Audience Response'. *Shakespeare Bulletin* 26.1 (2008): 43–62.

Osman, Arthur. 'Engineering Workers to Join Miners' Picket Line Today as 35,000 Hold Token Strike'. *The Times* 10 February 1972.

Papp, Joseph. 'The Shakespeare Marathon: The Coach's View'. *New York Times* 19 February 1989.

Parker, R.B. Introduction. *Coriolanus*. By William Shakespeare. Ed. R.B. Parker. Oxford: Oxford University Press, 1994. 1–148.

Parmet, Herbert S. *George Bush: The Life of a Lone-Star Yankee*. New York: Scribner, 1997.

Peacock, D. Keith. *Thatcher's Theatre: British Theatre and Drama in the Eighties*. Westport, CT and London: Greenwood Press, 1999.

Pearce, G.M. 'Coriolanus'. *Cahiers Élisabéthains* 26 (October 1984): 96–98.

Polowy, Kevin. 'Q & A: Ralph Fiennes on His Bard Badass "Coriolanus"'. *NextMovie* 30 (November 2011). www.nextmovie.com/blog/ralph-fiennes-interview-coriolanus. Accessed 8 February 2012.

Potter, Lois. 'Shakespeare Performed: Assisted Suicides: *Antony and Cleopatra* and *Coriolanus* in 2006–7'. *Shakespeare Quarterly* 58.4 (2007): 509–529.

Preece, Julian. *The Life and Work of Günter Grass: Literature, History, Politics*. Basingstoke and New York: Palgrave, 2001.

Prescott, Paul. 'Inheriting the Globe: The Reception of Shakespearean Space and Audience in Contemporary Reviewing'. *A Companion to Shakespeare and Performance*. Eds Barbara Hodgdon and W.B. Worthen. Oxford: Blackwell, 2005. 359–375.

Preussner, Arnold. 'Antony and Cleopatra and Coriolanus'. *Shakespeare Bulletin* 24.4 (2006): 115–123.

Production Notes for *Coriolanus*. www.districtpr.ca/coriolanus/coriolanus_productionnotes.pdf. Accessed 1 February 2012.

Prouvost, Christelle. 'En Québécois dans le Texte'. *Le Soir* 23 September 1992.

Purse, Lisa. *Contemporary Action Cinema*. Edinburgh: Edinburgh University Press, 2011.

Rebellato, Dan. *1956 and All That*. London and New York: Routledge, 1999.

Reuss, Gabriella. '(Re)Turning to Shakespeare or Imitating the Shakespeare Cult in Hungary? The Nineteenth-century Theatres of Gábor Egressy and William Charles Macready'. *The Globalization of Shakespeare in the Nineteenth Century*. Eds Krystyna Kujawinska Courtney and John M. Mercer. Lewiston, NY: Edwin Mellen Press, 2003. 97–115.

Rich, Frank with Lisa Aronson. *The Theatre Art of Boris Aronson*. New York: Knopf, 1987.

Richardson, Tony. *The Long-Distance Runner: An Autobiography*. New York: William Morrow, 1993.

Ripley, John. *Coriolanus on Stage in England and America, 1609–1994*. London and Cranbury, NJ: Associated University Presses, 1998.

Robertson, Roland. 'Glocalization: Time-space and Homogeneity-heterogeneity'. *Global Modernities*. Eds Mike Featherstone, Scott Lash and Roland Robertson. London: Sage, 1995. 25–44.

Róna, Katalin. 'Másssut is van Világ?' *Film, Színház, Muzsika* 28 September 1985: 4.

Rosen, Craig. *Creating the Berkovian Aesthetic: An Analysis of Steven Berkoff's Performance Style*. Dissertation University of Colorado, 2001. Ann Arbor: UMI 2001. ATT 9995765.

Rothstein, Mervyn. 'Trims and New Twists for a "Coriolanus"'. *New York Times* 30 November 1988.

Royal Shakespeare Company. *Coriolanus*. Basic programme. Stratford-upon-Avon, 1972.

—— *Coriolanus*. Commemorative programme. Stratford-upon-Avon, 1972.

—— *Coriolanus*. Programme. Stratford-upon-Avon, 1977.

—— *Coriolanus*. Prompt-book. Stratford-upon-Avon, 1972.

—— *Coriolanus*. Prompt-book. Stratford-upon-Avon, 1973.

—— *Coriolanus*. Prompt-book. Stratford-upon-Avon, 1977.

—— *Coriolanus*. Sound recording. London, 1973.

—— *Coriolanus*. Sound recording. Stratford-upon-Avon, 1977.

—— *The Plebeians Rehearse the Uprising*. Production photographs. London, 1970.

—— *The Plebeians Rehearse the Uprising*. Programme. London, 1970.

—— *The Plebeians Rehearse the Uprising*. Prompt-book. London, 1970.

—— *The Plebeians Rehearse the Uprising*. Sound recording. London, 1970.

—— *Royal Shakespeare Theatre Company 1960–1963*. Ed. John Goodwin. London: Max Reinhardt, 1964.

Rutter, Carol Chillington. *Enter the Body: Women and Representation on Shakespeare's Stage*. London and New York: Routledge, 2001.

Sachs, Jonathan. *Romantic Antiquity: Rome in the British Imagination, 1789–1832*. Oxford: Oxford University Press, 2010.

Salter, Denis. 'Between Wor(l)ds: Lepage's Shakespeare Cycle'. *Theater Sans Frontières: Essays on the Dramatic Universe of Robert Lepage*. Eds Jospeh I. Donohue Jr and Jane M. Koustas. East Lansing, MI: Michigan State University Press, 2000. 191–204.

—— 'Borderlines: An Interview with Robert Lepage and Le Théâtre Repère'. *Theatre* 24 (1993): 71–79.

Sanders, Eve Rachele. 'The Body of the Actor in *Coriolanus*'. *Shakespeare Quarterly* 57 (2006): 387–412.

Schandl, Veronika. *Socialist Shakespeare Productions in Kádár-Regime Hungary: Shakespeare Behind the Iron Curtain*. Lewiston, NY: Edwin Mellen, 2009.

Schofield, Martin. 'Drama, Politics, and the Hero: Coriolanus, Brecht, and Grass'. *Comparative Drama* 24 (1990–1991): 322–341.

Sesay, Mo. 'Rehearsal Notes: 5'. www.globe-education.org/print/626. Accessed 13 May 2011.

Setje-Eilers, Margaret. '"*Wochenend und Sonnenschein*": In the

Blind Spots of Censorship at the GDR's Cultural Authorities and the Berliner Ensemble'. *Theatre Journal* 61 (2009): 363–386.

Shakespeare Memorial Theatre. *Coriolanus*. Prompt-book. Stratford-upon-Avon, 1959.

—— *Coriolanus*. Sound recording. Stratford-upon-Avon, 1959.

Shakespeare, William. *Coriolanus*. Dir. Elijah Moshinsky. Videorecording. London: British Broadcasting Corporation, 1984.

—— *Coriolanus*. Ed. Reuben Brower. New York: Signet, 1966.

—— *Coriolanus*. Ed. G.R. Hibbard. Harmondsworth: Penguin, 1967.

—— *Coriolanus*. Ed. R.B. Parker. Oxford: Oxford University Press, 1994.

—— *Coriolanus*. Ed. John Dover Wilson. Cambridge: Cambridge University Press, 1958.

Shakespeare's Globe Theatre. *Coriolanus*. Performance video. London: 2006.

—— *Coriolanus*. Programme. London: 2006.

Sharp, Buchanan. 'Shakespeare's *Coriolanus* and the Crisis of the 1590s'. *Law and Authority in Early Modern England: Essays Presented to Thomas Garden Barnes*. Eds Buchanan Sharp and Mark Charles Fissel. Cranbury, NJ: Associated University Presses, 2007. 27–63.

Shaugnessy, Robert, ed. *Shakespeare in Performance*. New York: St Martin's, 2000.

Sheridan, Thomas. *Coriolanus: Or, The Roman Matron. A Tragedy.* 1755.

Sherman, Jon Foley. 'Steven Berkoff, Choral Unity, and Modes of Governance'. *New Theatre Quarterly* 26.3 (August 2010): 232–247.

Shrank, Cathy. 'Civility and the City in *Coriolanus*'. *Shakespeare Quarterly* 54 (2003): 406–423.

Silverstone, Catherine. 'Shakespeare Live: Reproducing Shakespeare at the "New" Globe Theatre'. *Textual Practice* 19 (2005): 31–50.

Simon, John. 'The Ignoblest Roman'. *New York Magazine* 5 December 1988: 194–195.

Sinclair, Andrew. *Arts and Cultures: The History of the 50 Years of the Arts Council of Great Britain*. London: Sinclair-Stevenson, 1995.

Sinfield, Alan. 'Royal Shakespeare: Theatre and the Making of Ideology'. *Political Shakespeare: New Essays in Cultural Materialism*. 2nd ed. Eds Jonathan Dollimore and Alan Sinfield. Manchester: Manchester University Press, 1994. 182–205.

Smith, James. 'Brecht, the Berliner Ensemble, and the British Government'. *New Theatre Quarterly* 22.4 (2006): 307–323.

Smith, Paul. *Clint Eastwood: A Cultural Production*. Minneapolis: University of Minnesota Press, 1993.

Sorge, Thomas. 'The Sixties: Hamlet's Utopia Come True?' *Redefining Shakespeare: Literary Theory and Theater Practice in the German Democratic Republic*. Eds J. Lawrence Gunter and Andrew M. McLean. Newark: University of Delaware Press, 1998. 98–110.

Spates, William Henry. 'Coriolanus'. *Theatre Journal* 59.2 (May 2007): 284–285.

Steen, Shannon and Margaret Werry. 'Bodies, Technologies, and Subjectivities: The Production of Authority in Robert Lepage's Elsinore'. *Essays in Theatre / Études théâtrales* 16.2 (1999): 139–153.

Sturgess, Kim C. *Shakespeare and the American Nation*. Cambridge: Cambridge University Press, 2004.

Subiotto, Arrigo. *Bertolt Brecht's Adaptations for the Berliner Ensemble*. London: The Modern Humanities Research Association, 1975.

Suvin, Darko. 'Brechtian or Pseudo-Brechtian: Mystical Estrangement in the Berliner Ensemble Adaptation of *Coriolanus*'. *ASSAPH Section 3: Studies in Theatre* 3 (1986): 135–58.

—— *To Brecht and Beyond: Soundings in Modern Dramatology*. Brighton: Harvester, 1984.

Tarján, Tamás. 'Sötét Van'. *Szinház* December 1985: 1–5.

Tasker, Yvonne. *Spectacular Bodies: Gender, Genre, and the Action Cinema*. London and New York: Routledge, 1993.

Tatlow, Antony. *Shakespeare, Brecht, and the Intercultural Sign*. Durham, NC: Duke University Press, 2001.

Taylor, Andrew. *The NUM and British Politics. Volume 2: 1969–1995*. Aldershot and Burlington, VT: Ashgate, 2005.

Taylor, Gary. 'Afterword: The Incredible Shrinking Bard'. *Shakespeare and Appropriation*. Eds Christy Desmet and Robert Sawyer. London and New York: Routledge, 1999. 197–205.

Terris, Olwen. 'The BBC Television Shakespeare: Weary, Stale, Flat, and Unprofitable?' *Walking Shadows: Shakespeare in the National Film and Television Archive*. Eds Luke McKernan and Olwen Terris. London: British Film Institute, 1994. 219–226.

Théâtre Repère. *Coriolan*. Production video. Montréal, May 1993.

Thomson, James. *Coriolanus, The Works of James Thomson*. 4 vols. 1773.

Thomson, Peter. 'No Rome of Safety: The Royal Shakespeare Season 1972 Reviewed'. *Shakespeare Survey* 26 (1973): 139–150.

Thorncroft, Anthony. 'National Theatre to Close Stage after Arts Council Setback'. *Financial Times* 8 February 1985.

Tőkés, Rudolf L. *Hungary's Negotiated Revolution: Economic Reform, Social Change, and Political Succession, 1957–1990*. Cambridge: Cambridge University Press, 1996.

Turan, Kenneth and Joseph Papp. *Free for All: Joe Papp, the Public, and the Greatest Theater Story Ever Told*. New York: Doubleday, 2009.

T.,W. 'Coriolanus or The Press War in London'. *The GDR Review* 17.2 (1972): 57–59.

Tynan, Kenneth. *Curtains: Selections from the Drama Criticism and Related Writings*. New York: Atheneum, 1961.

—— *Profiles*. Ed. Kathleen Tynan and Ernie Eban. London: Nick Hern Books, 1990.

Ustinov, Peter. *Dear Me*. Boston: Little Brown, 1977.

Valuch, Tibor. 'Changes in the Structure and Lifestyle of the Hungarian Society in the Second Half of the XXth Century'. *Social History of Hungary From the Reform Era to the End of the Twentieth Century*. Eds Gábor Gyáni et al. Trans. Mario Fenyo. Boulder, CO: Social Science Monographs, 2004. 511–671.

Vickers, Brian. *Coriolanus*. London: Edward Arnold, 1976.

Vinen, Richard. *Thatcher's Britain: The Politics and Social Upheaval of the Thatcher Era*. London and New York: Simon & Schuster, 2009.

Völker, Klaus. *Brecht: A Biography*. Trans. John Nowell. New York: Seabury, 1978.

Walsh, Lawrence E. *Final Report of the Independent Counsel for Iran/Contra Matters*. www.fas.org/irp/offdocs/walsh/.

Warren, Roger. 'Shakespeare in England'. *Shakespeare Quarterly* 35 (1984): 334–340.

Weinstein, Charles E. 'Olivier's Coriolanus: The Unknown Sound Recording'. *Shakespeare Bulletin* 11 (1993): 35–36.

Wekwerth, Manfred. 'Experiments at the Berliner Ensemble'. *World Theatre / Le théâtre dans le monde* 15.3–4 (1966): 210–214.

Wekwerth, Manfred and Joachim Tenschert. 'Bearbeitung von Shakespeare's *"Coriolan"'*. *Spectaculum*: VIII. Frankfurt: Suhrkamp Verlag, 1966. 7–70, 332–337.

Wells, Robin Headlam. '"Manhood and Chevalrie" *Coriolanus*, Prince Henry, and the Chivalric Revival'. *The Review of English Studies*, New Series, 51 (2000): 395–422.

Wells, Stanley. *Royal Shakespeare: Four Major Productions at Stratford-upon-Avon*. Manchester: Manchester University Press, 1977.

Wheeler, David. 'To Their Own Purpose: The Treatment of *Coriolanus* in the Restoration and Eighteenth Century'. *Coriolanus: Critical Essays*. Ed. David Wheeler. New York and London: Garland, 1995. 273–297.

Whelehan, Imelda and Deborah Cartmell. 'Through a Painted Curtain: Laurence Olivier's *Henry V*'. *War Culture: Social Change and Changing Experience in World War Two Britain*. Eds Pat

Kirkham and David Thoms. London: Lawrence & Wishart, 1995. 49–60.

Whitehead, Philip. *The Writing on the Wall: Britain in the Seventies*. London: Joseph, 1985.

Willems, Michèle. 'Verbal-visual, Verbal-pictorial or Textual-televisual? Reflections on the BBC Shakespeare Series'. *Shakespeare and the Moving Image: The Plays on Film and Television*. Eds Anthony Davies and Stanley Wells. Cambridge: Cambridge University Press, 1994. 69–85.

Williamson, Nicol. 'Saying Who You Are'. *Plays and Players* 21.1 (October 1973): 20–23.

Willis, Susan. *The BBC Shakespeare Plays: Making The Televised Canon*. Chapel Hill, NC and London: The University of North Carolina Press, 1991.

Wilsher, Peter et al. *Strike: Thatcher, Scargill and the Miners*. London: André Deutsch, 1985.

Wilson, Richard. 'Against the Grain: Representing the Market in *Coriolanus*'. *Seventeenth Century* 6.2 (1991): 111–148.

Witts, Richard. *Artist Unknown: An Alternative History of the Arts Council*. London: Little, Brown and Co., 1998.

Worth, Irene. 'Never Stick with the Same Guru'. *The Times* 13 December 1984.

Worthen, W.B. *Shakespeare and the Force of Modern Performance*. Cambridge: Cambridge University Press, 2003.

Zeeveld, W. Gordon. '"Coriolanus" and Jacobean Politics'. *The Modern Language Review* 57.3 (1962): 321–334.

Index

Lightning Source UK Ltd.
Milton Keynes UK
UKHW020738190519
342860UK00006B/306/P